I0812126

IMAGES
of America

ALBION

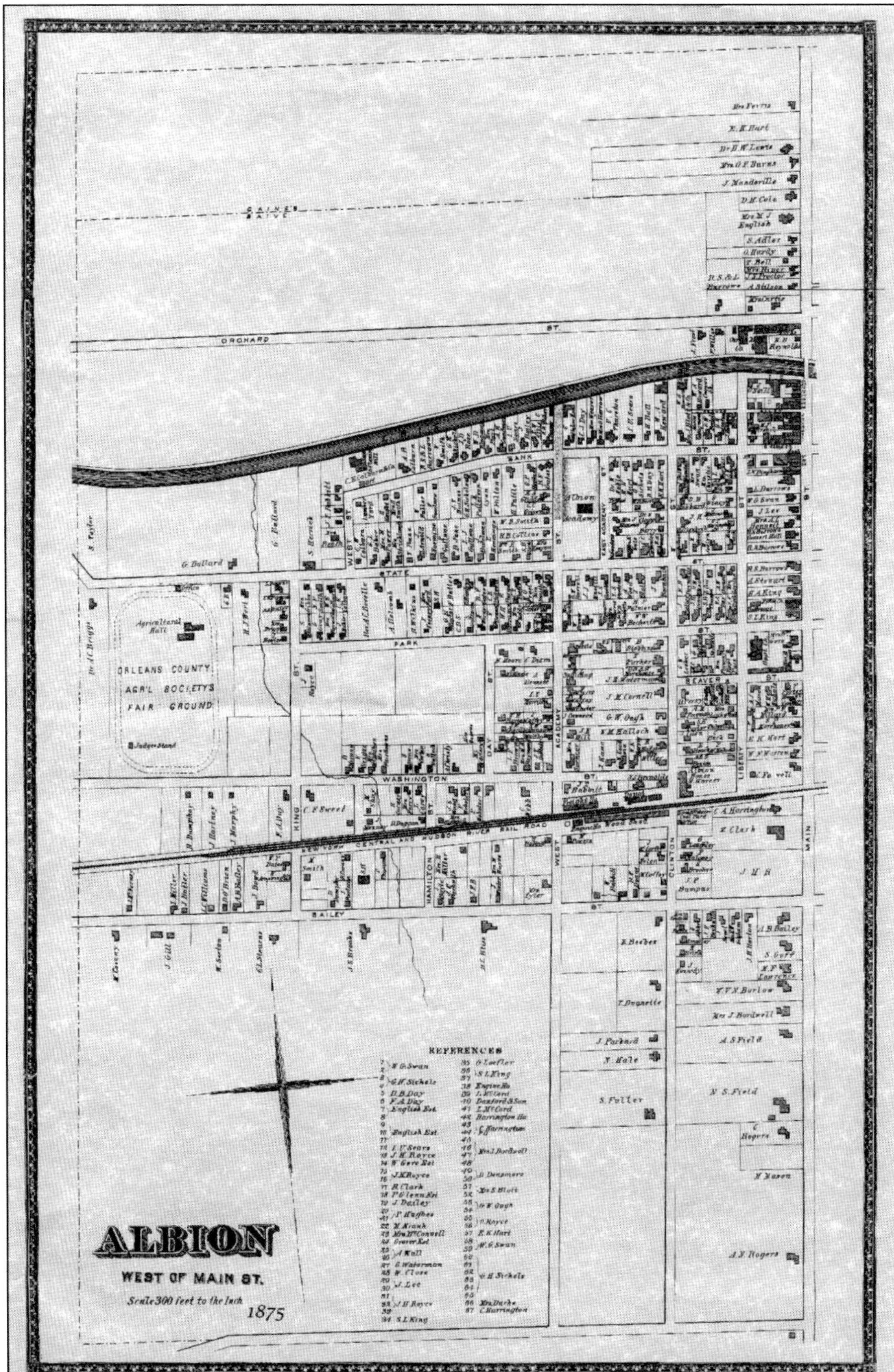

ALBION, WEST OF MAIN STREET, 1875. This map shows the various school districts and boundary lines within the town of Albion, west of Main Street around 1875. Note the fairgrounds at the left. (Courtesy of Historicaltownmaps.com.)

IMAGES
of America

ALBION

Avis A. Townsend

ARCADIA
PUBLISHING

ISBN 978-0-7385-3929-4

Published by Arcadia Publishing
Charleston, South Carolina

Printed in the United States of America

Library of Congress Catalog Card Number: 2005931669

For all general information contact Arcadia Publishing at:
Telephone 843-853-2070
Fax 843-853-0044
E-mail sales@arcadiapublishing.com
For customer service and orders:
Toll-Free 1-888-313-2665

Visit us on the Internet at www.arcadiapublishing.com

Contents

FOREWORD

It has often been stated that a picture is worth a thousand words. To tell the story of Albion in the written word would take volumes. Here, however, at a glance through photographers' lenses of long ago, we see a compelling visual history. Many of the photographs from the 19th century bring to life an era of living we can only imagine in the 21st century. Indeed, time flies mercilessly. These images, presented here for our edification, put into perspective a rich and voluminous heritage. Many of the pictures show Albion at its best, giving us a true sense of transition through the decades. In our own mind's eye we cannot help but compare what we know today with this historic visual record. Through this calculation the past teaches us and gives us a sturdy foundation to better understand and appreciate our inherent legacy of Albion, its lore, and abiding lure.

Do we see through this volume the character of aesthetics and the value of preservation? One can only hope. By ongoing publications of this nature, we come to the realization that history is a cohesive factor in our lives and an element not to be dismissed. We can learn by it and reap its manifestations when we come to recognize its best offerings. Historic Albion is surely rejuvenated on the pages that follow through images of the past.

—C. W. Lattin
Orleans County historian

Albion, may thy sons ne'er forget thee,
And to thy name we ever will be loyal.
And through all our days we will sing thy praise,
In times of victory or in times of toil.
We'll cheer for Albion and our cheers will re-echo,
As high above the sea our colors fly,
One, two, three great big cheers for thee,
Dear Old Albion.

"Alma Mater," written in 1913 by Frank R. Wassung
Principal, Albion High School

INTRODUCTION

Albion is located in Orleans County, its borders being Genesee County to the south and Lake Ontario to the north. The hamlets of Carlton, Childs, Eagle Harbor, Gaines, and Oak Orchard all share the same postal code as Albion. Gaines is the home of the Cobblestone Museum located in Childs. History abounds in every area, and one does not have to look far to find a piece of the past.

In pioneer times, the area north of what is now Gaines was known as the Black North because of all the dense timber growing from the Ridge to Lake Ontario. There were so many trees, settlers could build numerous log cabins and line their roadways, and still there was so much timber it was burned to make potash.

The first residents of what is now Gaines were the Gilberts, who settled in what is now Childs on March 3, 1807. Gradually, more settlers came. By 1812, there was a sawmill on Otter Creek, and by 1816, there was a post office and school. Albion was originally called Newport, but with the advent of the postal service, it had to be changed, as New York State already had a Newport. The first newspaper came off the presses in 1822, and by 1825, Albion had become the county seat for Orleans County. Gaines was the original choice for county seat, but the location of the Erie Canal made Albion the unanimous choice. Between 1826 and 1836, Albion grew faster than in any other decade since its existence. It became incorporated as a village in 1828 with a population of 400. People from all over visited to do business.

The Erie Canal was the most significant factor in the quick settlement of this area. In addition, the soil and climate made farmers wealthy as they grew fruit, vegetables, grain, and livestock. Beautiful homes were constructed on large expanses of land, and many are still standing.

Legend suggests that because of the Erie Canal masons, cobblestone houses were built from Batavia to Lewiston, with over 100 of these homes built in Orleans County. When the masons died, their secret died with them. Yet most of these lovely homes, barns, and buildings are there today, looking brand new, thanks to the craftsmanship of the stone mason. The area on the corner of Ridge Road, Route 104, and Route 98 features the Cobblestone Museum, which is made up of several cobblestone buildings designated as national historic landmarks. The museum offers information and tours daily from May to October. The Cobblestone Society was formed to preserve these unique buildings and to disseminate information on cobblestone masonry.

The area was a melting pot of Irish laborers who stayed after the canal was widened, English stonecutters imported to do the canal's stone work, and Italian and Polish immigrants who came to work the quarries. Work was plentiful. During World War II, when men left home, Jamaicans were imported to fill the slack for harvesting.

In 1824, Medina sandstone was discovered in Oak Orchard Creek while the canal was being dug, and quarrying became a commercialized industry by 1837. In the early 20th century, Orleans County had 48 quarries employing 1,200 men, with a payroll of $3,000 a day. The stone was shipped all over the eastern United States and was used for road paving and building construction. As the years passed, it became easier to pour cement than cut stone. Thus, quarries closed and cement businesses took over.

Canning factories sprang up. Orleans mucklands, resulting from swamp drainage over the centuries, have produced millions of dollars' worth of lettuce, carrots, potatoes, spinach, onions, and celery.

A trolley crossed the area every half hour from 6 a.m. to midnight from 1909 to 1931. The New York Central Railroad passenger trains ran daily from 1852 to 1957. However, the things that made Albion prosper eventually contributed to its decline in popularity. The quarry business waned, as did the trolley and passenger train. Canal shipping disappeared with the advent of tractor trailer trucks. Small farms gave way to large conglomerates. Industry moved to big cities and seaports, and the people who worked those jobs followed to the new areas. Today two prisons are now the sources of employment, not only for Albion residents but also for workers from outlying towns.

The residents of the Albion area are proud of their heritage. They strive to keep the town quaint, while welcoming the modern conveniences and today's electronic age. The aura of the 19th century is preserved in the cemeteries, the Cobblestone Society, the lands along the canal, and in many local businesses. Just recently, the Orleans County Genealogical Society purchased an early freight house for a library and museum and hired a preservation architect to make sure all renovations maintain the historic integrity of the building. The freight house, located on the railroad tracks off Academy Street, will be open to the public as a genealogical research library and as a museum of memorabilia related to the orphan trains from New York City, trains that in the 19th century carried hundreds of orphans westward so they could be adopted by the families here and beyond.

An 1876 Orleans County Directory described Albion as "situated on the Erie Canal, the principal station on the New York Central Railroad between Rochester and Lockport, and about midway between these two places. It contains six churches, county buildings, Phipps Union Female Seminary, Albion Academy, two newspaper offices, two banks, several manufacturies and about 5,000 inhabitants. . . . The streets are ornamented with beautiful rows of shade trees. There are several large business blocks and many beautiful private residences. . . . Considering the beauty of the surrounding scenery, the facilities for communication with its literary institutions, and the healthfulness of its location, it is one of the most desirable places for residence in Western New York. . . ." Most people visiting Albion find that description true today.

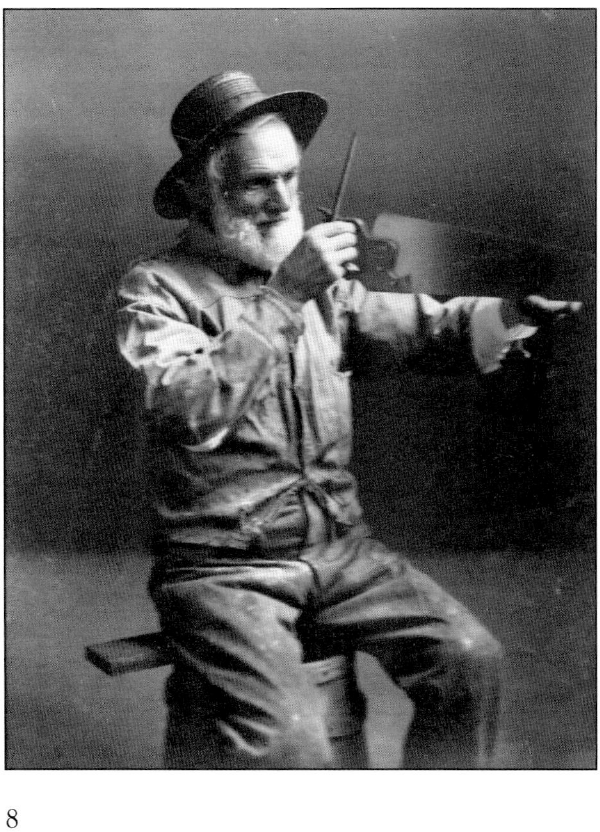

SIGHTING A SAW. William V. N. Barlow was an architect and builder who designed many buildings in Albion, including the courthouse in 1857 to 1858. Here he is sighting a saw, peering down the blade, making sure the teeth are situated properly for a correct alignment. (Courtesy of Orleans County Department of History.)

One

EARLY YEARS AND PIONEERS

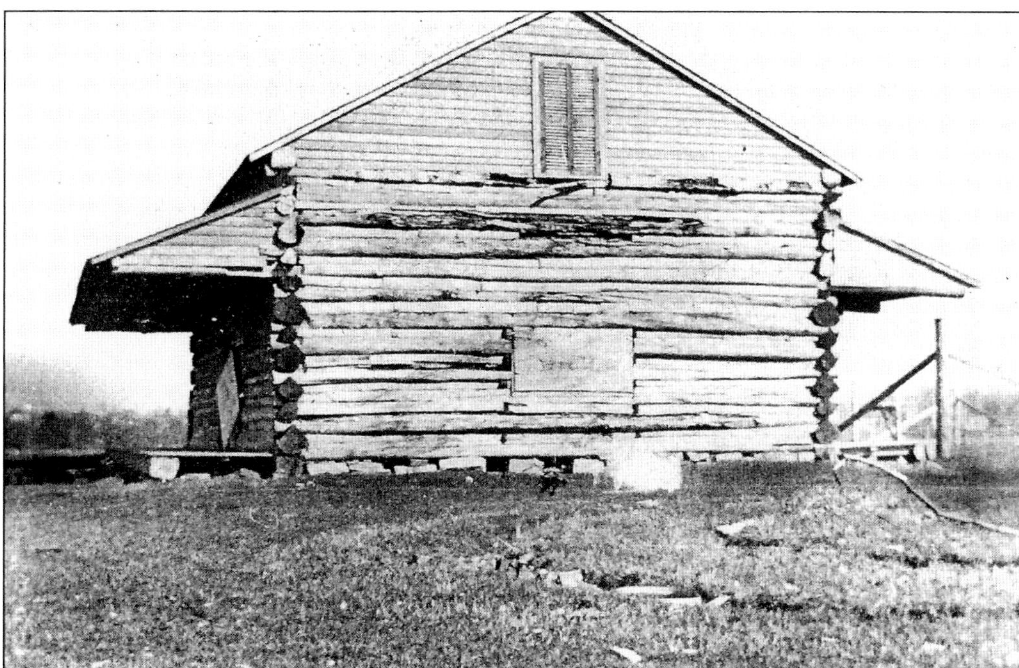

FIRST CABIN. The first log cabin in Albion was built on what is now Courthouse Square by William McCallister in 1811. When a foundation was dug for the county clerk's office addition in 1957, the skeletal remains of Mrs. McCallister were discovered, as she had been buried on the property when she died. The photograph above is a replica, built in 1882 to be used as a museum on the Orleans County Fairgrounds. It was torn down in the early 20th century. (Courtesy of Orleans County Department of History.)

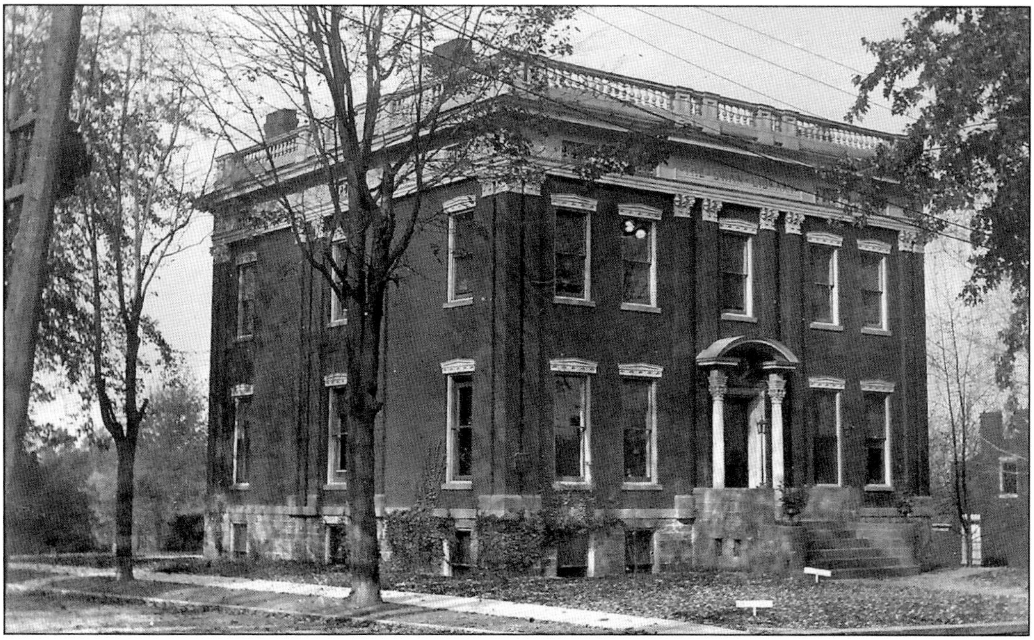

SWAN LIBRARY. A prominent Albion resident for many years, William G. Swan was well traveled and eventually became the superintendent of the Niagara Railway Suspension Bridge at the town of Suspension Bridge. He never forgot his roots, nor did he give up his property in Albion. He was treasurer and commissioner of Mount Albion Cemetery prior to his death in 1896. In his will, he gave an endowment of $35,000 to establish the Swan Library, which carries his name today. (Courtesy of Orleans County Department of History.)

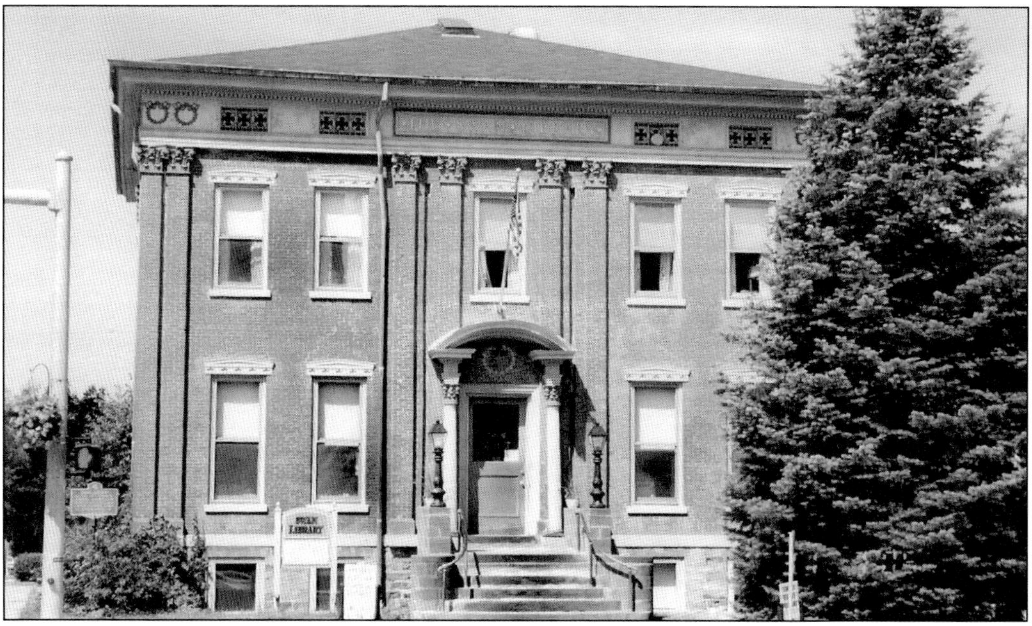

SWAN LIBRARY TODAY. The library was chartered on December 21, 1899, and opened on March 17, 1900. It remains open to this day. Not much has changed. A historical marker to the south of the building tells its history, and a sign in front identifies it. Its brick is clean and casts a pinkish hue.

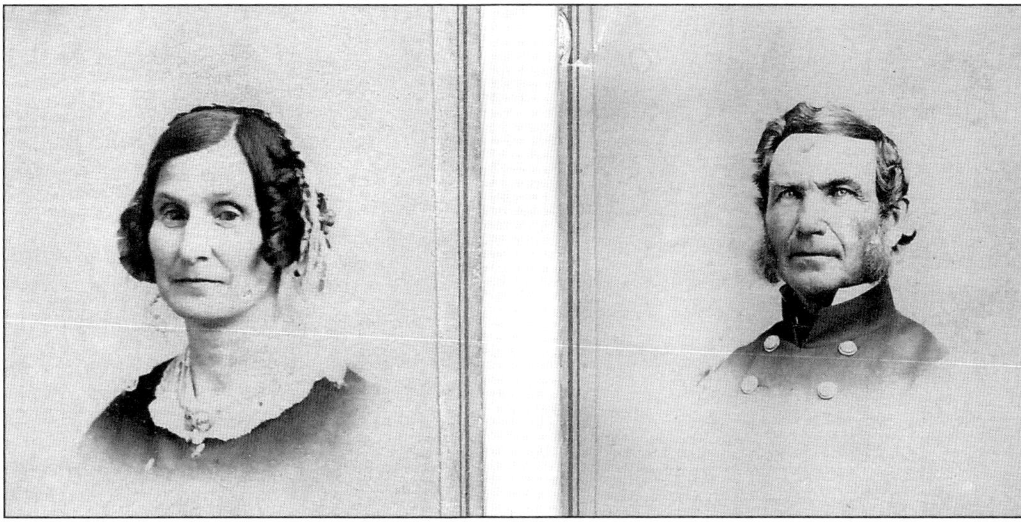

Seminary Founders. In 1836, Caroline Phipps borrowed $4,100 from some of Albion's citizens and founded a female seminary school for young adult women. She ran the school with her husband, Henry Achilles, until it burned in 1875. She then built a boys' school on Academy Street. That school became the Union Free School and, eventually, a high school. (Courtesy of Orleans County Department of History.)

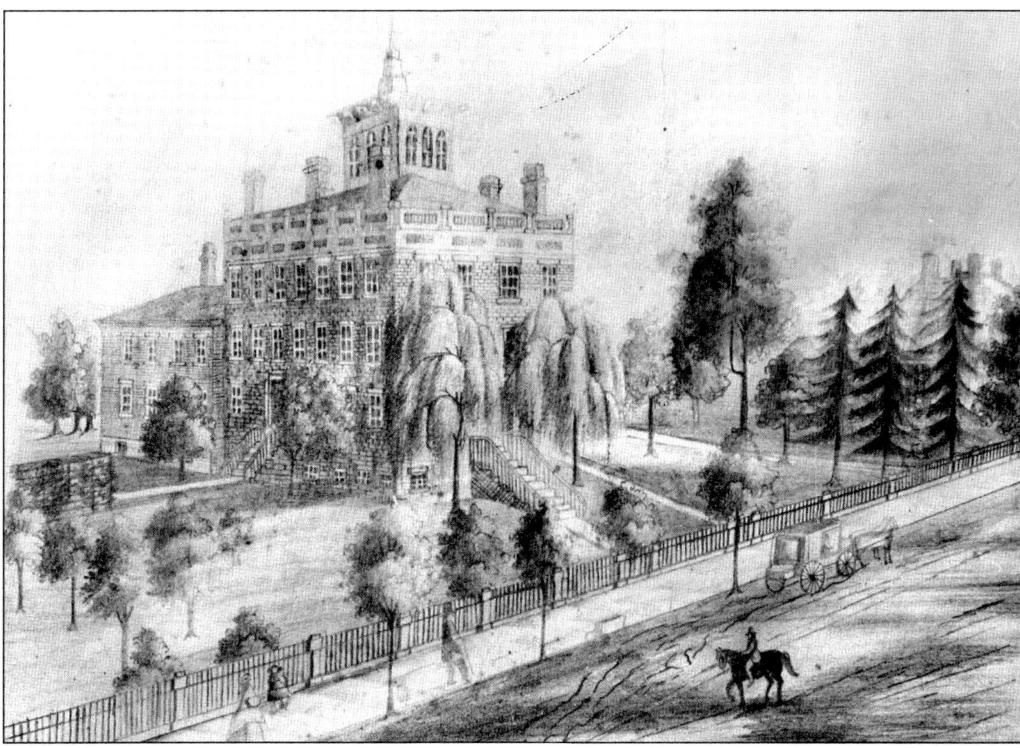

Phipps Union Seminary The Phipps Female Academy was in operation from 1837 until 1875. It was demolished in 1882 and was replaced by the Orleans County Clerk's Office. (Courtesy of Orleans County Department of History.)

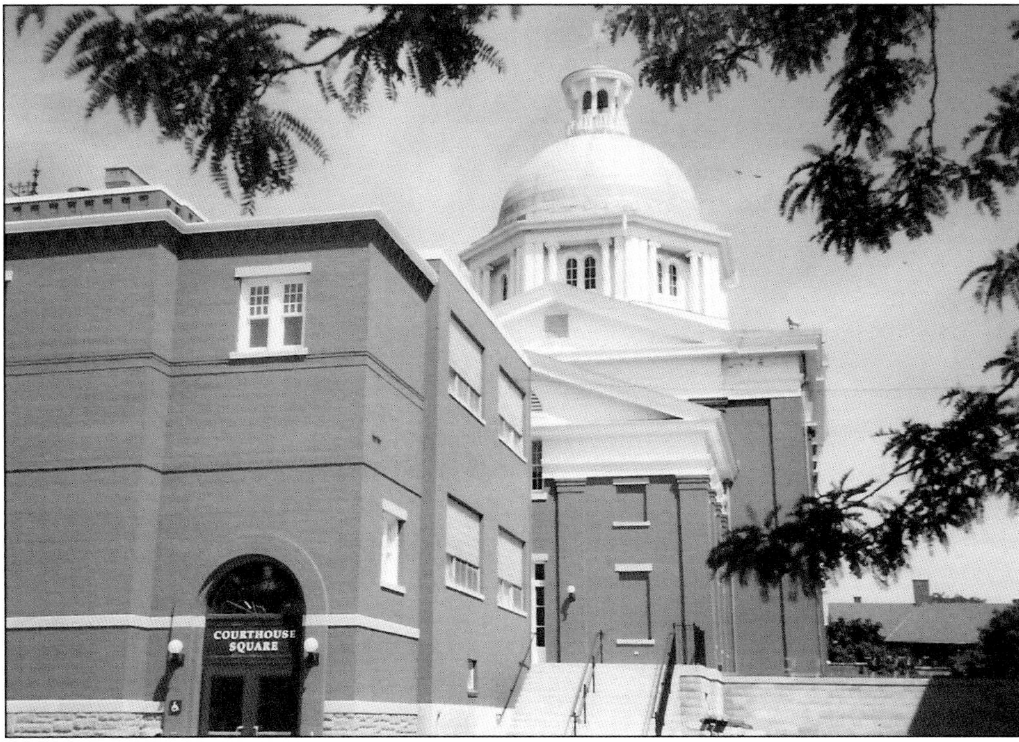

COURTHOUSE SQUARE. The courthouse was built in 1859 of red brick with white Greek Revival columns 50 feet high. Its silver dome, 100 feet high and 36 feet in diameter, can be seen from miles away. At the top is a cupola, from which visitors once viewed Lake Ontario, 10 miles away. Residents say the courthouse is especially impressive at Christmastime, when it is lit at night.

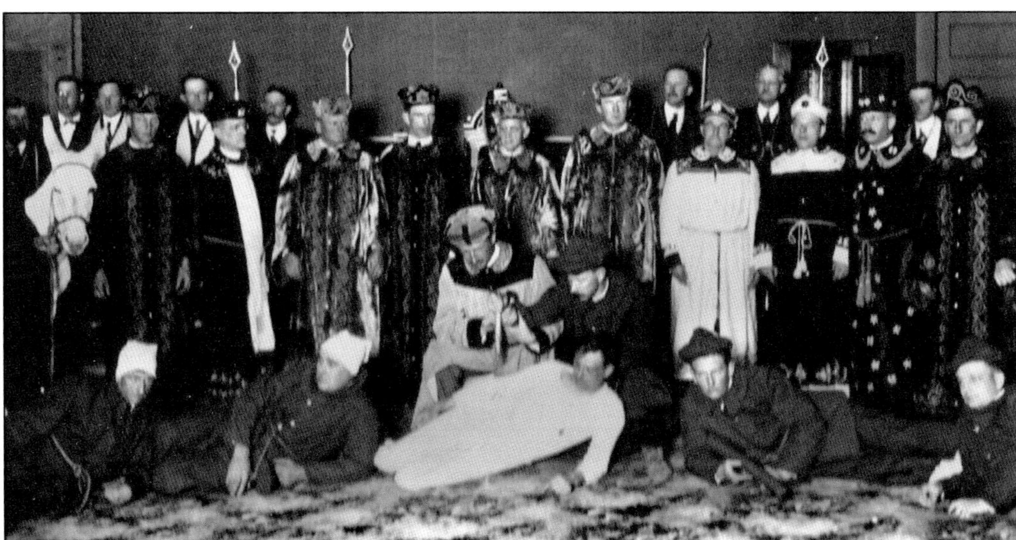

ODD FELLOWS AND A DONKEY. Members of the Independent Order of Odd Fellows lodge are in costume for one of their many pageants around 1910. Performances were conducted at Albion Temple No. 58, and even a donkey was allowed in the lodge as part of the ceremony, which was not sanctioned by the Grand Lodge. (Courtesy of Mark Tillman.)

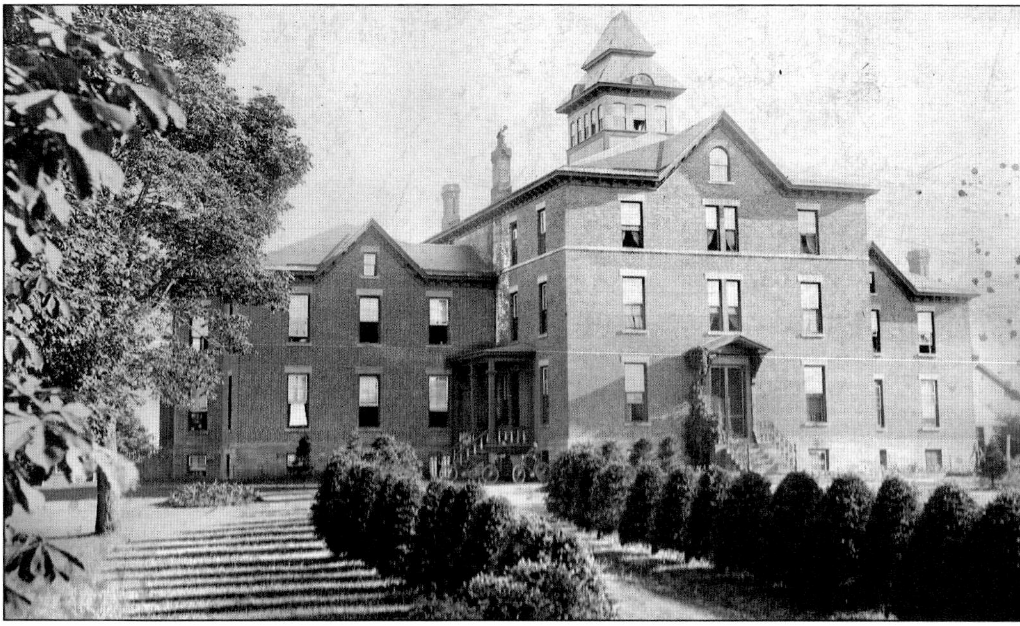

THE POORHOUSE. The Orleans County Almshouse, known by locals as the Poorhouse, took in destitute people who could not afford to live on their own. The county building committee, consisting of H. D. Waldo, Gates Sherwood, and Berton Keys, approved the construction, and the almshouse was erected in 1878 by Cornelius Finucan and George Clark. The building was demolished in 1962. (Courtesy of Orleans County Department of History.)

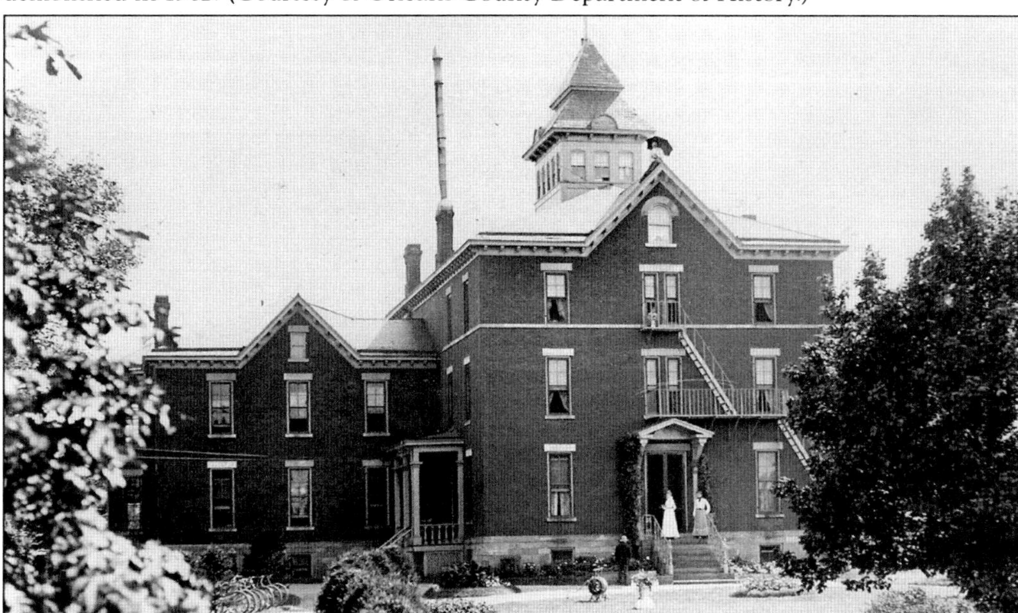

ANOTHER VIEW. The almshouse was built on County House Road in 1878, and a hospital was added to the east side in 1903. Note the new fire escapes, which are not in the previous photograph. In 1960, a new county home and infirmary was built on a 20-acre site west of Albion's village. Patients were transferred to the new facility from the old county home. (Courtesy of Orleans County Department of History.)

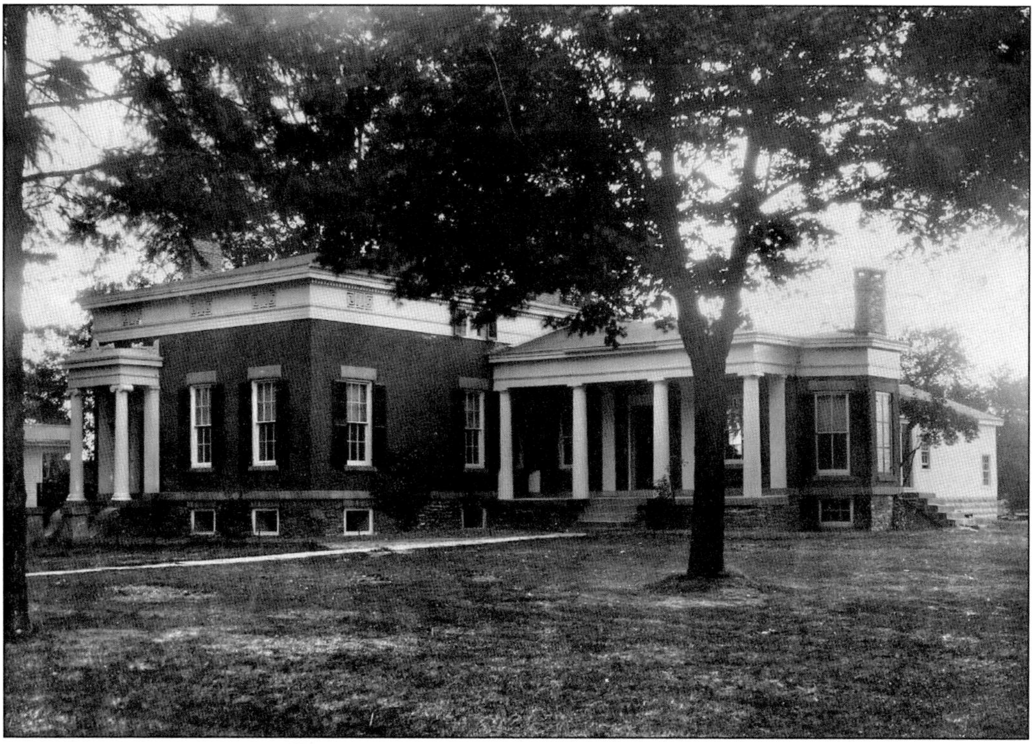

ORLEANS CHAPTER HOUSE. This beautiful structure, built in 1846, stands on North Main Street. Formerly a private home, the house has been used by the Daughters of the American Revolution since 1929. (Courtesy of Orleans County Department of History.)

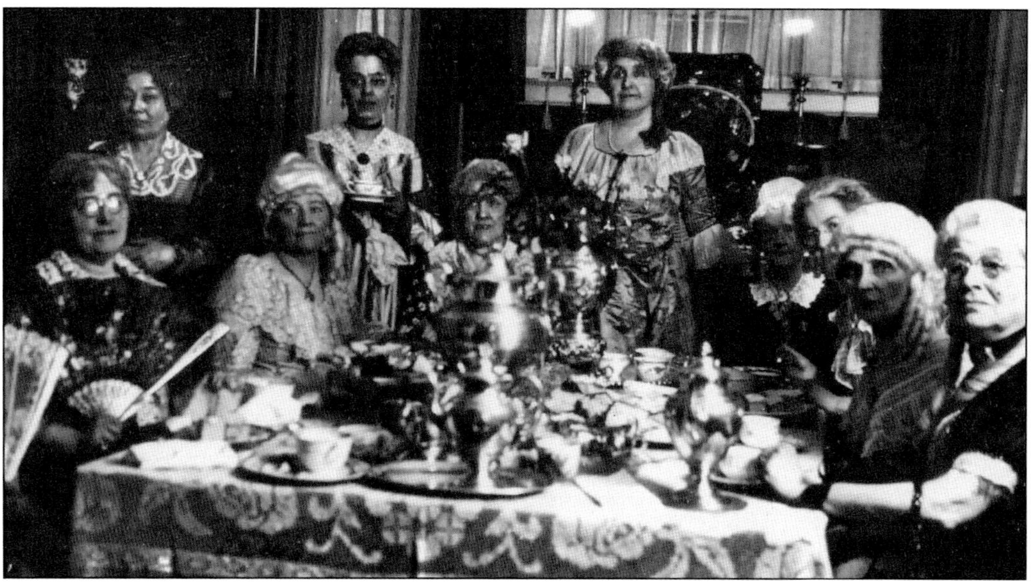

SILVER TEA PARTY. Dressed in costumes, members of the Daughters of the American Revolution hold a silver tea party at the home of Mrs. Sanford T. Church in 1927, before they had the Orleans Daughters of the American Revolution chapter house. (Courtesy of Mark Tillman.)

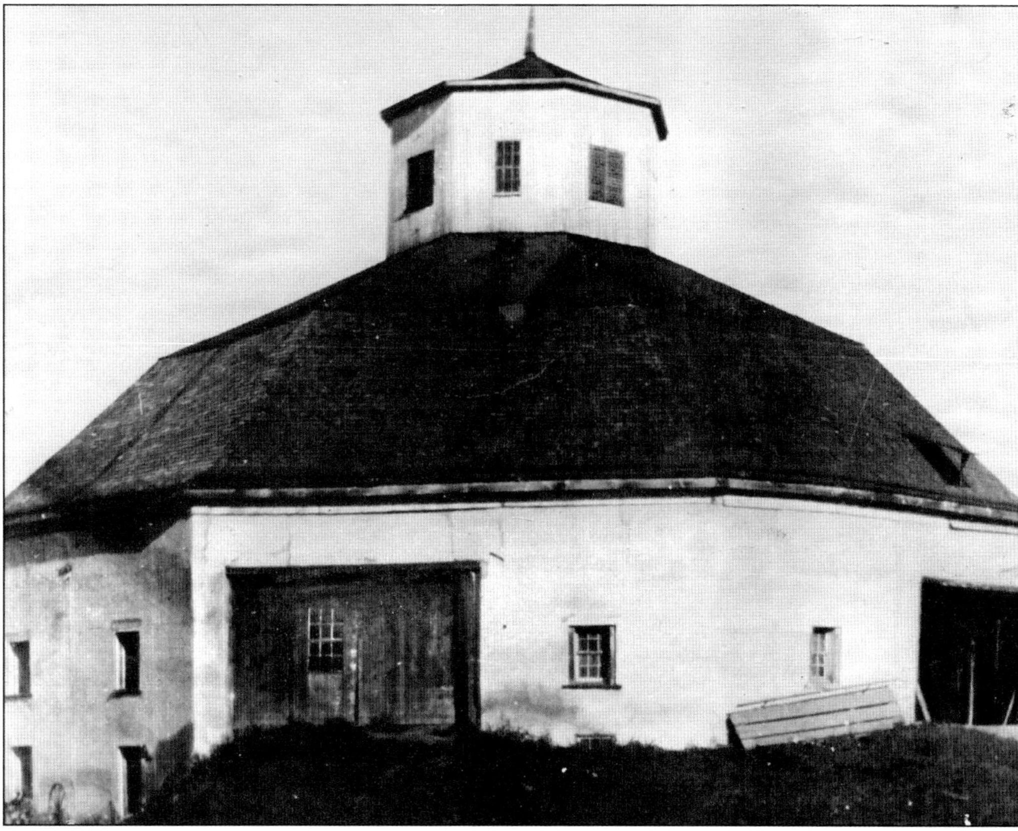

OCTAGON BARN. This barn was built by Lucius Sanford about 1845. It remained a working barn until it was destroyed by fire in 1936. The farm is still a working farm, situated about a mile north of the hamlet of Gaines. (Courtesy of Donna Kay Belmont.)

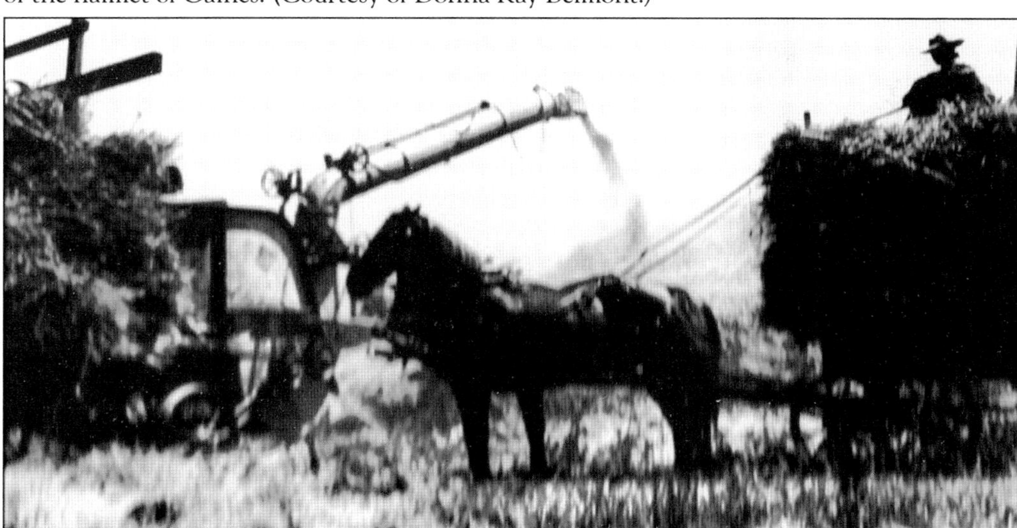

THRESHING WHEAT. A solitary farmer sits on a bed of wheat straw, watching the thresher separate the wheat from the chaff. By 1910, modern equipment helped farmers and horses do tasks that were not possible before. (Courtesy of Tillman's Village Inn.)

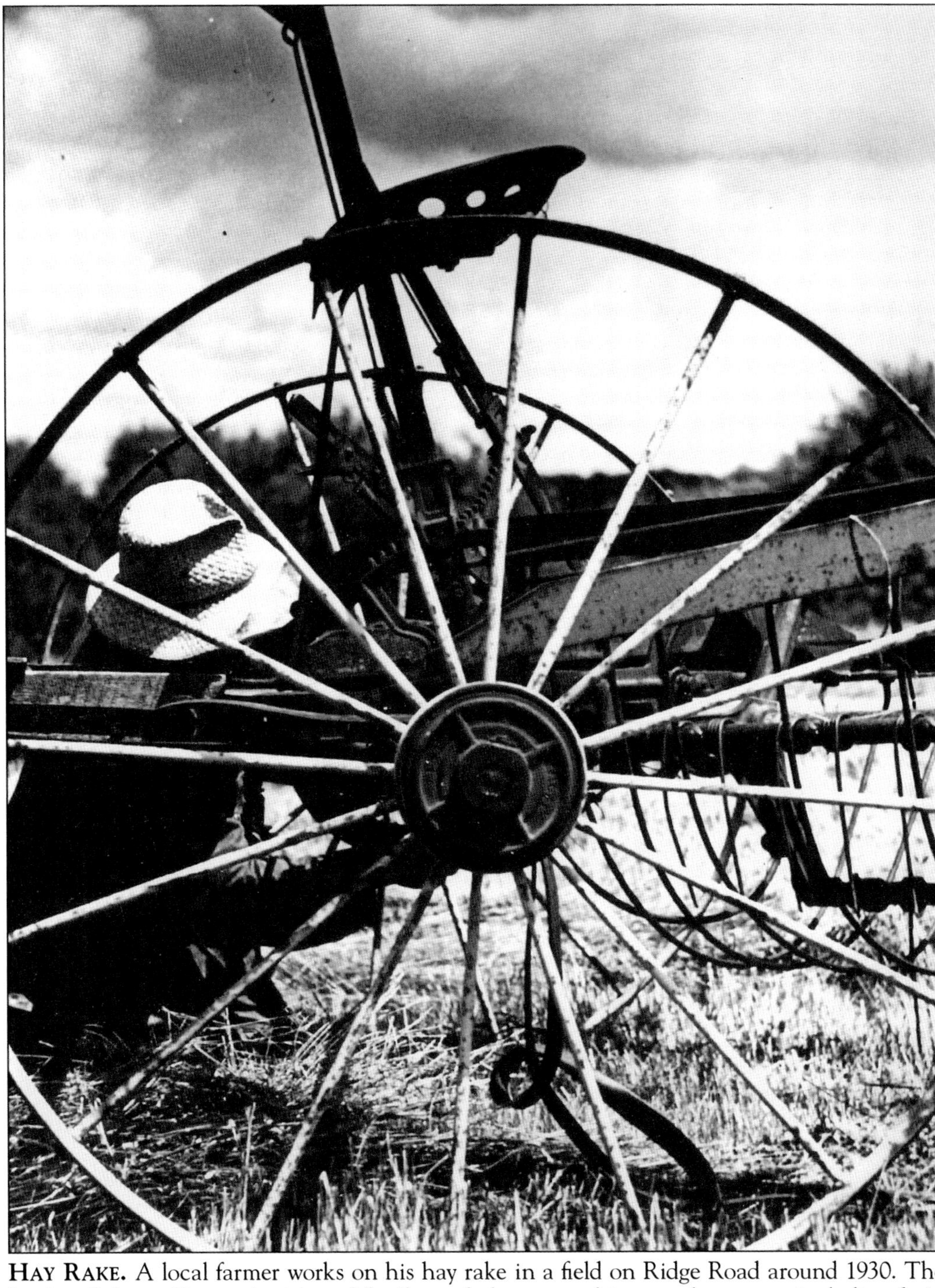

HAY RAKE. A local farmer works on his hay rake in a field on Ridge Road around 1930. The land in Orleans County is rich and fertile, and almost anything can be grown, including fruit, vegetables, and hay crops. (Courtesy of Tillman's Village Inn.)

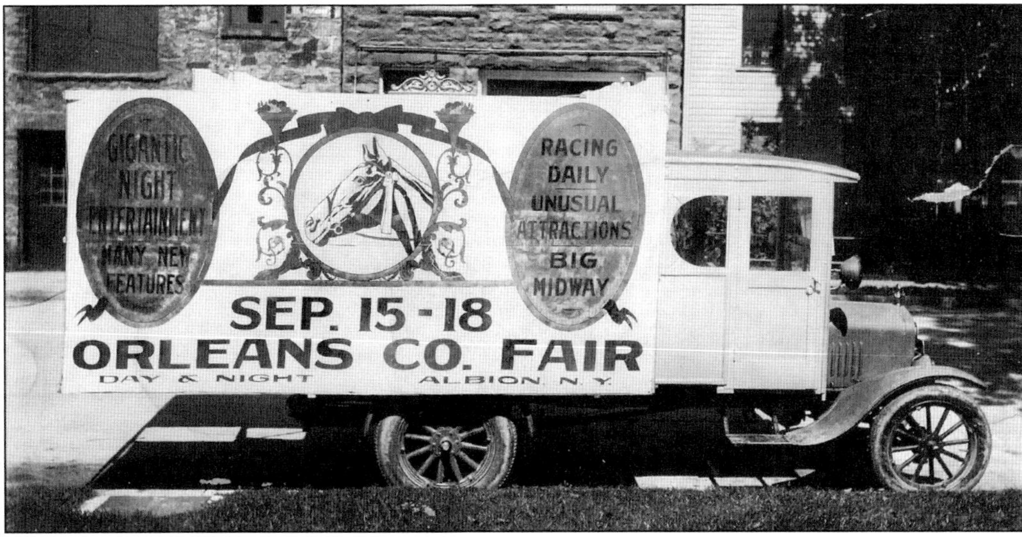

ANNOUNCING THE FAIR. A truck advertises the upcoming Orleans County Fair, September 15–18, around 1925. The sign inside the left oval reads, "Gigantic night entertainment. Many new features." The one in the right oval reads, "Racing daily. Unusual attractions. Big midway." The Orleans County Fair ran from 1856 to 1942 at the fairgrounds on West State Street. The fair ceased in 1942 with the advent of World War II. (Courtesy of Orleans County Department of History.)

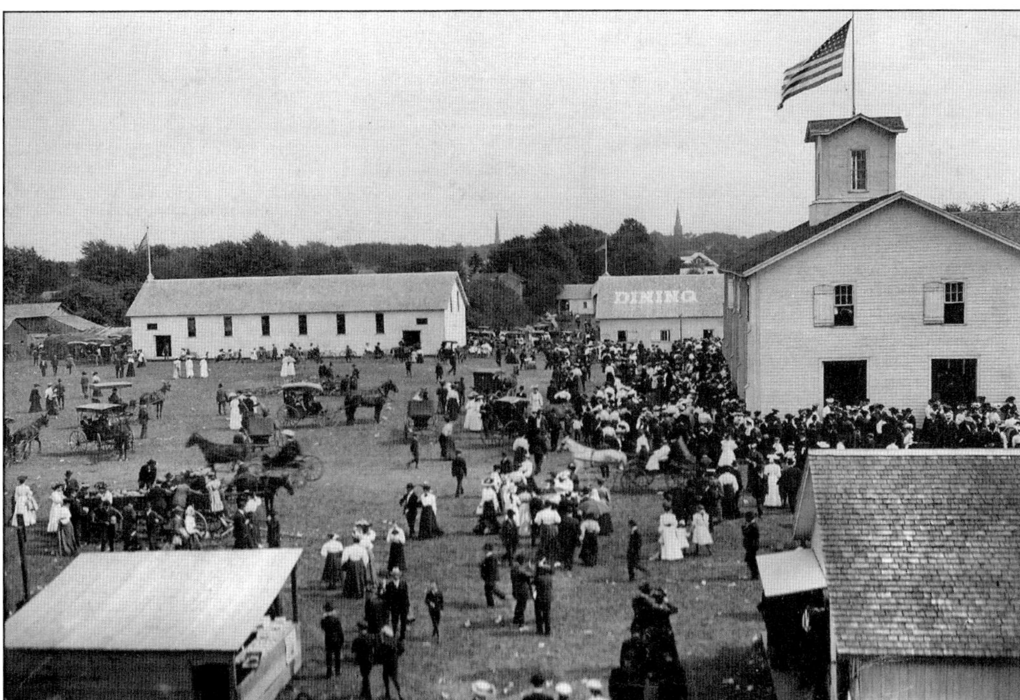

FAIR CROWDS. Crowds gather at the Orleans County Fair around 1910. Note the large dining building. The 63rd annual fair, in 1919, advertised horse races, a baseball game, and good band music. In 1928, there were four bands, a carnival, and a circus. (Courtesy of Orleans County Department of History.)

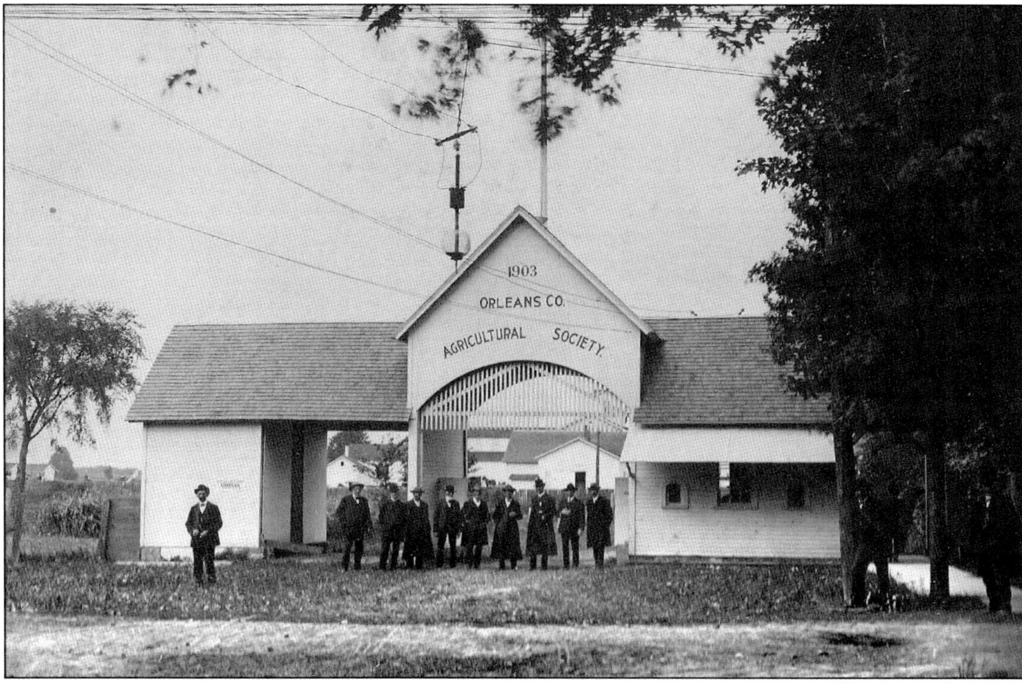

THE 1903 GATEHOUSE. Members of the Orleans County Agricultural Society stand outside the gatehouse and entrance to the Orleans County Fairgrounds, off King Street. In 1874, admission prices were individual 25¢, double-carriage team with driver 75¢, single horse and driver 50¢, and a horse with rider 40¢. (Courtesy of Orleans County Department of History.)

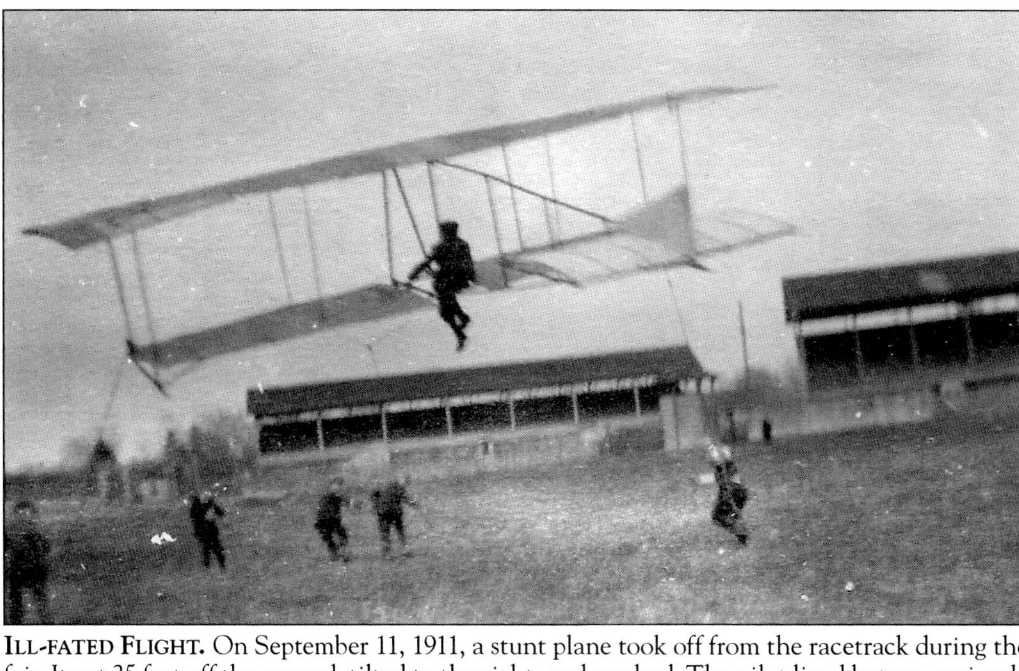

ILL-FATED FLIGHT. On September 11, 1911, a stunt plane took off from the racetrack during the fair. It got 25 feet off the ground, tilted to the right, and crashed. The pilot lived but was seriously injured. (Courtesy of Orleans County Department of History.)

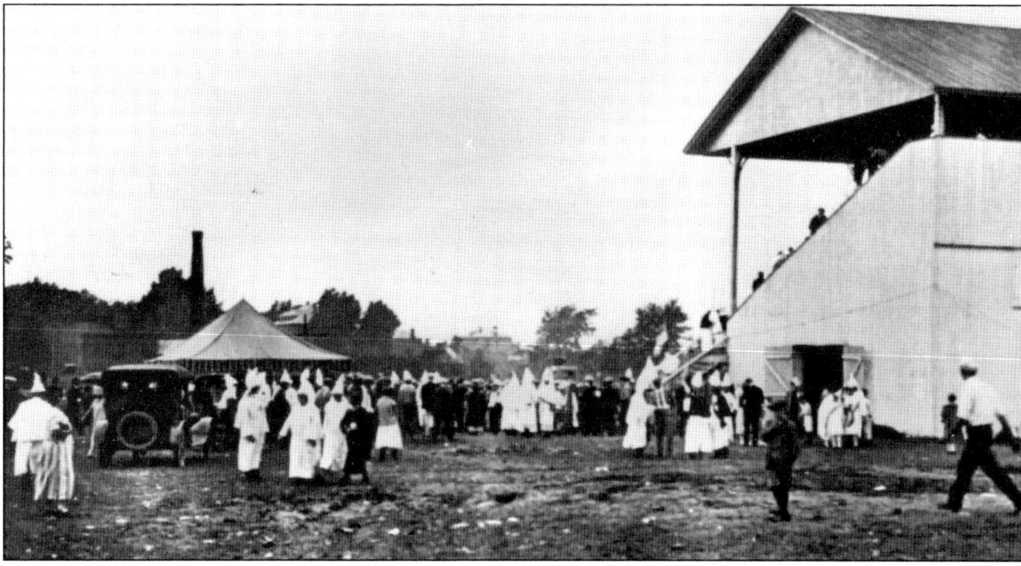

KLAN MEETING. A Ku Klux Klan rally was held at the Orleans County Fairgrounds in September 1925, and a large cross was burned at night. Albion was not the only town with Klan meetings. The Klan put on parades, complete with children dressed in white capes, all over New York State. (Courtesy of Tillman's Village Inn.)

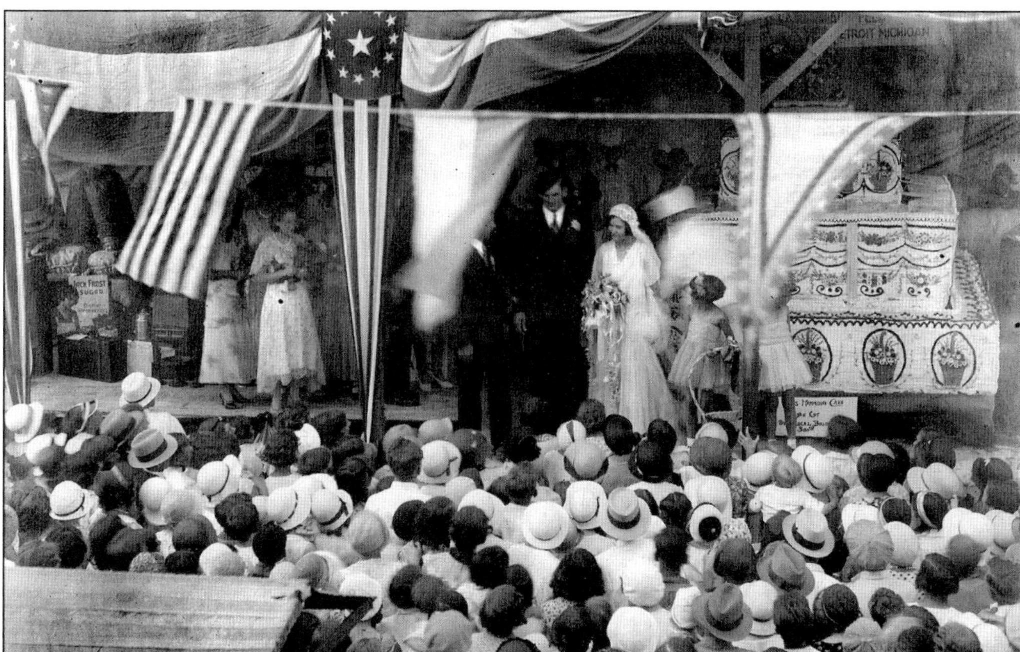

WORLD'S LARGEST WEDDING CAKE. This couple decided to marry at the Orleans County Fair and had the world's largest cake in 1931. That followed the world's largest pie, an apple pie crafted by blacksmith Joseph Dibley in 1929. The dough for the 3-ton pie was rolled out with the world's largest rolling pin, a 60-pound, 4-foot-long rolling pin, with 8-inch-long handles. The cake was made to celebrate the diamond jubilee of the fair. (Courtesy of Orleans County Department of History.)

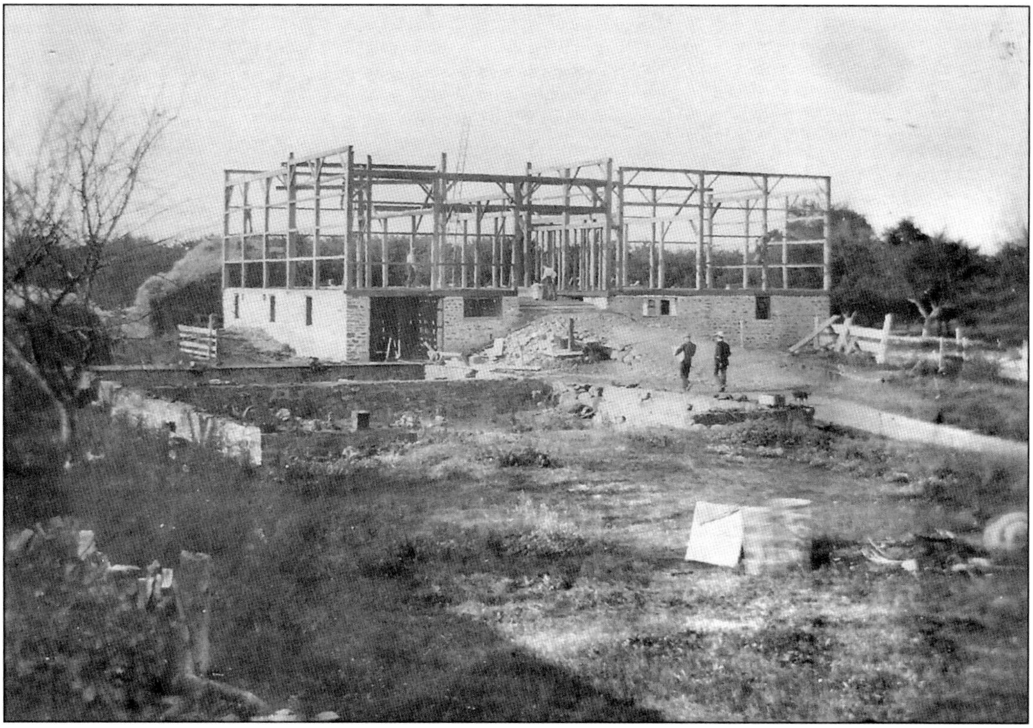

Barn Raising. This huge barn was constructed about 1880 at the Arnold Gregory Farm, on West County House Road. Years later, the Arnold Gregory Hospital was built with an endowment provided by Arnold Gregory. (Courtesy of Orleans County Department of History.)

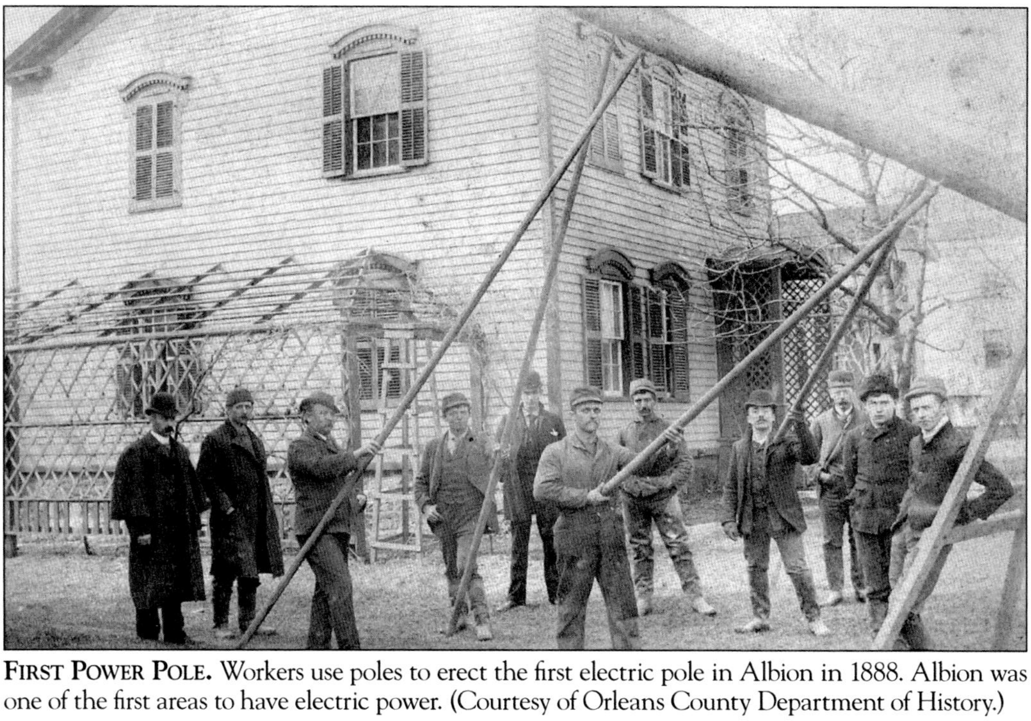

First Power Pole. Workers use poles to erect the first electric pole in Albion in 1888. Albion was one of the first areas to have electric power. (Courtesy of Orleans County Department of History.)

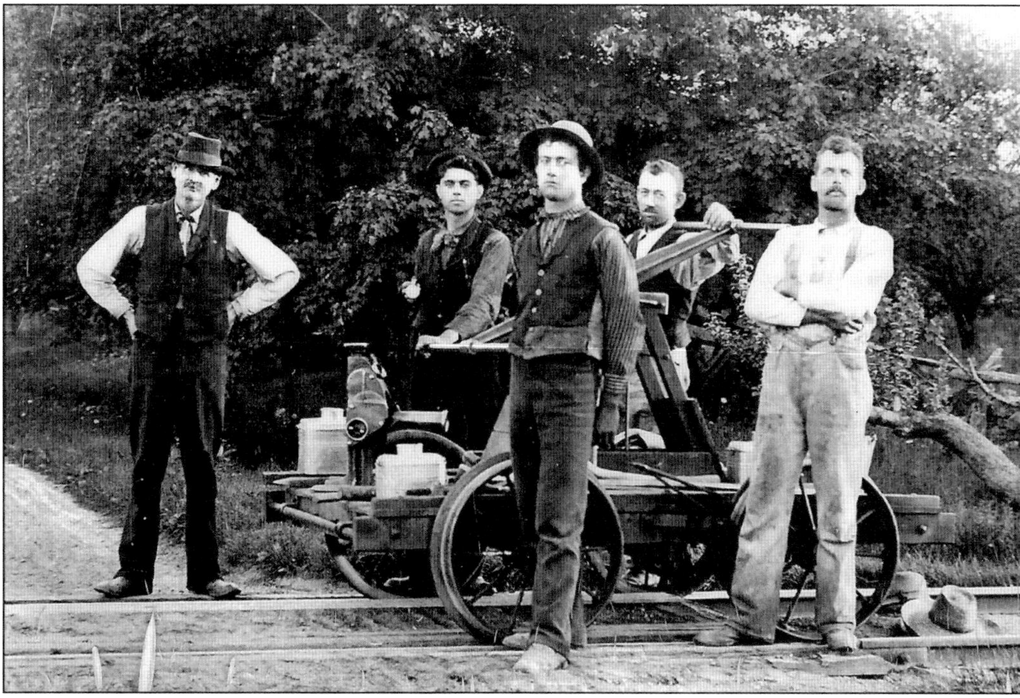

Working on the Railroad. A section gang poses for the camera around 1890 on the Hojack rail line. Note the lunch boxes on the front of the handcar. Apparently, a woman who left just before the photograph was taken had dropped off food for the workers' lunch. (Courtesy of Tillman's Village Inn.)

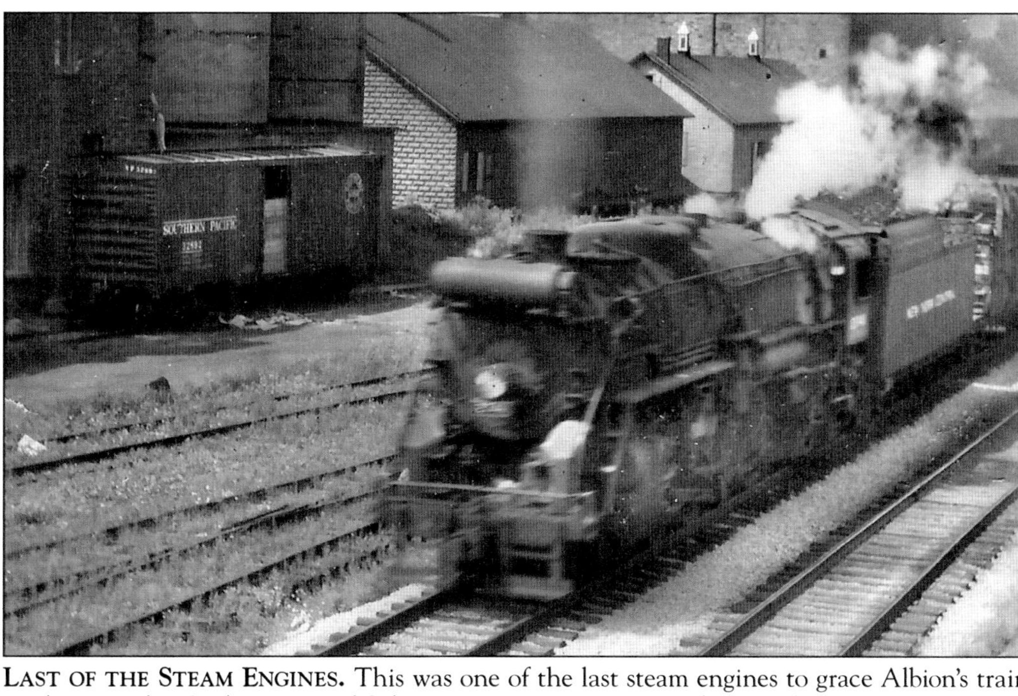

Last of the Steam Engines. This was one of the last steam engines to grace Albion's train tracks around 1950. (Courtesy of Orleans County Department of History.)

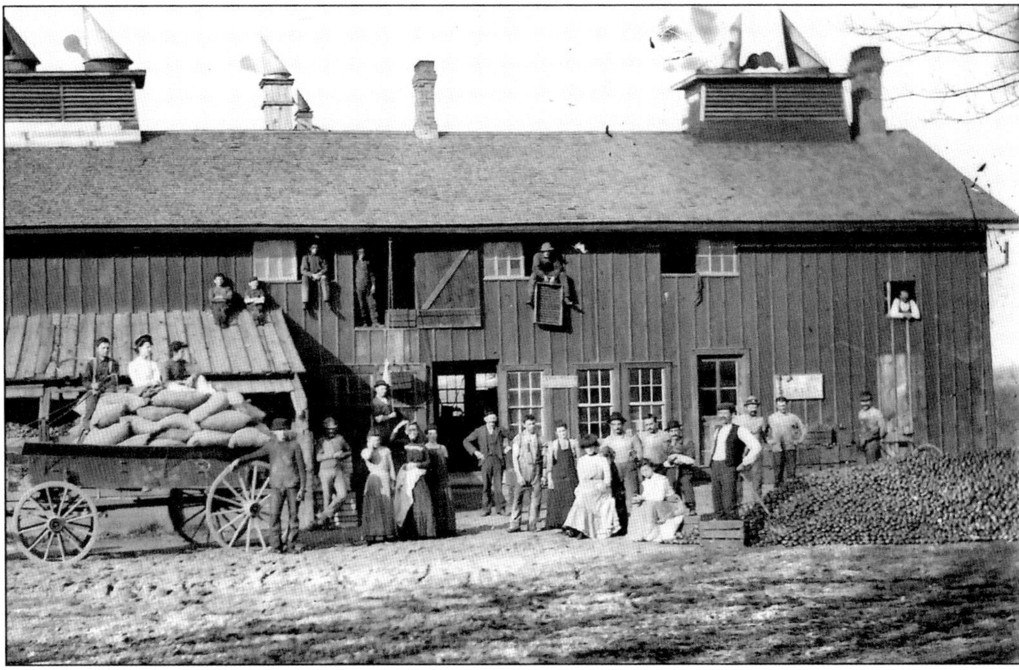

Dry House. Prior to canning factories, dry houses were abundant and provided seasonal work for women. People took their perishables to the dry house to have them dried and preserved. Also, the owner of a dry house often sold dried fruit in bulk to stores. (Courtesy of Orleans County Department of History.)

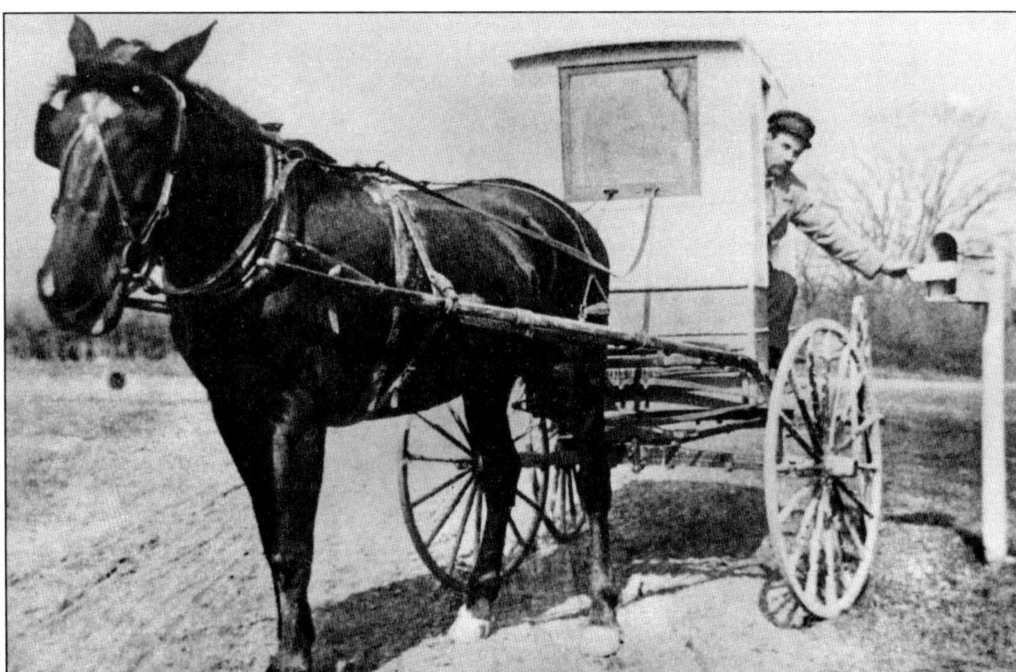

Mail Route. Mail is delivered by horse and buggy on a rural free delivery route in Albion's countryside around 1905. (Courtesy of Orleans County Department of History.)

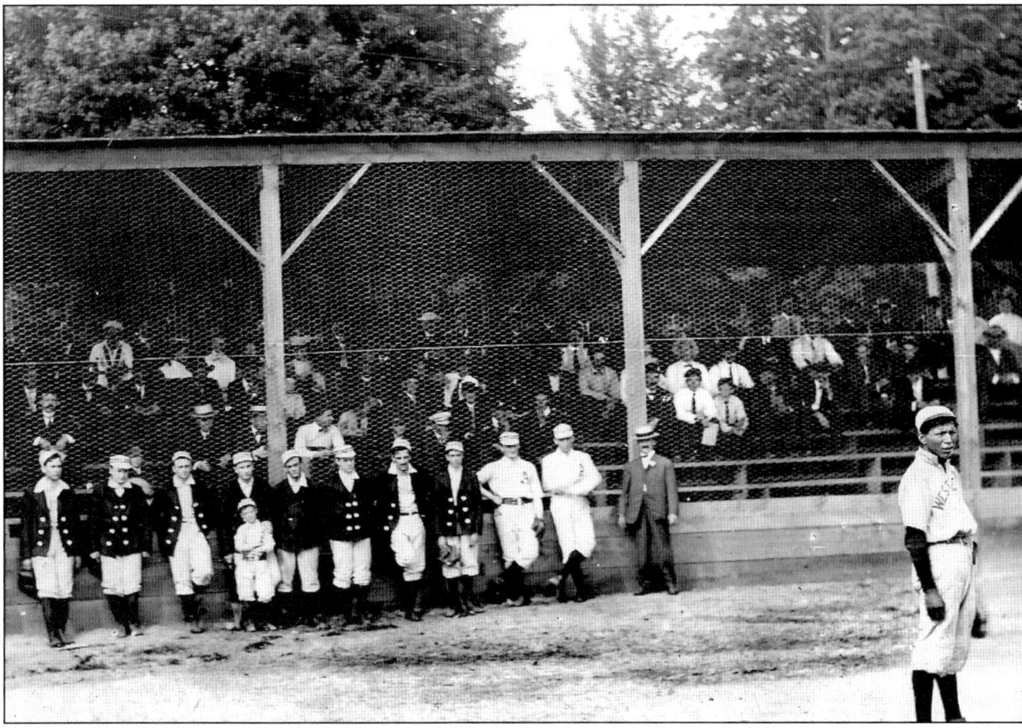

NEW BALLPARK. Players pose in front of the grandstand on their new ball diamond around 1900. The ballpark was located on the south side of Caroline Street, east of the intersection with Ingersoll Street. (Courtesy of Orleans County Department of History.)

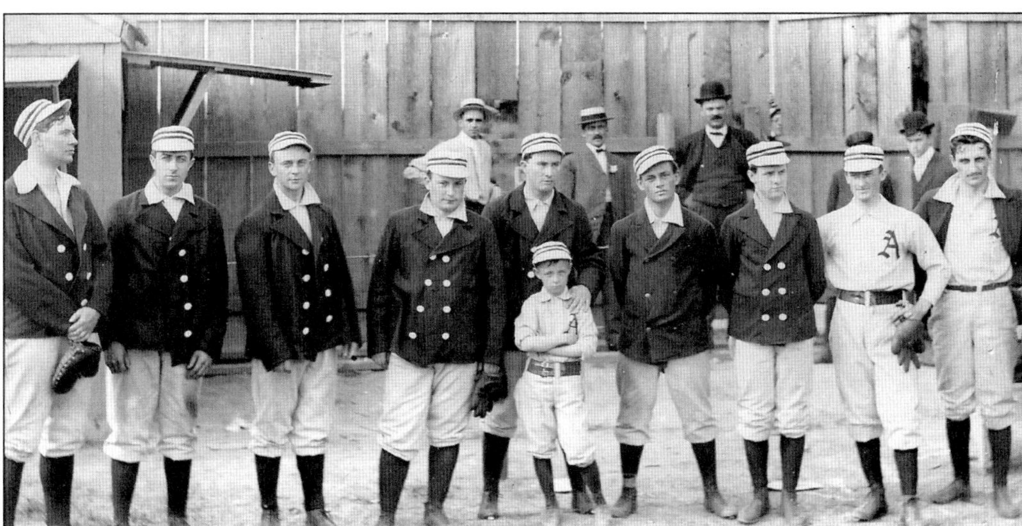

BALL TEAM AND MASCOT. Players pose in uniform in their ballpark around 1900. (Courtesy of Orleans County Department of History.)

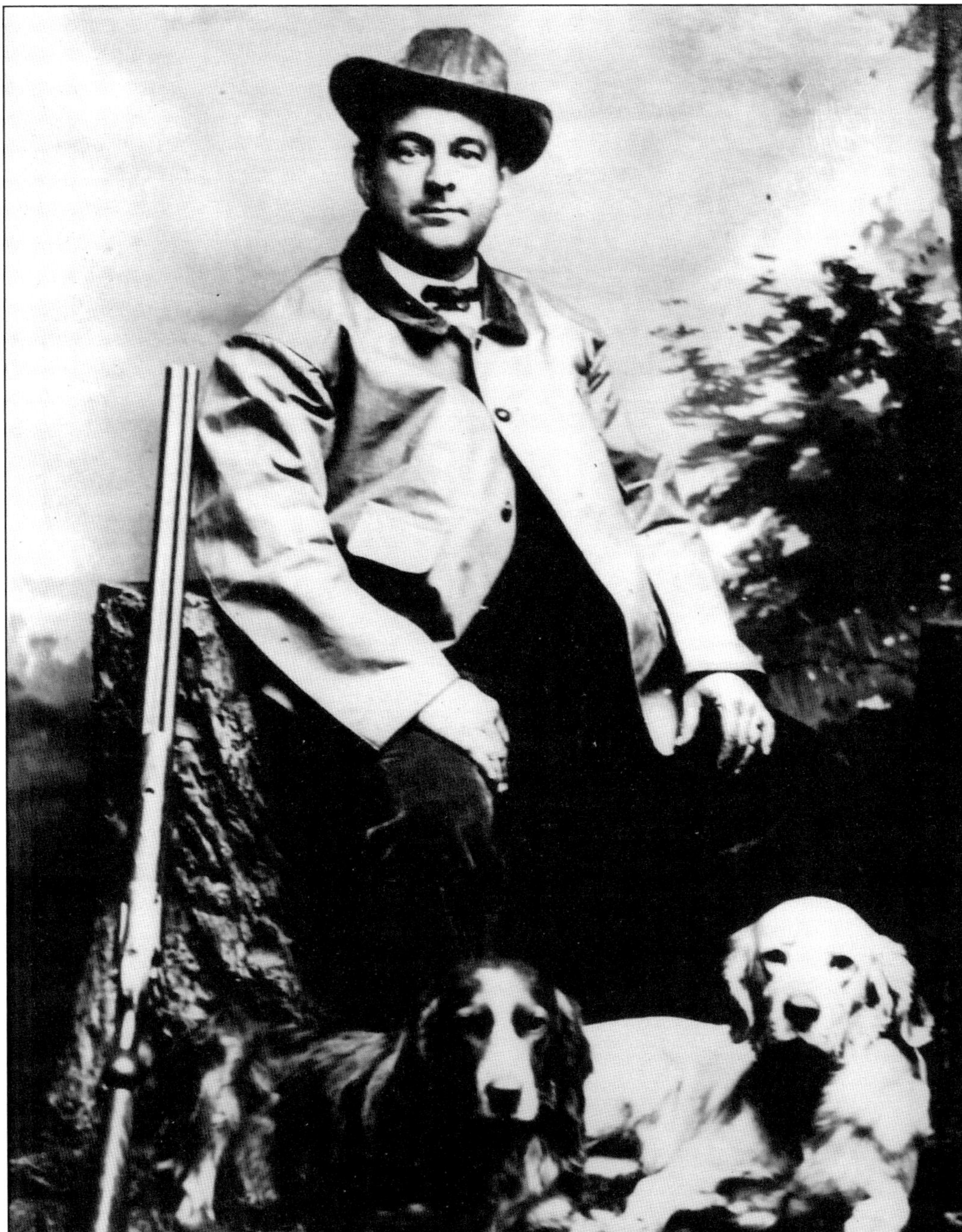

FORMAL PORTRAIT. Proud of his hunting abilities, George Lattin poses with his rifle and two hunting dogs around 1910. (Courtesy of Tillman's Village Inn.)

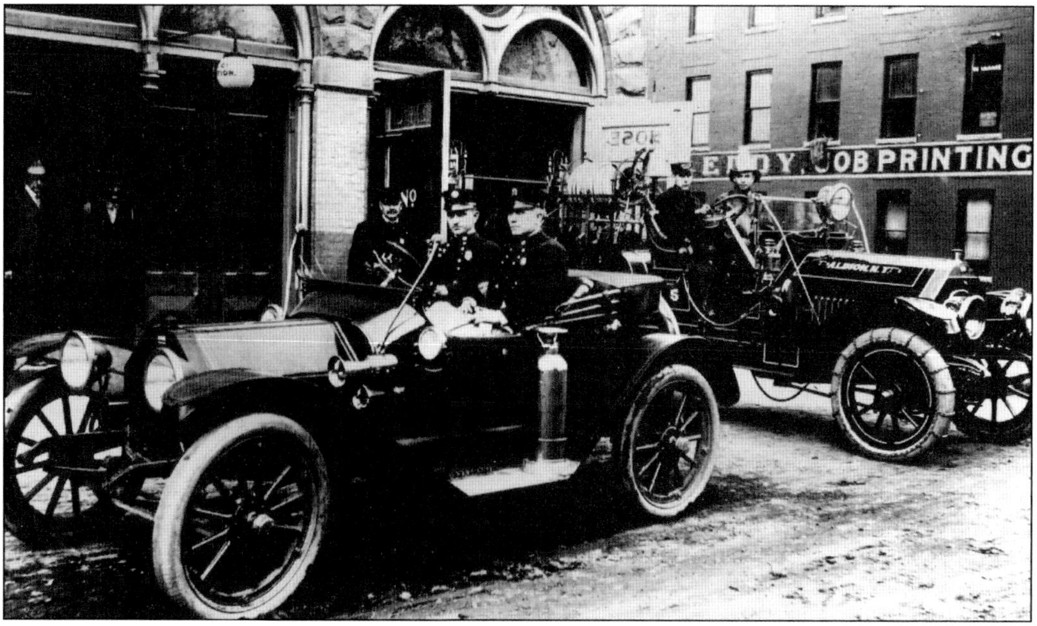

FIREFIGHTERS TO THE RESCUE. This 1912 photograph was taken outside the firehouse. The automobile is the fire chief's car, and the truck behind it is a chemical hose vehicle. (Courtesy of Mark Tillman.)

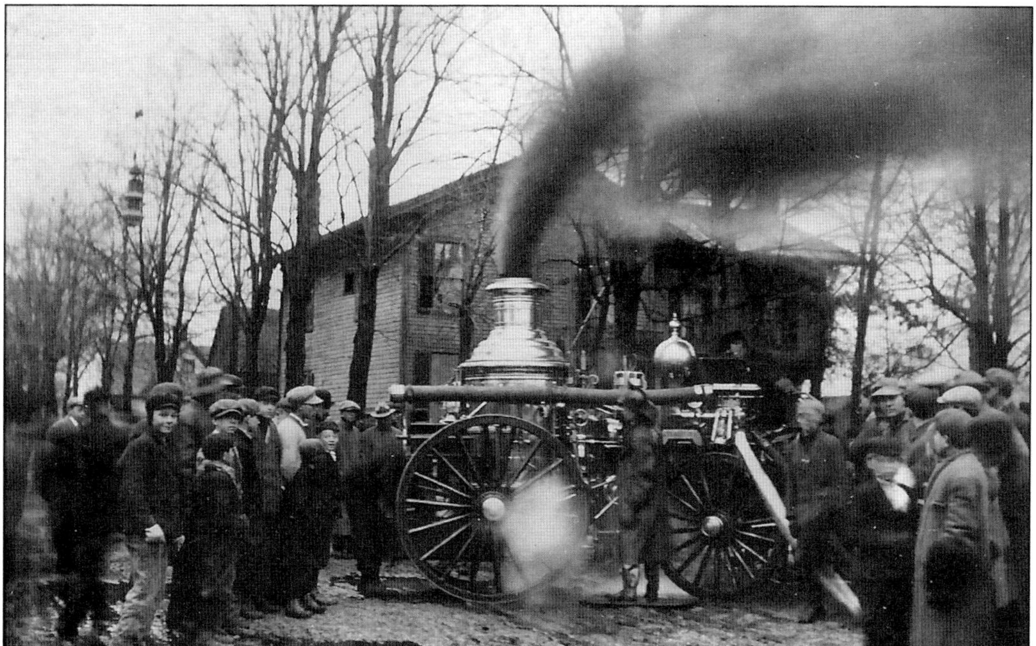

STEAM FIRE ENGINE. When this steam engine arrived in Albion shortly before the photograph was taken in 1910, the whole town came out to see how it worked. Steam engines replaced horse-drawn fire vehicles as the world became more mechanized. Horses were not completely out of the picture, however, until about 1920. (Courtesy of Orleans County Department of History.)

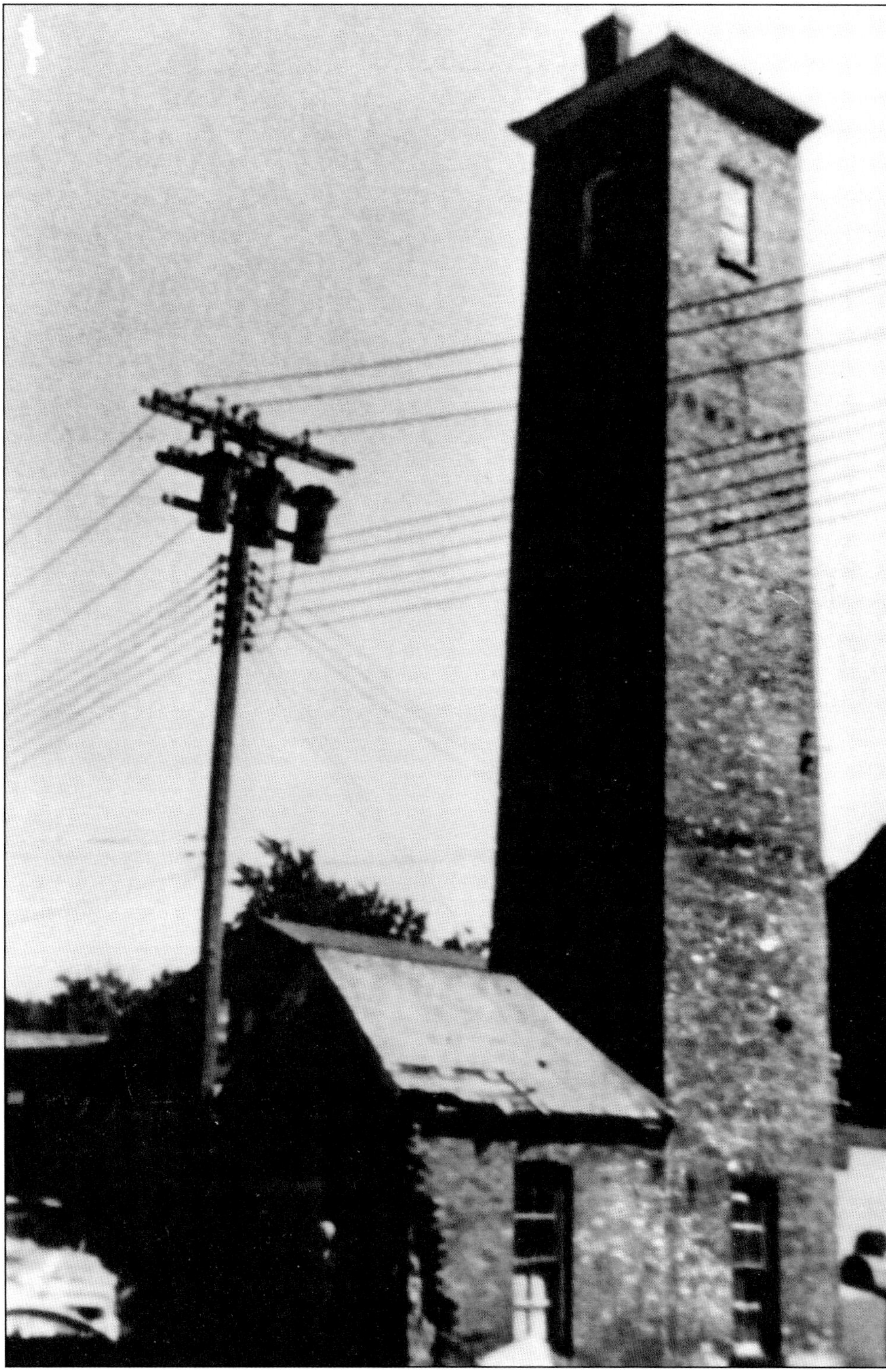

HOSE TOWER. The Albion Fire Department Hose Tower stood as a distinctive landmark from the time it was erected in 1882 until it was demolished in 1959. (Courtesy of Tillman's Village Inn.)

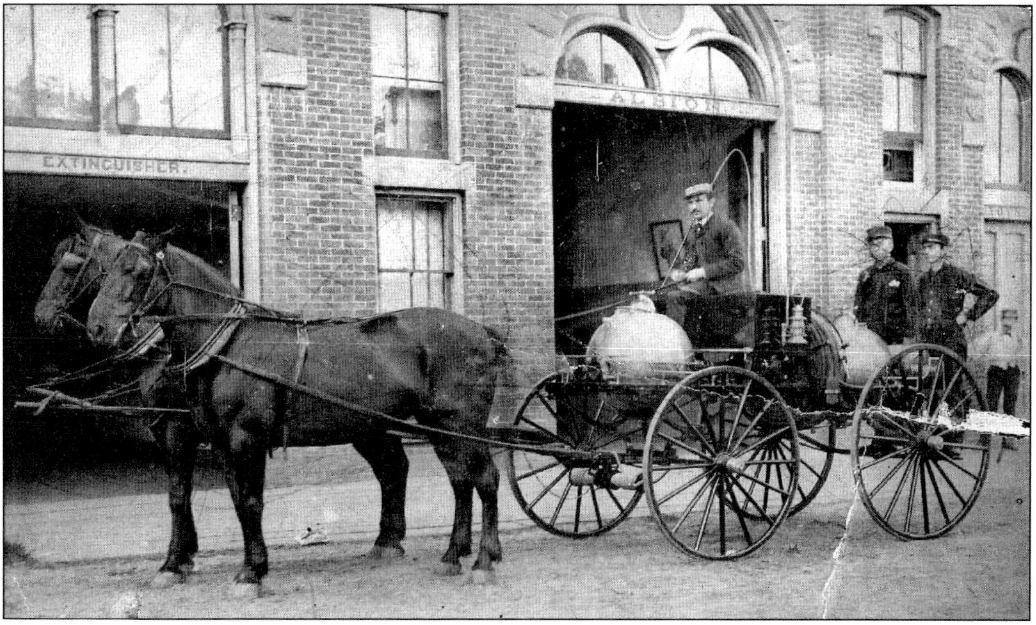

WARNER CHEMICAL TRUCK. Horses are used to pull fire equipment on February 12, 1899. From left to right are driver P. Sullivan, William Eggleston, and Mr. Graves. (Courtesy of Orleans County Department of History.)

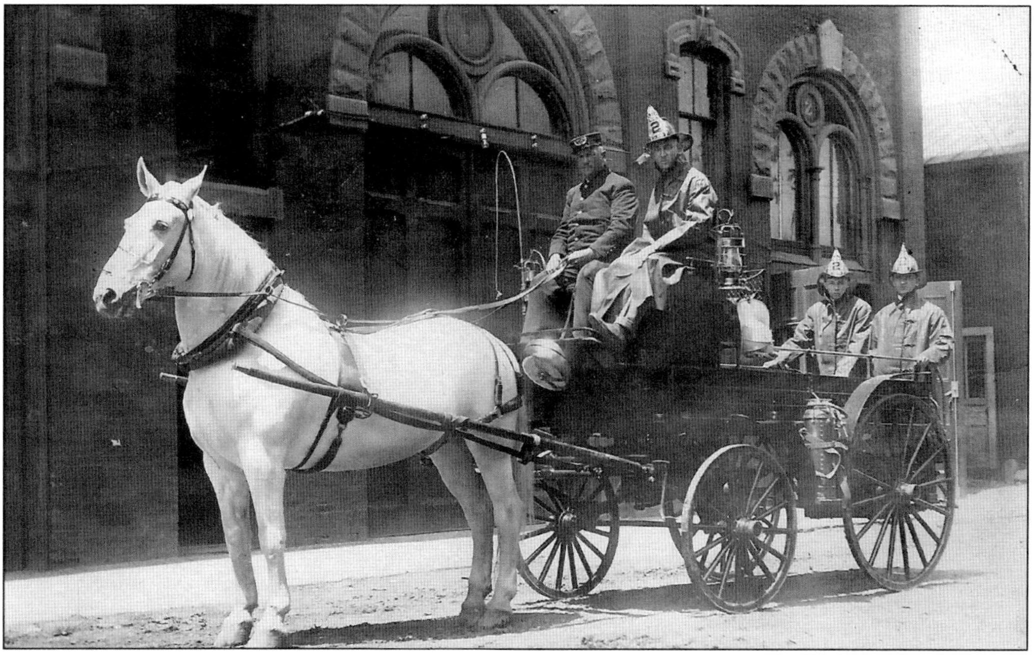

FIRE WAGON. A great white horse pulls four firemen on the wagon in 1909. From left to right are driver Fremont Herrick, John Donahue, Jimmie Downey, and Wallace Eggleston. (Courtesy of Orleans County Department of History.)

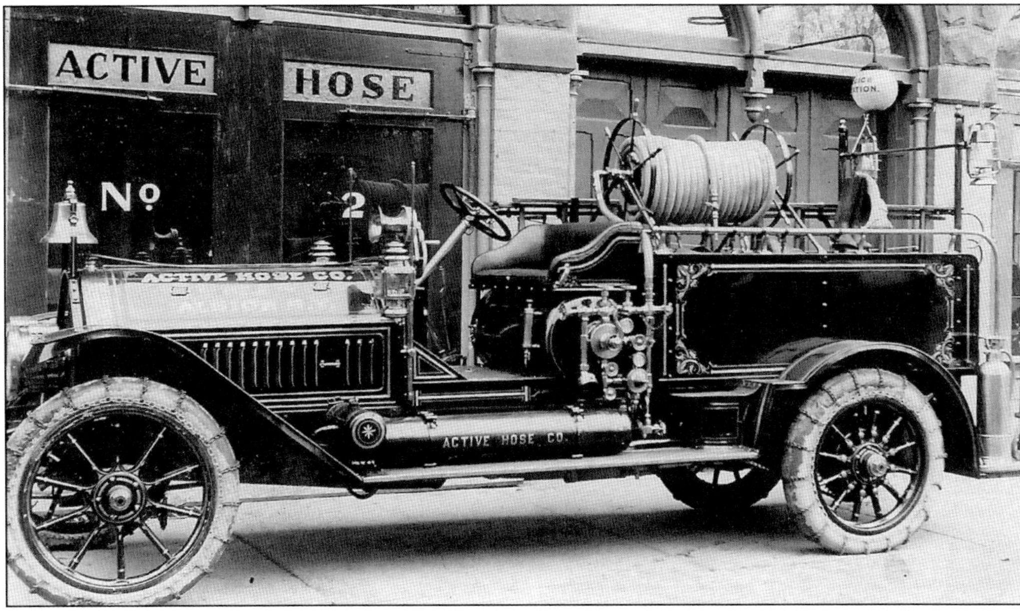

Replacing the Horse. A new truck sits outside the fire station sits around 1925. (Courtesy of Orleans County Department of History.)

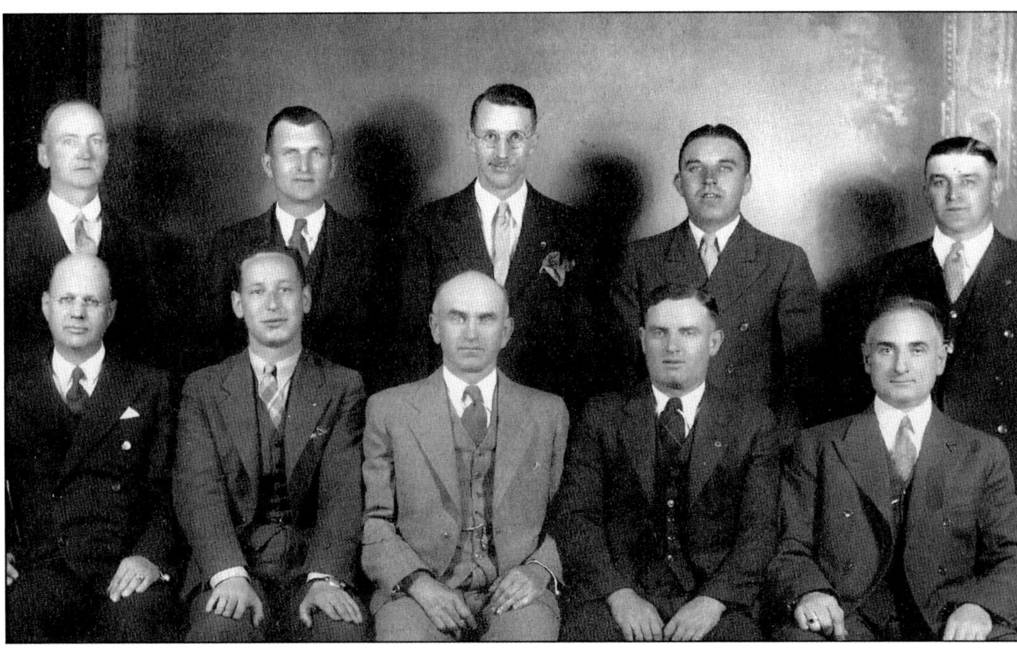

Firemen's Convention. In 1935, the general committee for the 36th convention of the Western New York Firemen consisted of, from left to right, the following: (first row) Harry Colburn, Stanley Landauer, J. Wallace Eggleston, Charles Irwin, and August Becker; (second row) Thomas McNally, Lewis Bloom, Clark Miller, Jack Breuilly, and Casimer Majewski. (Courtesy of Orleans County Department of History.)

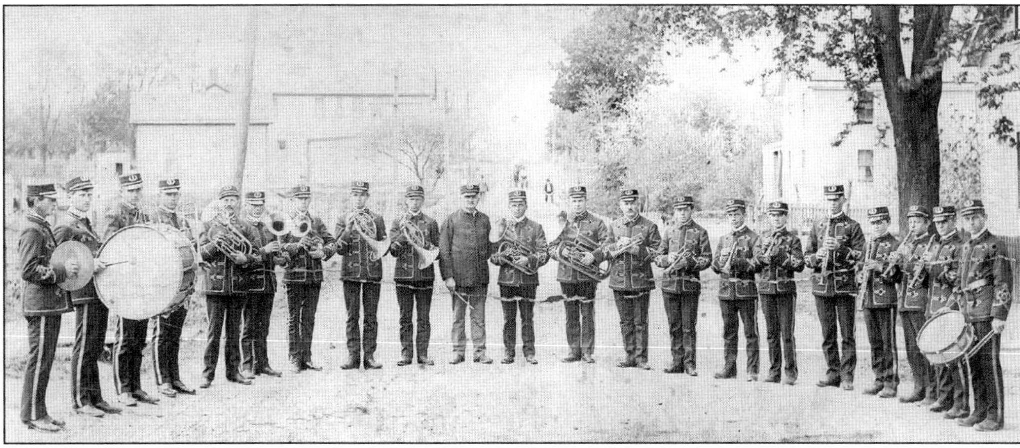

POLISH BAND. St. Mary's Church had its own Polish band, with uniforms of dark green accented with gold braid trim. Pictured in 1914 are, from left to right, ? Kaminski, ? Cichocki, C. Kaminski, John Button, August Major, Joe Wright, S. Rytowski, John Nayman, D. Jaworski, ? Reynolds (bandmaster), T. Zwifka, James Kaniecki, Ignatius Rice, Stanley Rice, Frank Furmanski, Frank Smith, Alex Rytlewski, Frank Bloom, Frank Jaworski, T. Jasnieski, and Max Warlawski. (Courtesy of Orleans County Department of History.)

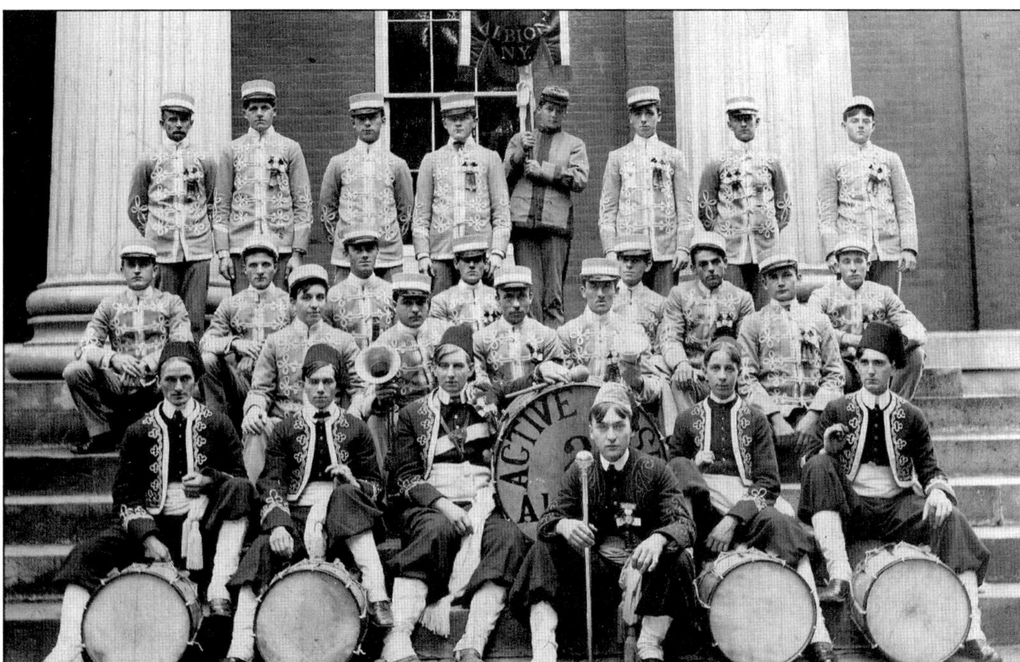

ALBION ACTIVE HOSE BAND. Pictured in 1902 are, from left to right, the following: (first row) Homer Galarneau, Walter Brown, Homer Heady, George Dhoman, Jesse English, and Dan Dugan; (second row) James English, John Wilson, Charles Kippendall, Ed Sullivan, and Arthur Nixon; (third row) Wallace Eggleston, Jay Doolittle, Thomas Neary, Owen Dickson, Robert Van Stone, Charles Terrill, and Joseph Dibley; (fourth row) William Ireland, Fred Sitzer, Henry Swartz, Ed Slattery, Herbert Hall, Leonard Simpson, Wallace Griswold, and William Miller. (Courtesy of Orleans County Department of History.)

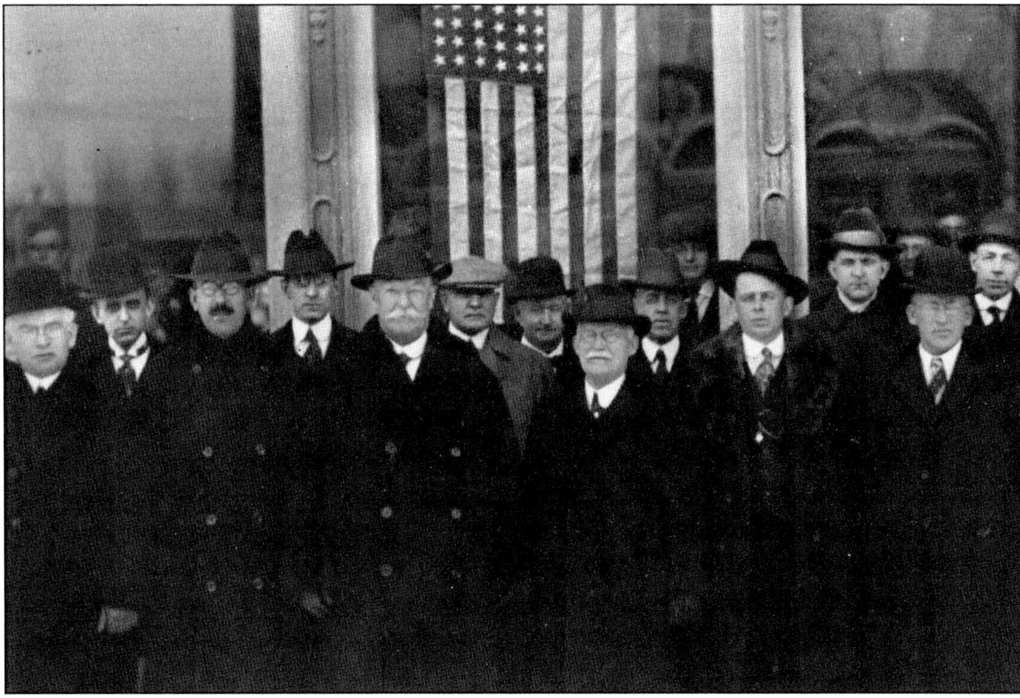

William Howard Taft. In 1920, William Howard Taft (fifth from the left, with the white mustache) visited Albion. He was campaigning, urging the country to support Pres. Woodrow Wilson in his proposed Covenant of the League of Nations. (Courtesy of Orleans County Department of History.)

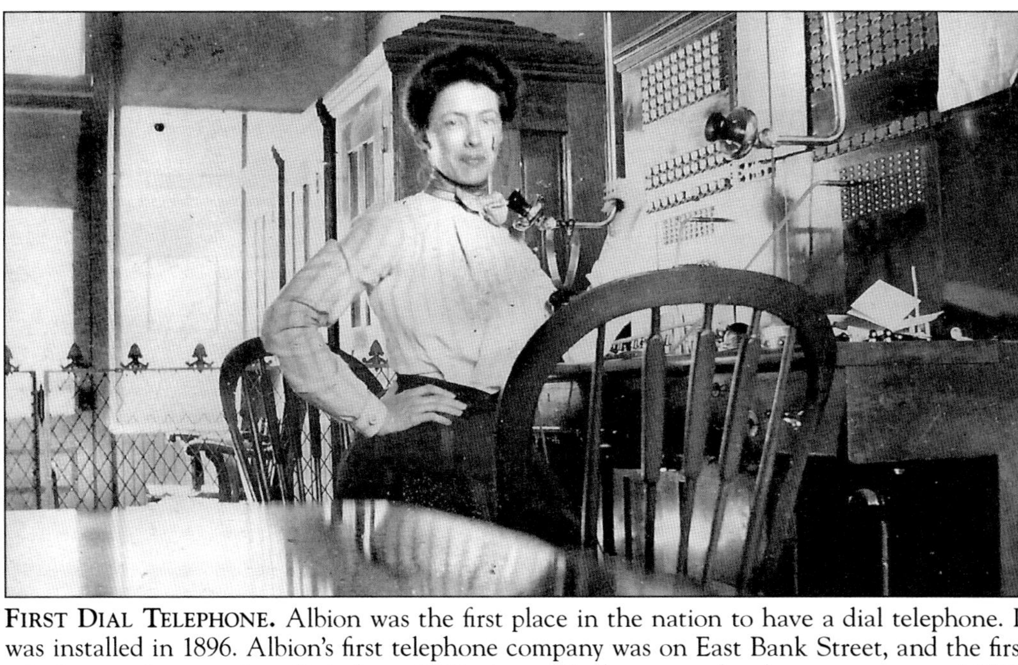

First Dial Telephone. Albion was the first place in the nation to have a dial telephone. It was installed in 1896. Albion's first telephone company was on East Bank Street, and the first telephone poles were installed about 1880. Anna Hughes poses for the camera around 1910. (Courtesy of Orleans County Department of History.)

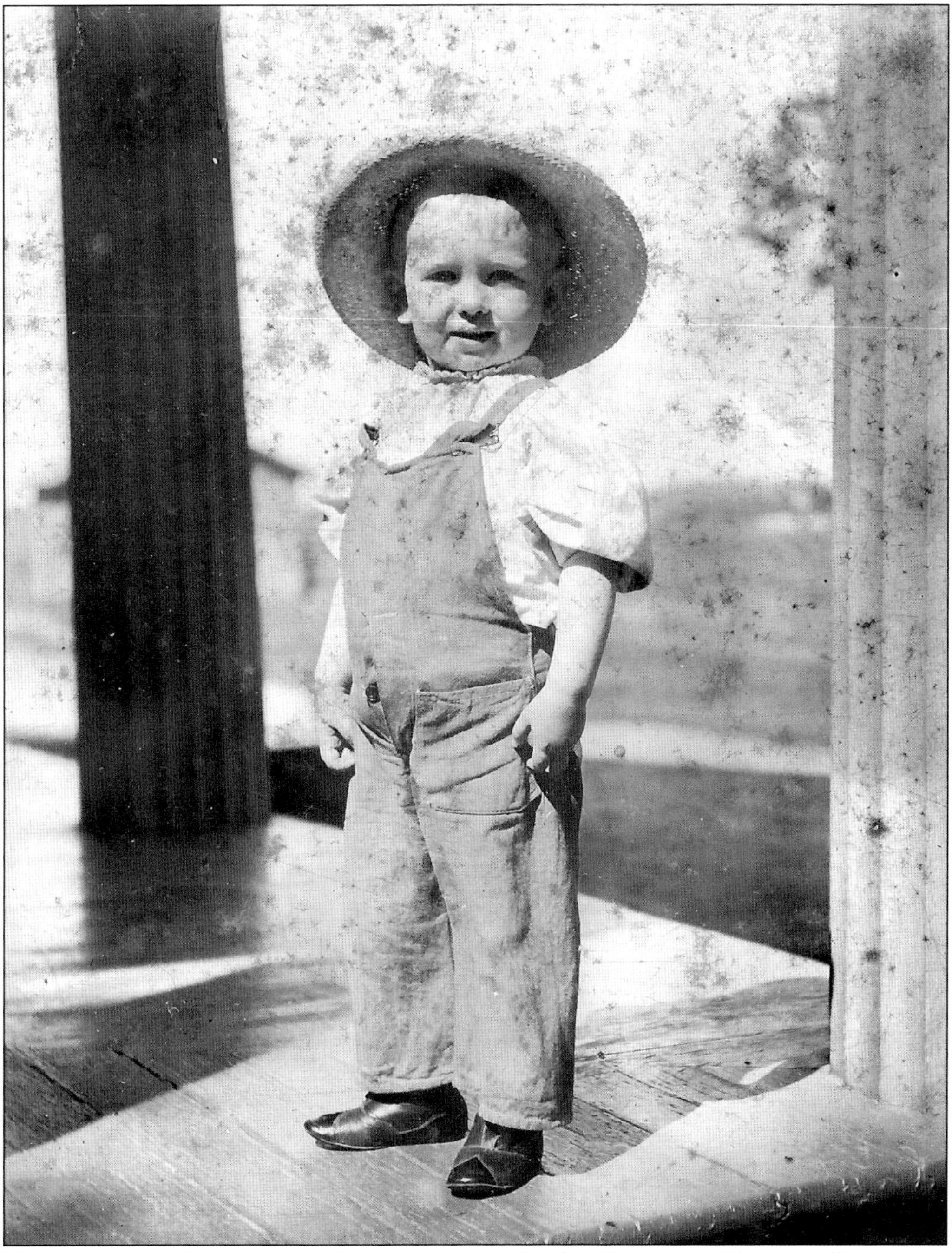

YOUNG SANTA. No one knew that two-year-old Charles Howard would eventually grow up to be Albion's own Santa and create a campus for the one and only Santa Claus School. The school opened in 1936 and not only trained men to be Santa but also handled the cleaning of Santa's clothing and elf clothes from all over the United States. Uniforms, wigs, and beards were manufactured here, and in 1956, Christmas Park—a mini–North Pole, complete with rides, toys, and reindeer—opened to the public. The park lasted until 1965. (Courtesy of Orleans County Department of History.)

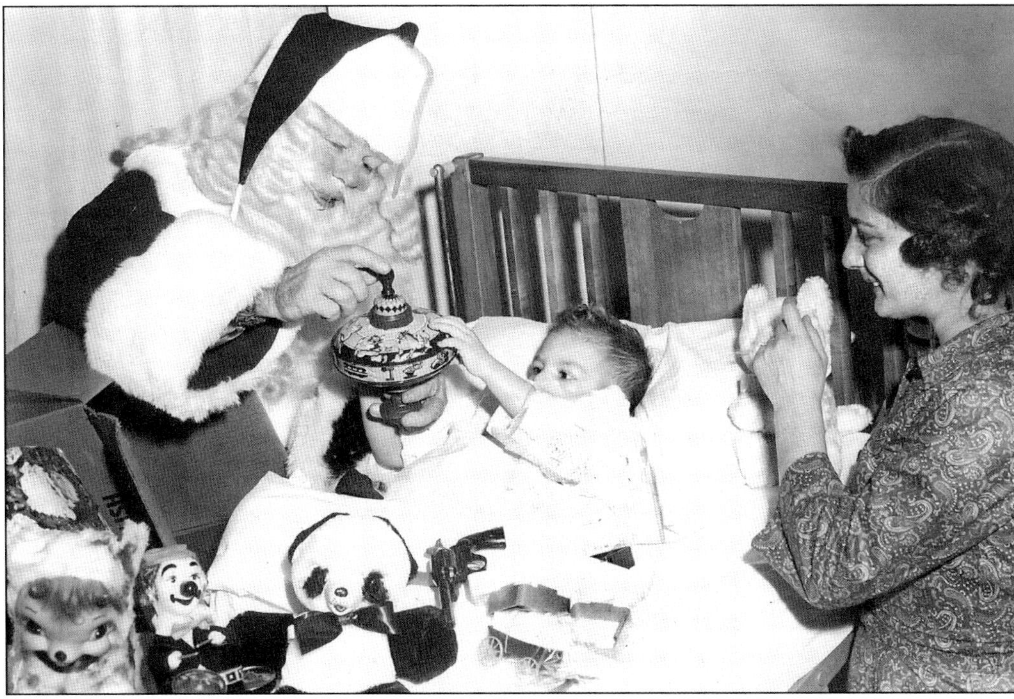

VISITING THE SICK. Albion's own Santa visits with Paul Reiferson and his mother at Buffalo Children's Hospital in December around 1955. (Courtesy of Orleans County Department of History.)

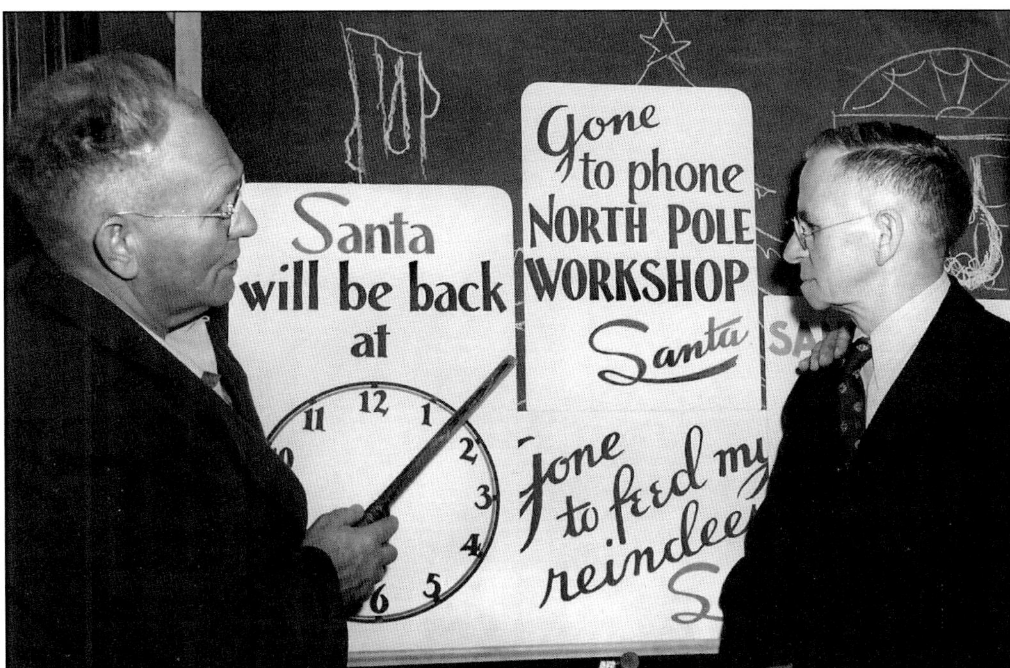

TEACHING SANTA. Charles Howard (left), without his Santa costume, shows Horace Bird various signs to use when department store Santas take a break. (Courtesy of Orleans County Department of History.)

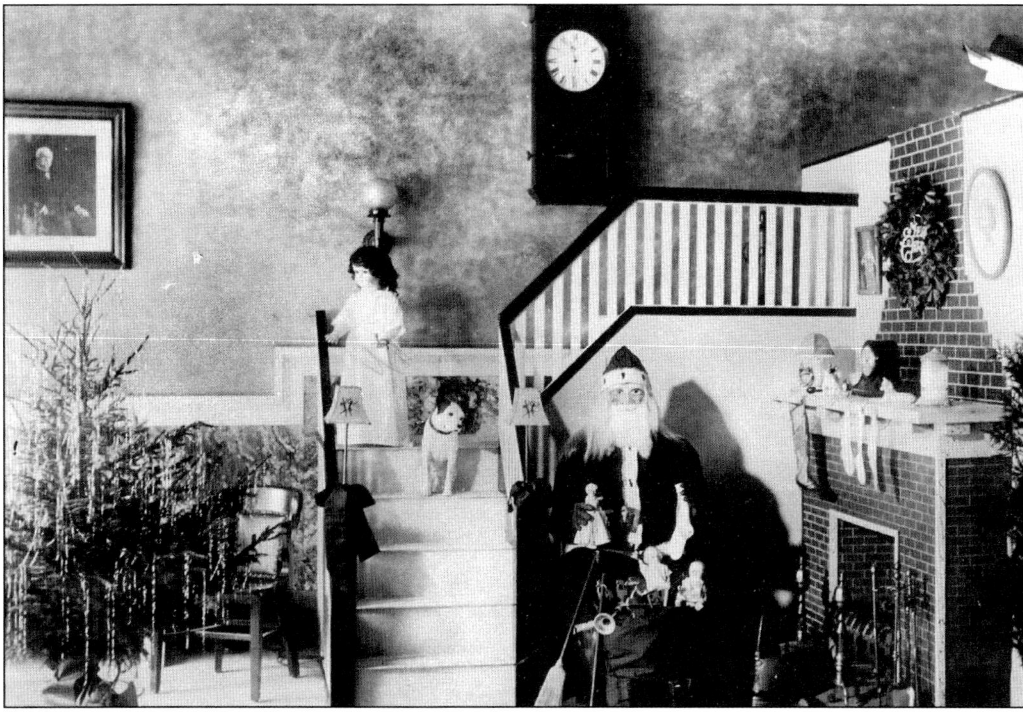

CHRISTMAS DISPLAY. Prior to the Santa Claus School, Charles Howard provided colorful displays at various businesses throughout Albion. This one, around 1928, was in the former Citizens Bank building, which is now the Albion Visitor's Center. (Courtesy of Orleans County Department of History.)

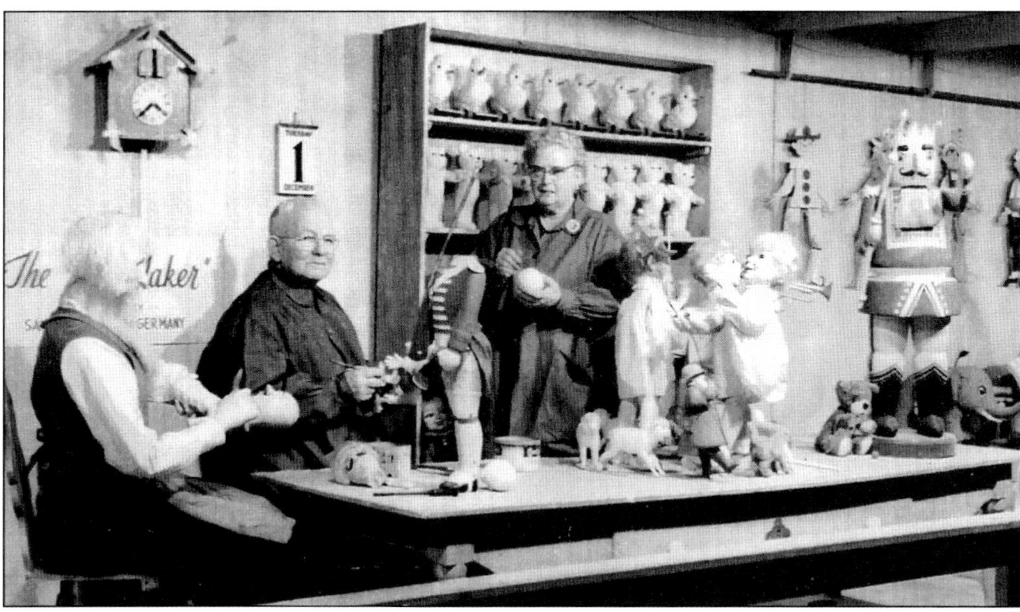

POSTCARD TO FRIENDS. Charles Howard and his wife, Ruth, mailed this postcard to friends in 1960. On the back of the card, the Howards asked people to guess who the dummy was. Many of the items they sold were imported from Germany. (Courtesy of C. W. Lattin.)

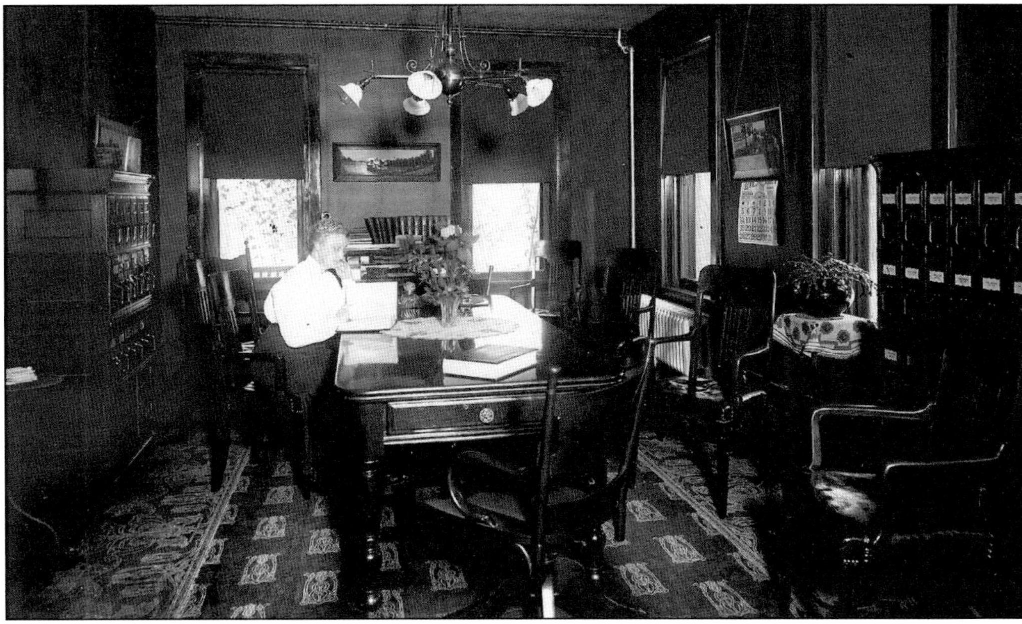

LADIES' PRISON SUPERINTENDENT. Miss Curtin, superintendent, sits at a desk in the Western House of Refuge for Women, Albion's reformatory for wayward women aged 16 to 30. There were many buildings for the inmates, whose fate lay with their crime. This photograph was taken in 1915. Today the facility is known as the Albion Correctional Facility. (Courtesy of Orleans County Department of History.)

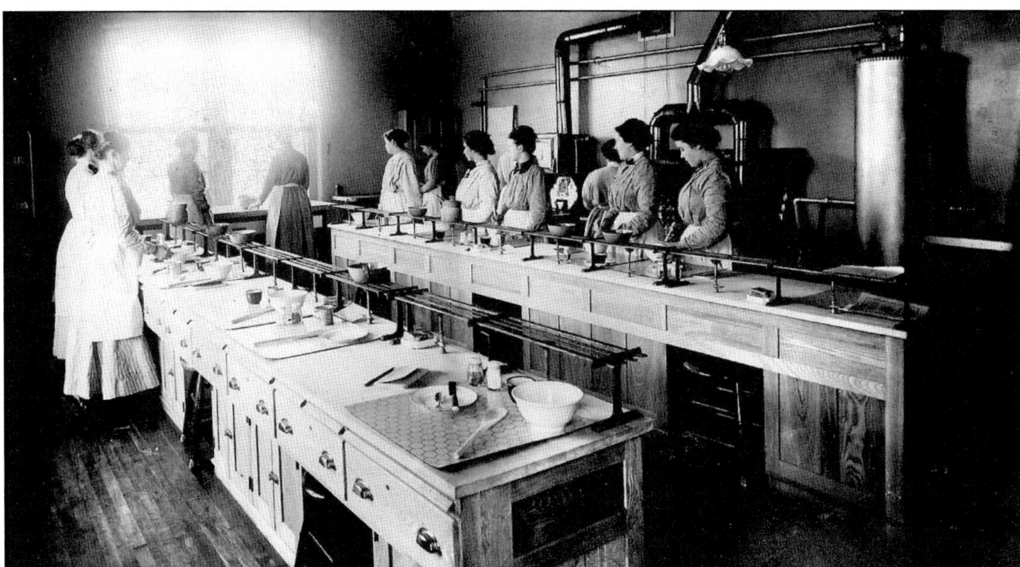

HOME ECONOMIC CLASS. In 1915, young women learn how to cook and clean in the Domestic Science Room at Albion's House of Refuge so that when they are released, they can work in households as maids and housekeepers. The room was very modern for its time, with gas burners on the counters and a coal range in the back. The facility became the Albion State Training School in 1923 and, eventually, the Albion Correctional Facility. (Courtesy of Orleans County Department of History.)

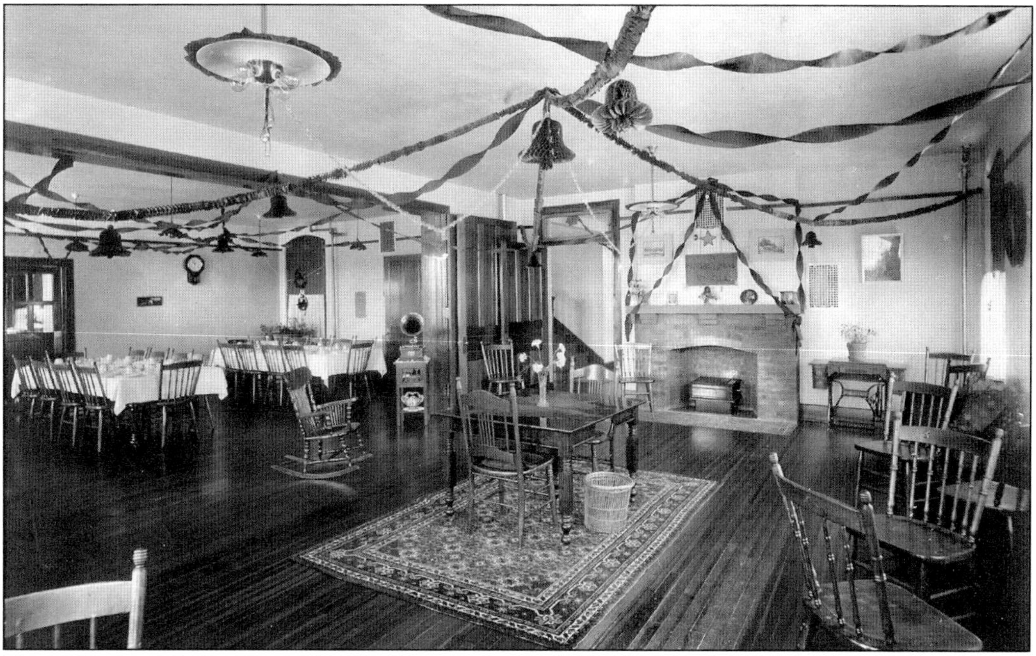

The Honors Cottage. This building was used for the best-behaved inmates, and it was considered an honor to be allowed to enjoy this room. Note the Victrola to the left of the center dining room table and the decorative streamers on the ceiling—preparations for a party. (Courtesy of Orleans County Department of History.)

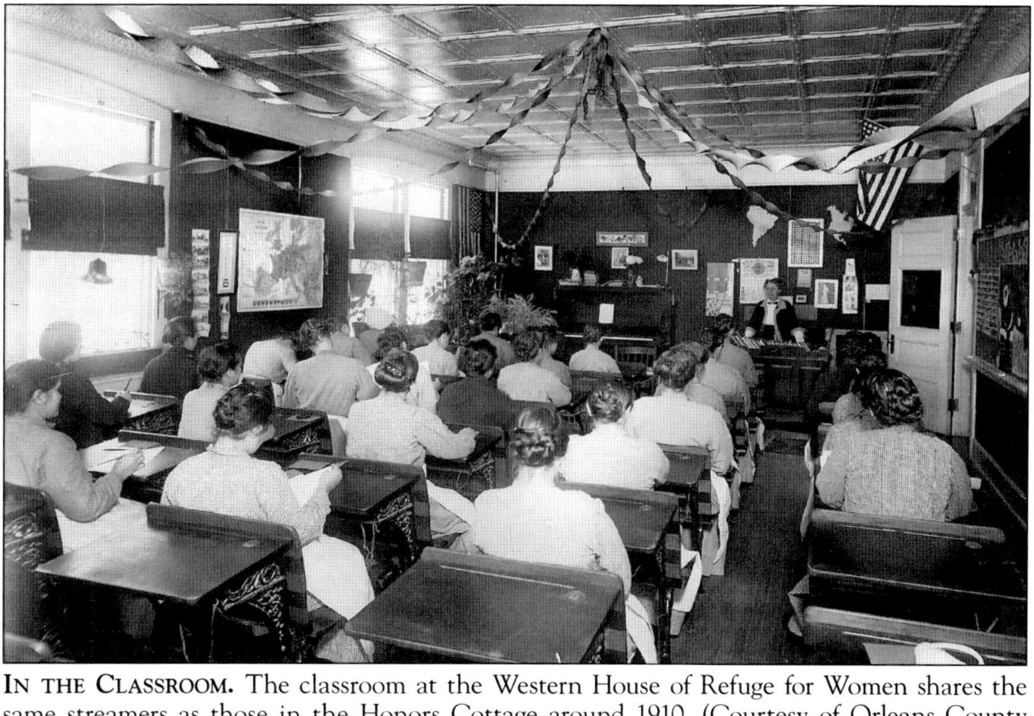

In the Classroom. The classroom at the Western House of Refuge for Women shares the same streamers as those in the Honors Cottage around 1910. (Courtesy of Orleans County Department of History.)

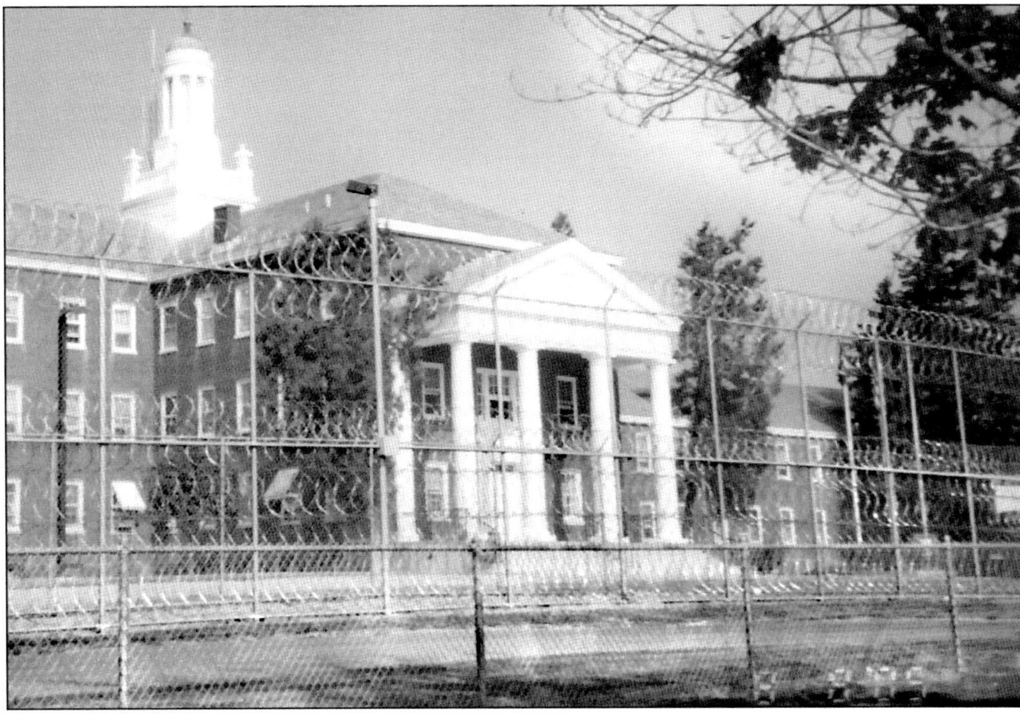

Albion Correctional Facility. Albion was a pioneer in the women's reformatory movement. Starting as the Women's House of Refuge, it was a rehabilitation center for drug addicts in the 1960s, a community preparation center for men in the 1970s, a coed facility in the 1980s, and is a general confinement facility for women today. Its most recent famous inmate was Amy Fisher, "the Long Island Lolita."

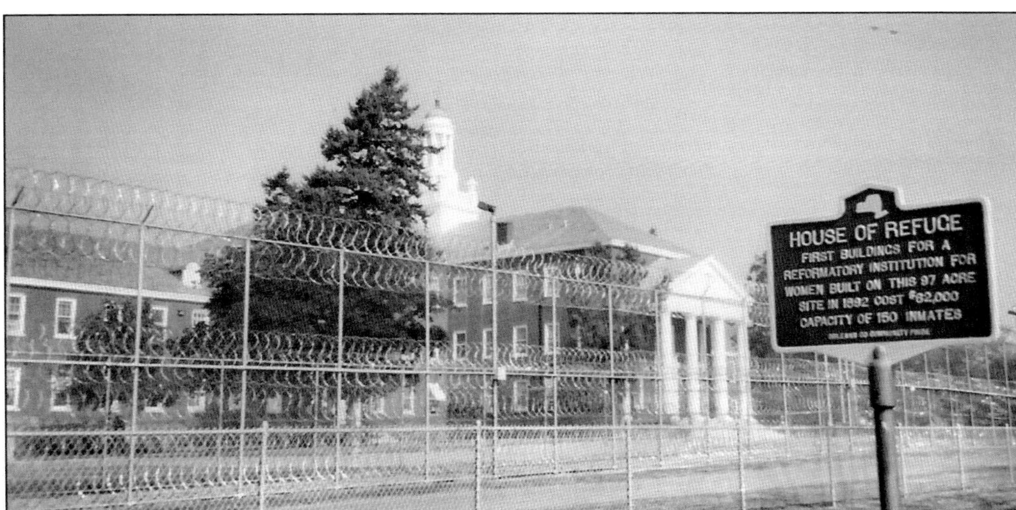

Former House of Refuge. Except for three rows of barbed wire, numerous electric lights, and an armed guard at the entrance gate, people would mistake this elegant building for a college. The sign explains that the "first buildings for a reformatory institution for women built on this 97 acre site in 1892 cost $62,000." The original building held 150 inmates. Now the complex can house 1,500 women.

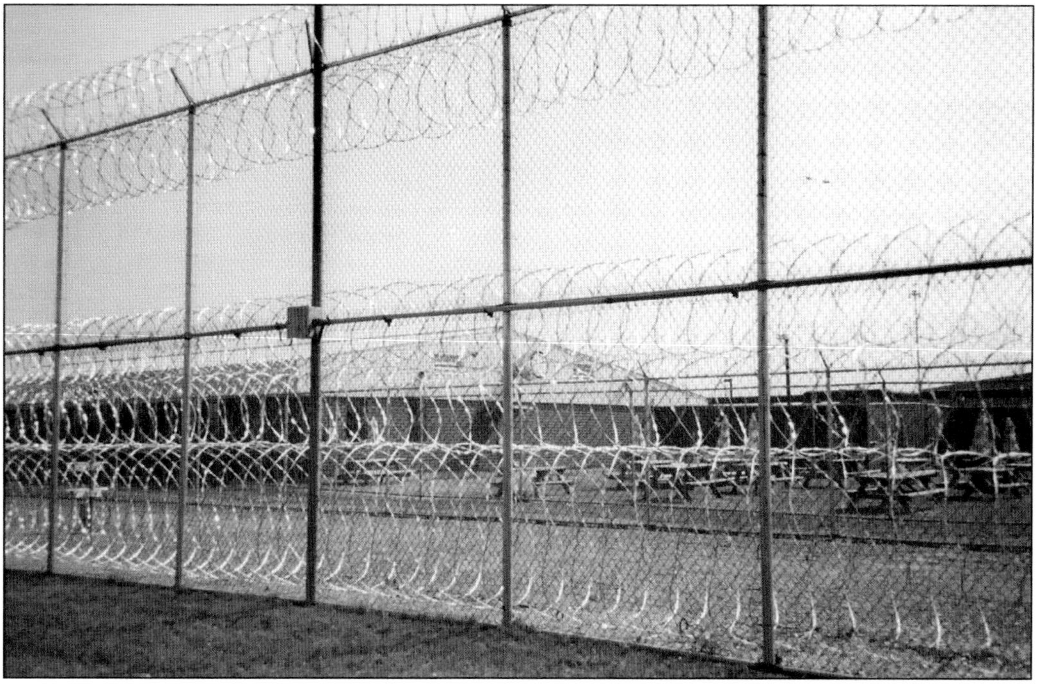

ORLEANS CORRECTIONAL FACILITY. After the Albion Correctional Facility ceased to be coed, a men's prison was constructed on 45 acres of land adjacent to the women's prison, facing Gaines-Basin Road. Erected as a 542-bed, 11-building medium-security facility, the complex was later enlarged to 33 buildings holding 1,500 prisoners. Almost hidden behind this wall of wire and steel are many modern buildings housing men prisoners.

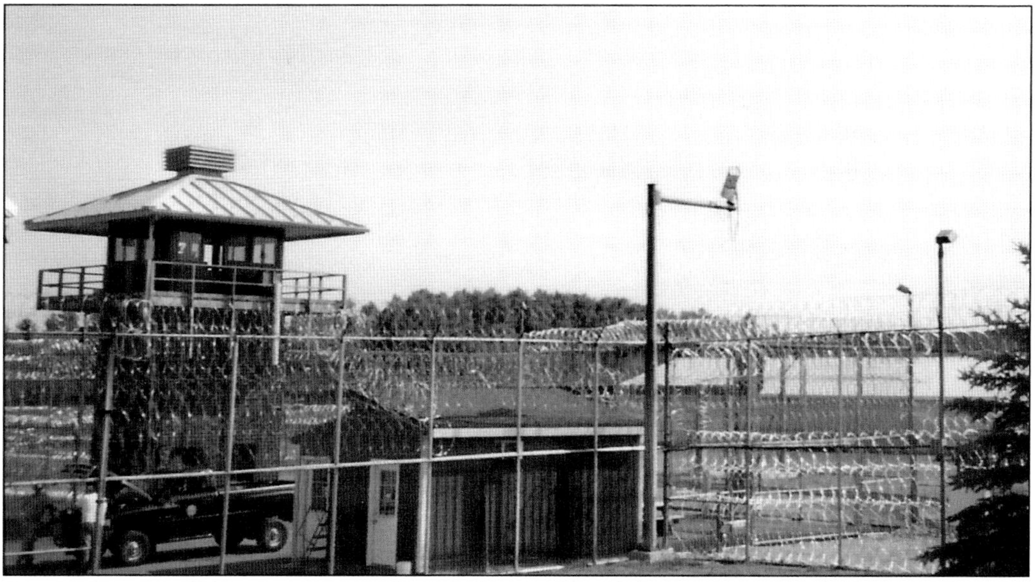

ARMED TOWER. This tower is on the northwest side of the men's prison facility. Inside is an armed guard patrolling the perimeter. The men's facility consists of many buildings, including not only holding cells but also education and training centers. Minimum-security prisoners are allowed to do gardening and janitorial work but are always watched by guards.

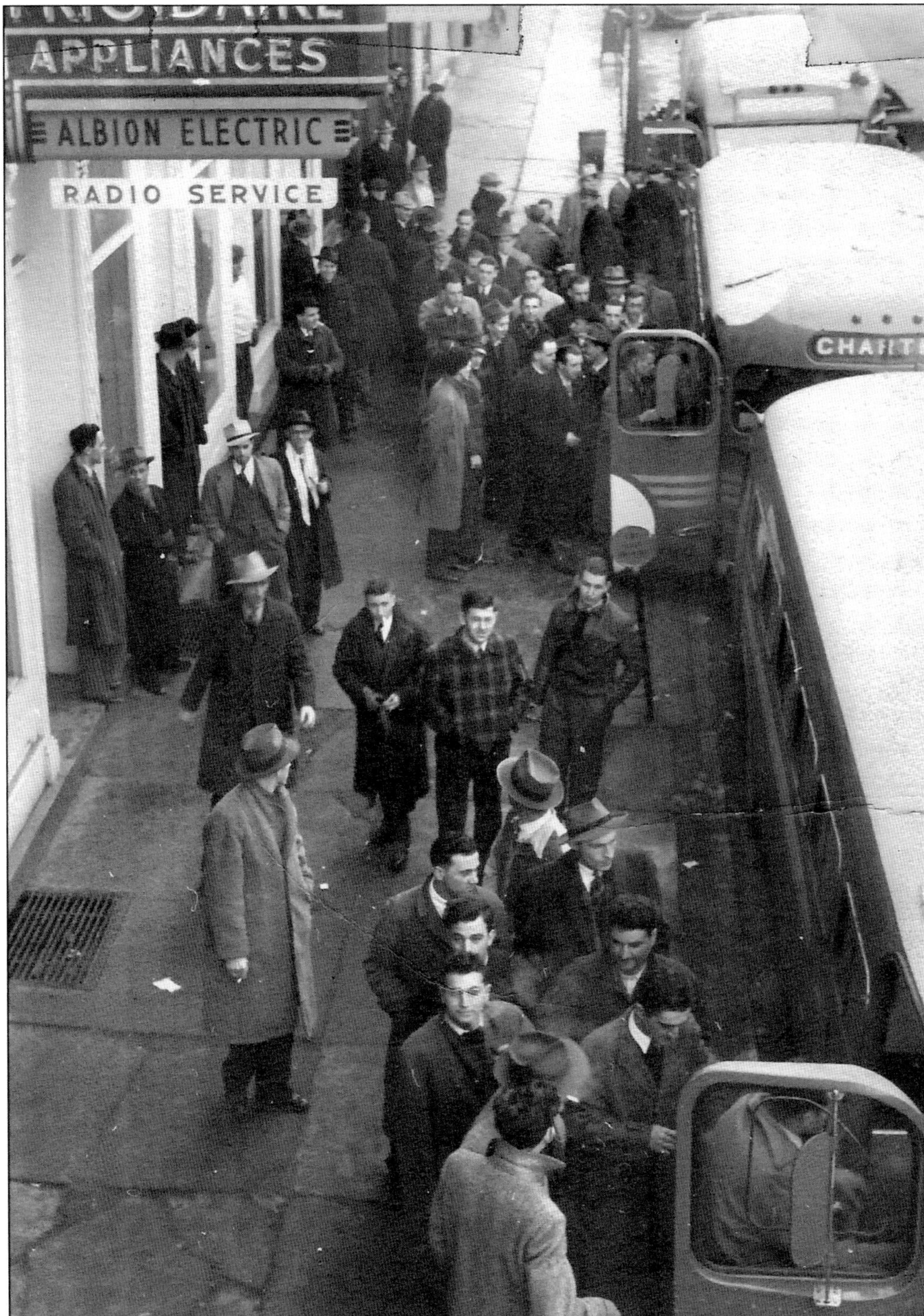

GOING TO WAR. These draftees prepare to board buses that will take them to boot camp around 1941. (Courtesy of Orleans County Department of History.)

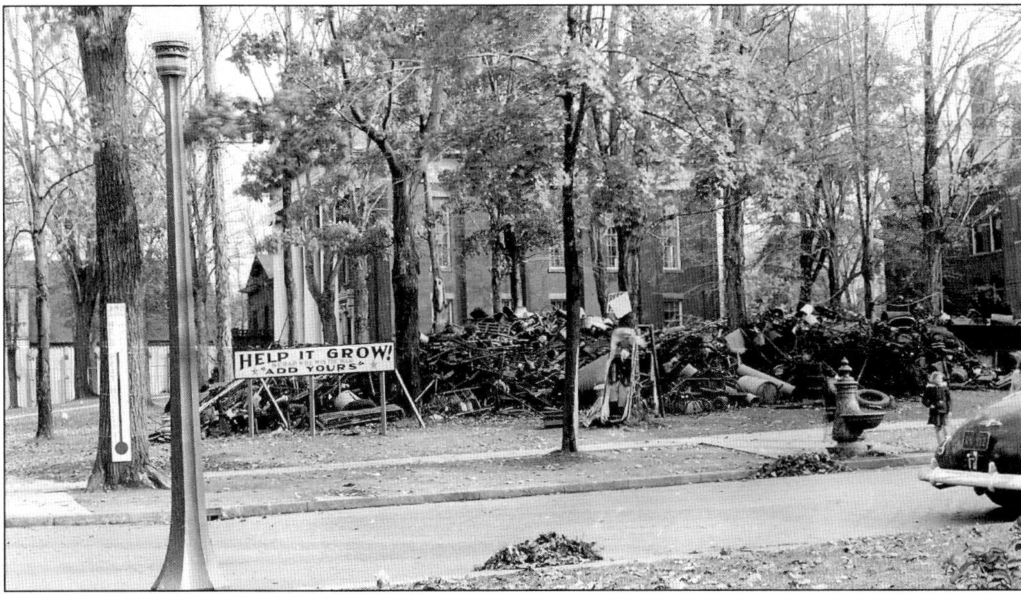

TRASH COLLECTION. During World War II, Orleans County residents were asked to contribute scrap metal to the war effort. The metal was collected on the front lawn of the courthouse. The sign states, "Help it grow. Scrap will win the war. Add yours." From the size of the pile, it appears people were eager to help. Note the drinking fountain for horses at the right on the curb. (Courtesy of Orleans County Department of History.)

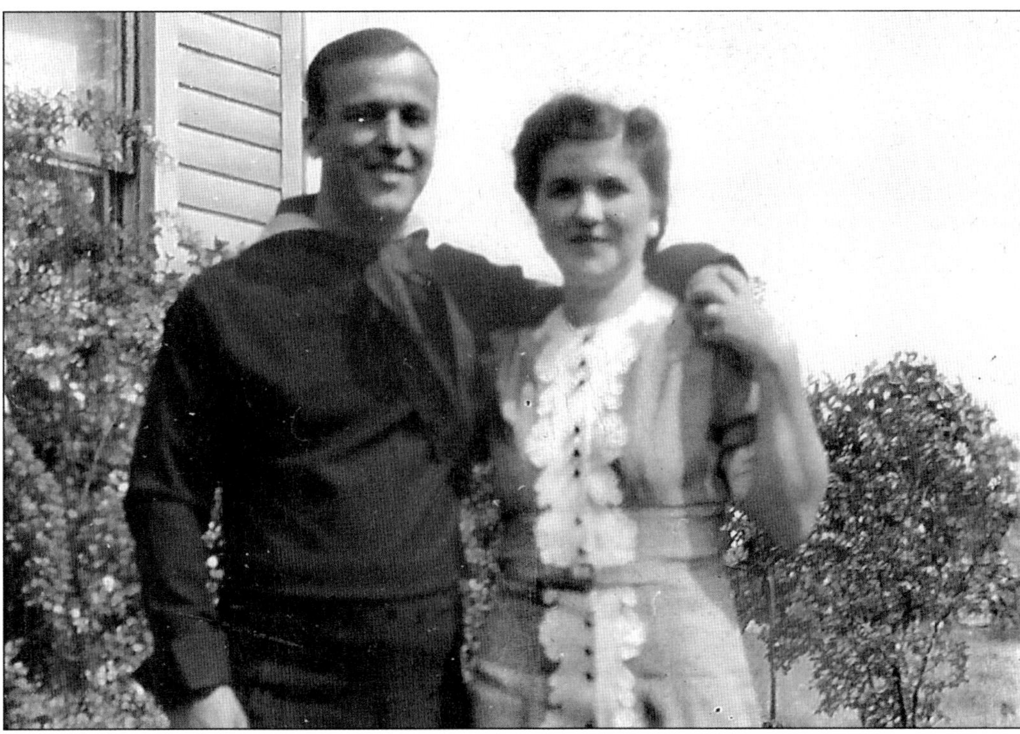

HOME ON LEAVE. Louis Monacelli visits his sister, Emily Monacelli Fortunato, when home on leave during World War II. (Courtesy of Susan Fuller.)

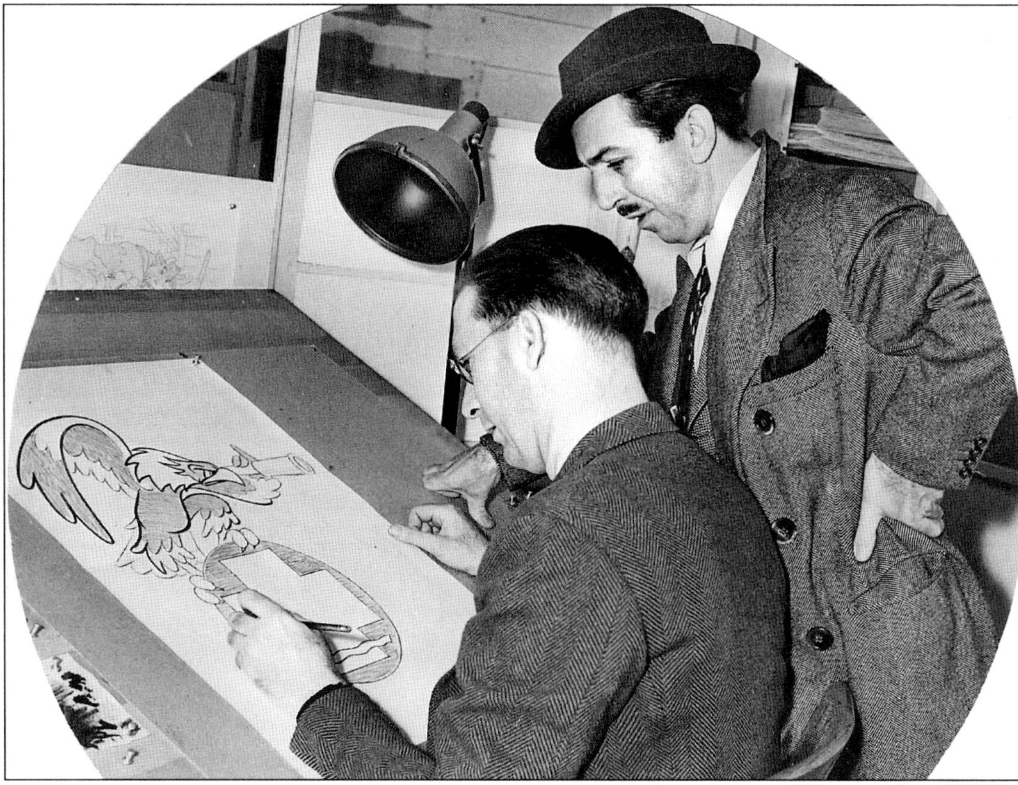

WORKING WITH WALT. Albion native Henry Porter was born in Albion in 1901. He left to work for Walt Disney, who watches over Porter's shoulder as he works on a sketch. In 1934, Porter created the cartoon character of Donald Duck, and in 1943, another Disney employee, Carl Barks, gave Donald Duck a clear voice and definite personality. (Courtesy of Orleans County Department of History.)

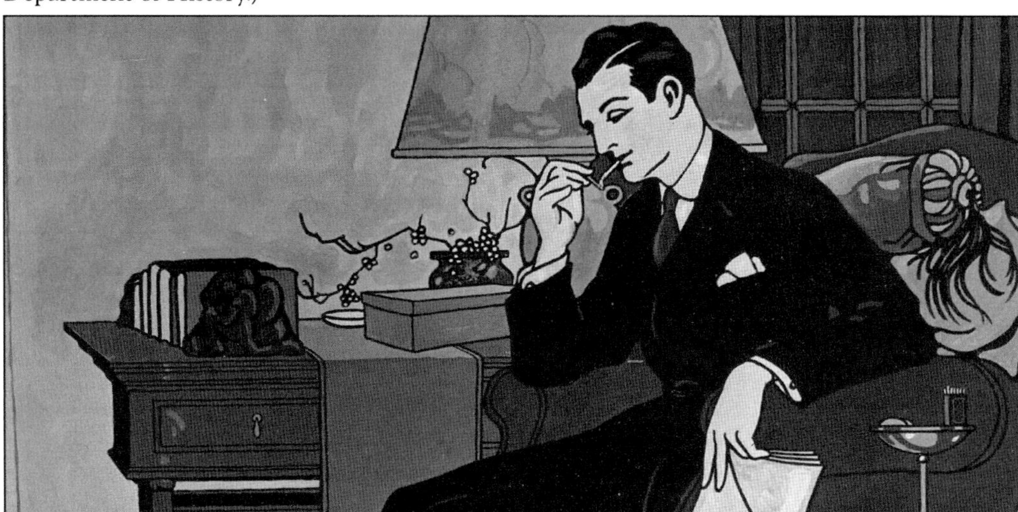

SELF-PORTRAIT. Henry Porter painted a self-portrait while in art school before working for Walt Disney Productions. Porter was born in Albion in 1901. (Courtesy of Orleans County Department of History.)

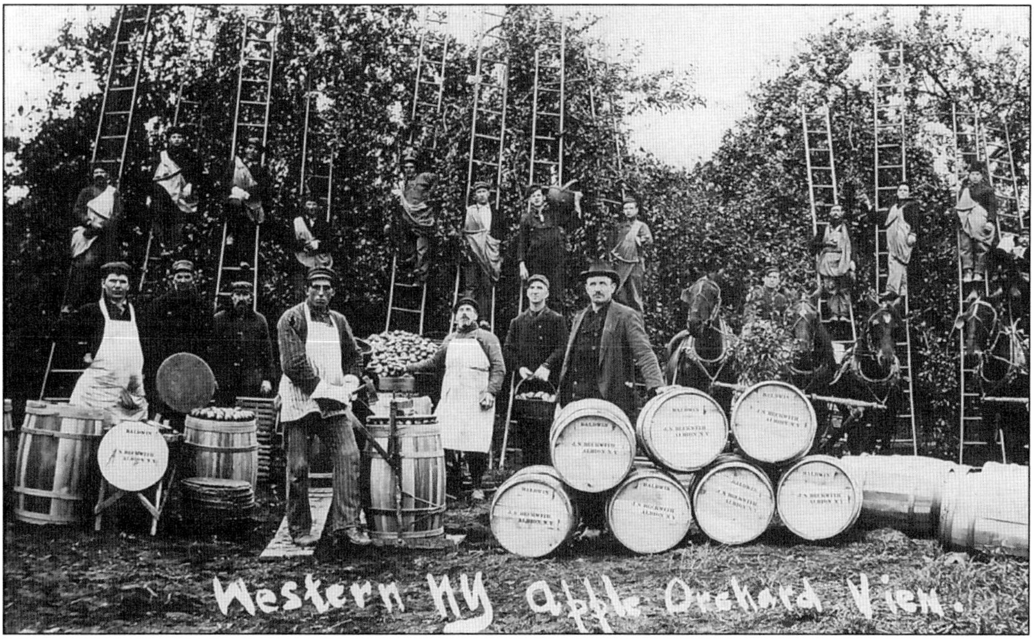

APPLE PICKERS AND HIGH LADDERS. Long before dwarf trees were propagated, men used very tall ladders to get to the tops of the apple trees in the orchards. Apples were packed in barrels and sent to market on the Erie Canal. (Courtesy of Orleans County Department of History.)

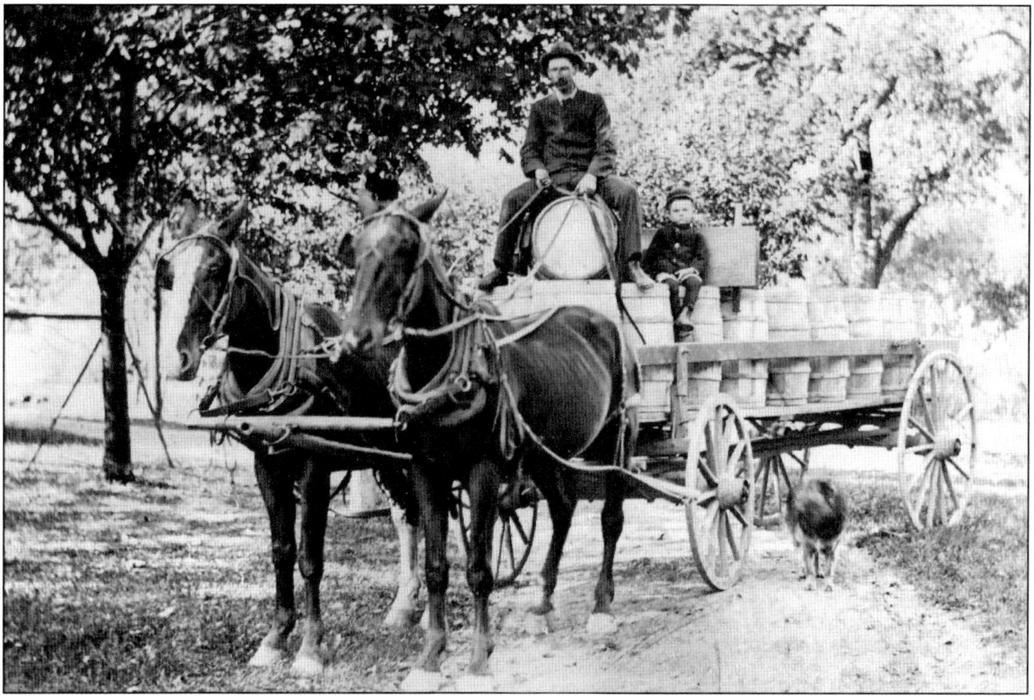

APPLE HARVEST. Nahum Lattin and his son, Cary Lattin, ride on barrels of apples as they prepare to go to the Albion Depot with the latest harvest around 1901. (Courtesy of Tillman's Village Inn.)

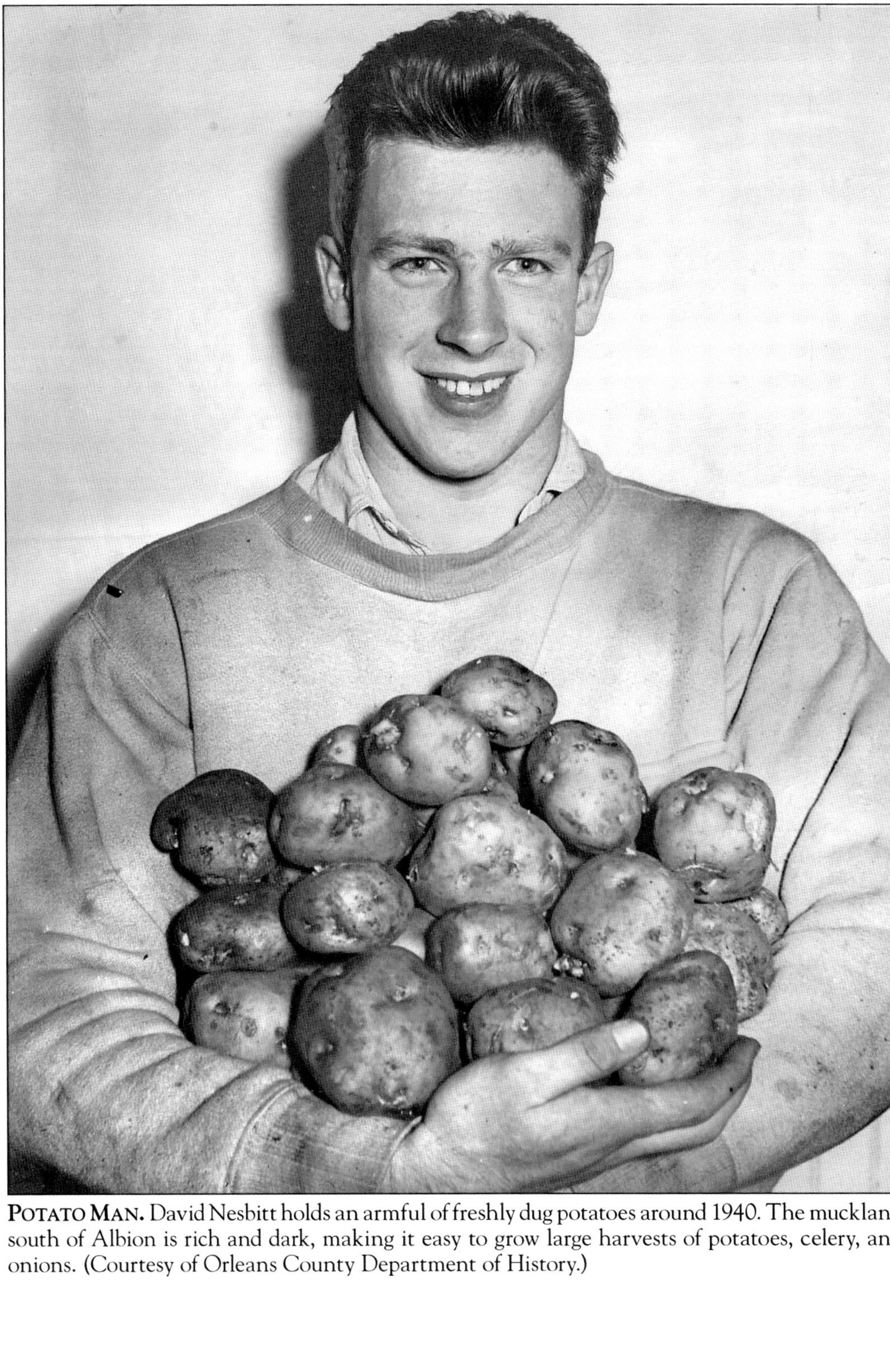

POTATO MAN. David Nesbitt holds an armful of freshly dug potatoes around 1940. The muckland south of Albion is rich and dark, making it easy to grow large harvests of potatoes, celery, and onions. (Courtesy of Orleans County Department of History.)

Two

FARMING AND BUSINESS

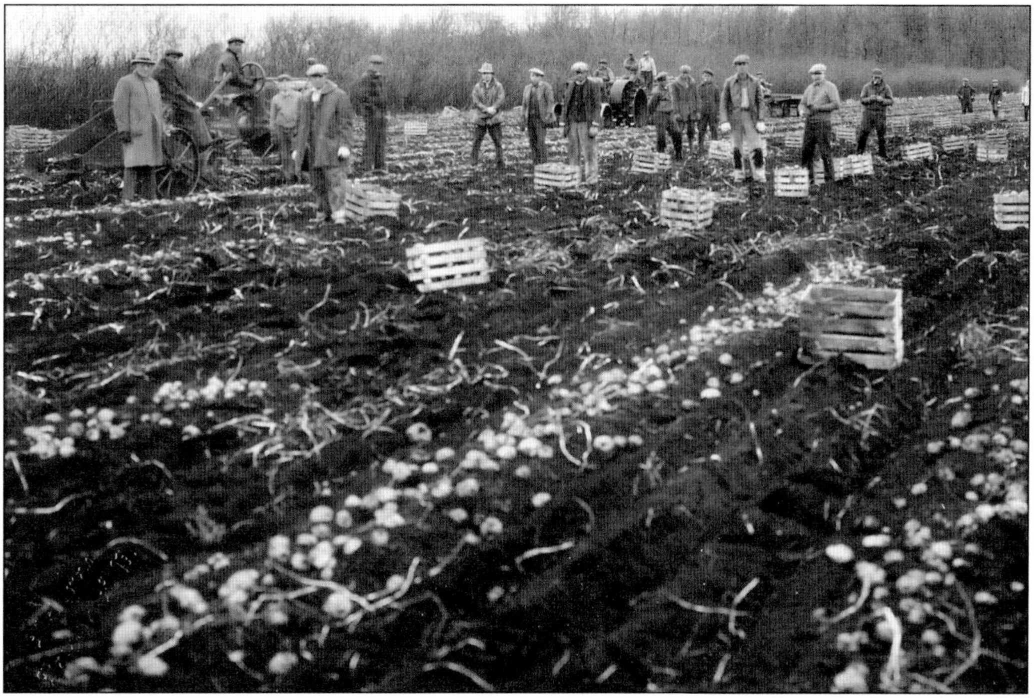

READY TO PACK. Freshly dug potatoes lie on the ground after being turned over by fork-wielding workers, who pose for the camera before bending their backs to begin packing the tubers into the large crates around 1930. (Courtesy of Orleans County Department of History.)

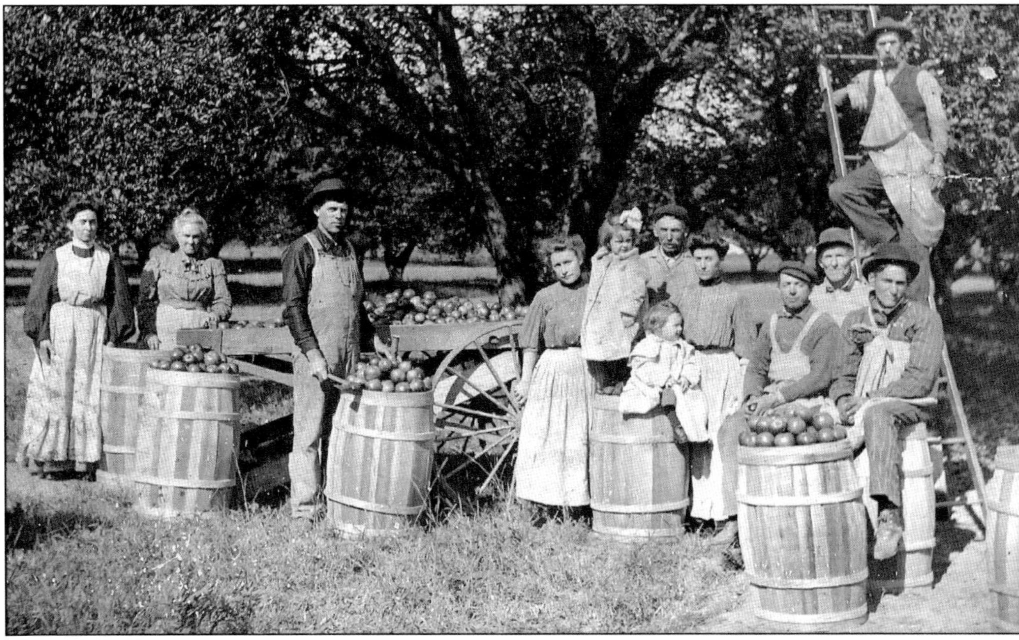

Barrels of Apples. People of all ages get into the spirit of apple picking in this photograph, taken around 1904 at the Hewitt Farm in the town of Gaines. (Courtesy of Orleans County Department of History.)

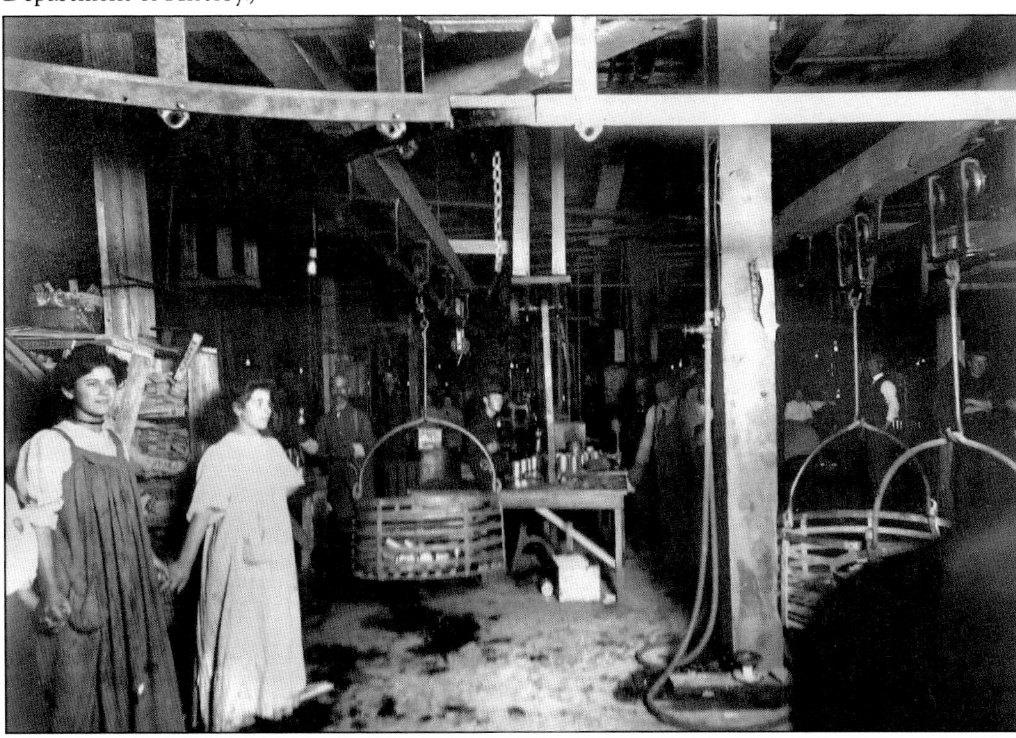

Inside the Canning Factory. Canning company employees pose beside their work inside the Burt Olney Canning Company, on East Avenue, in 1903. The canned products was carried along overhead conveyors in baskets. (Courtesy of Orleans County Department of History.)

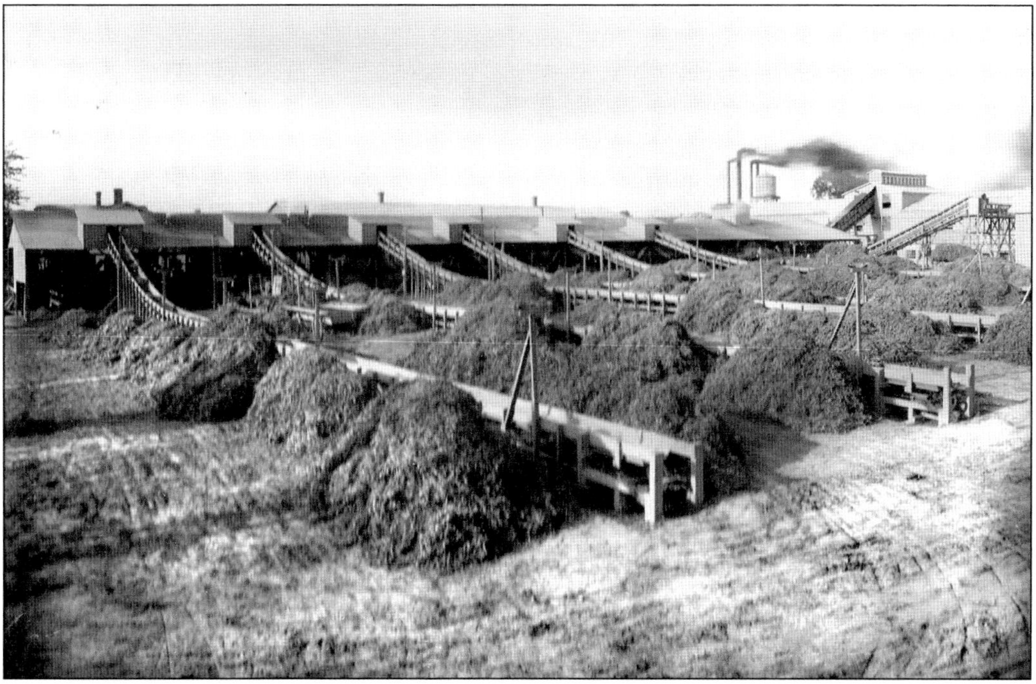

PEA VINES OUTSIDE THE CANNERY. Peas on the vine wait to be transported up the conveyor chutes into the cannery. Peas were a popular canned product during the heyday of the Burt Olney Canning Company, which was from 1903 to 1920. (Courtesy of Orleans County Department of History.)

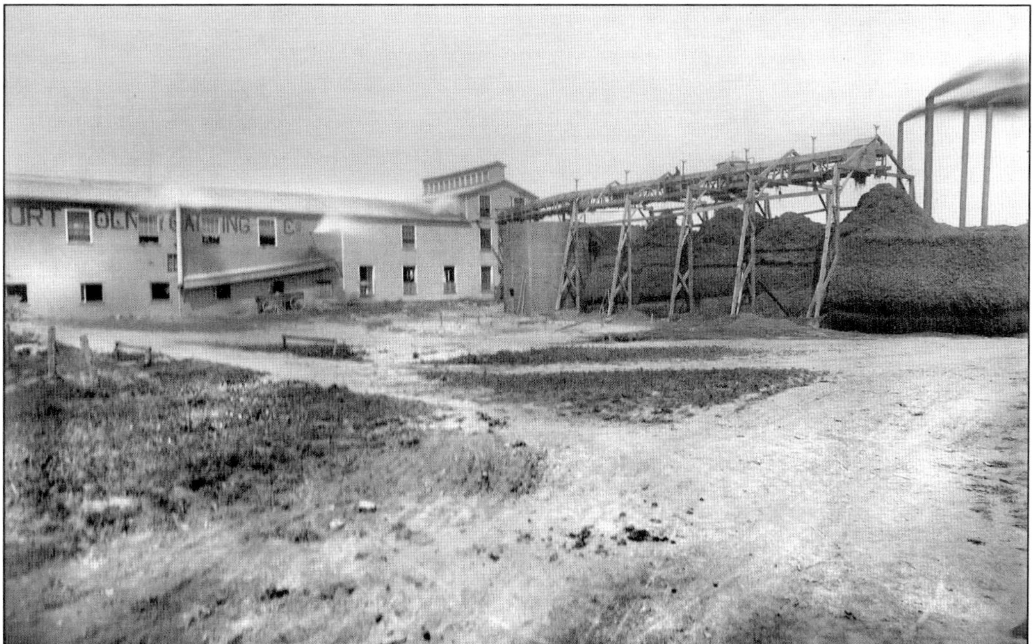

SMOKING STACKS. Steam rises from the stacks, indicating that the boilers are working inside the Burt Olney Canning Company. (Courtesy of Orleans County Department of History.)

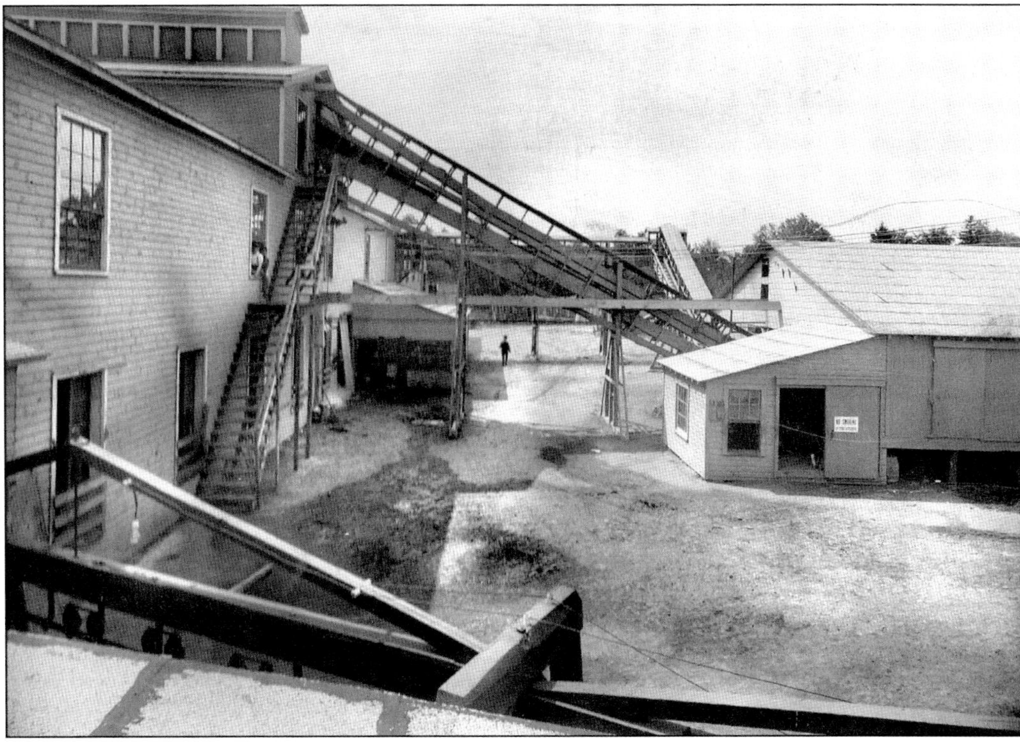

Chutes and Ladders. A solitary man stands outside the canning factory on East Avenue during the 1920s. (Courtesy of Orleans County Department of History.)

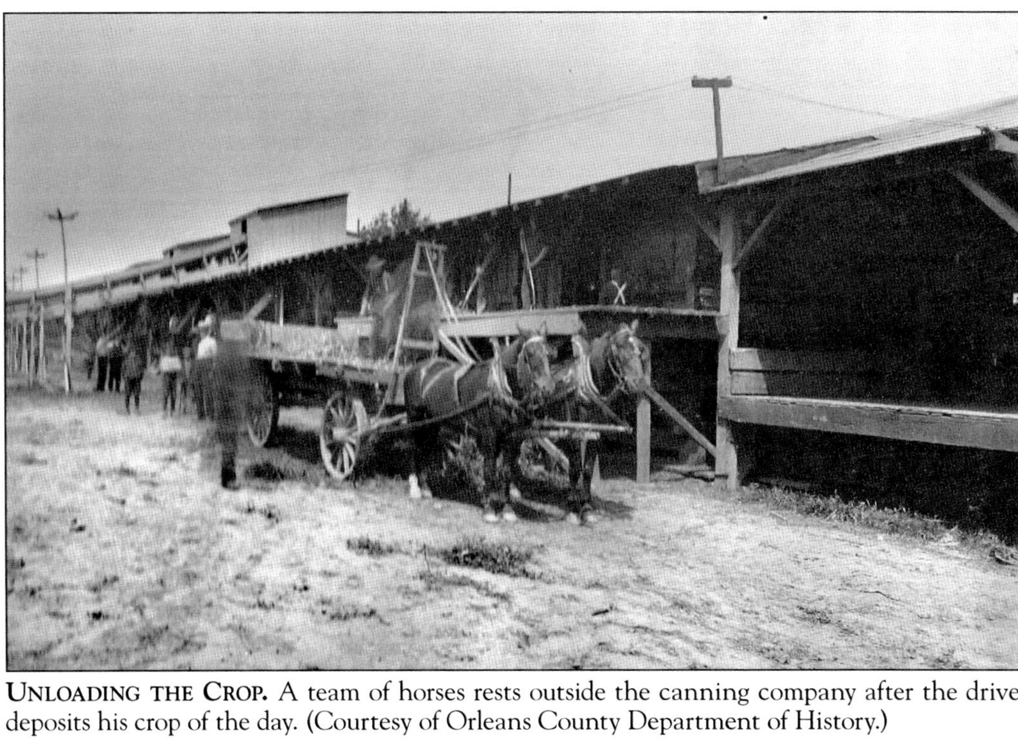

Unloading the Crop. A team of horses rests outside the canning company after the driver deposits his crop of the day. (Courtesy of Orleans County Department of History.)

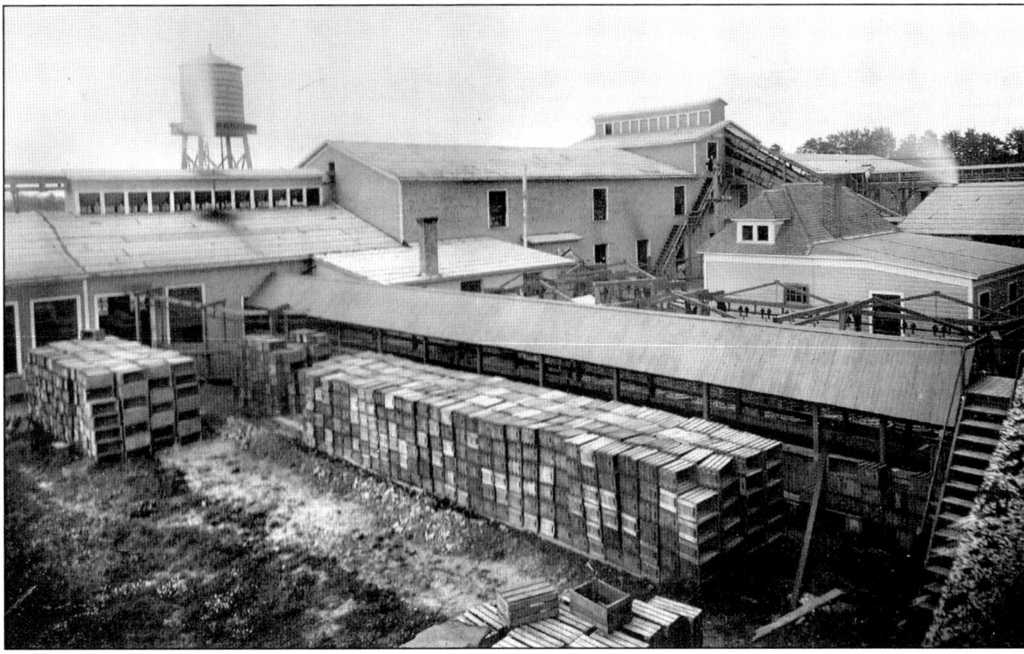

EMPTY CRATES. Hundreds of empty crates are piled high outside the Olney canning factory after a long day's harvesting. (Courtesy of Orleans County Department of History.)

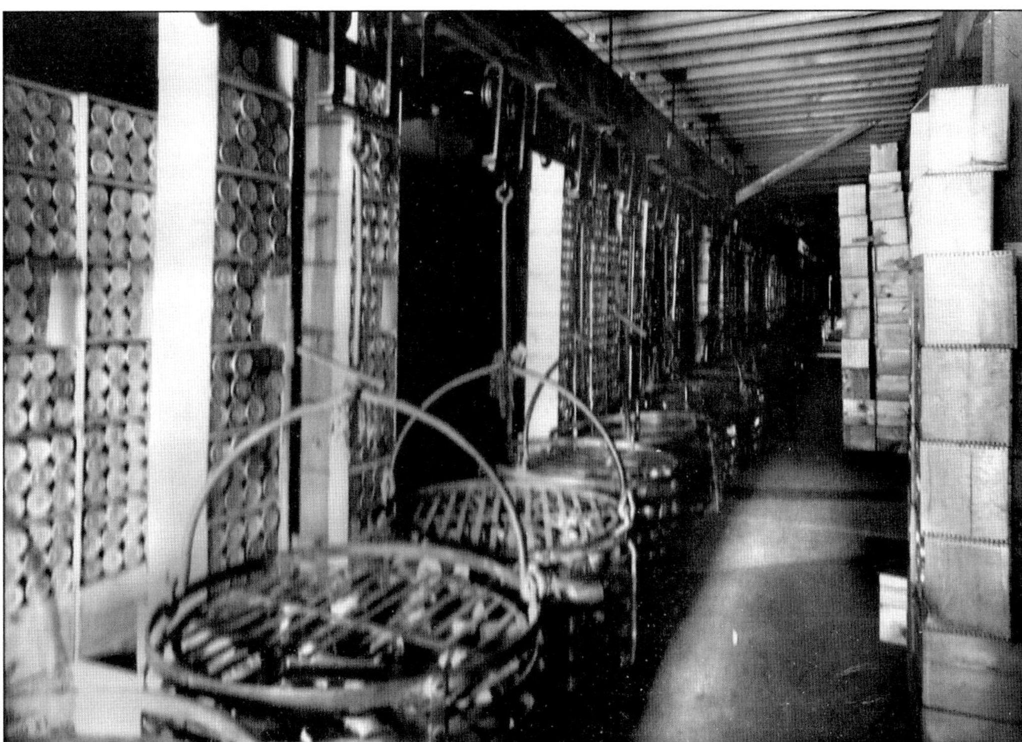

INSIDE THE FACTORY. Interesting baskets were used to haul the cans along at the Burt Olney Canning Company around 1905. (Courtesy of Orleans County Department of History.)

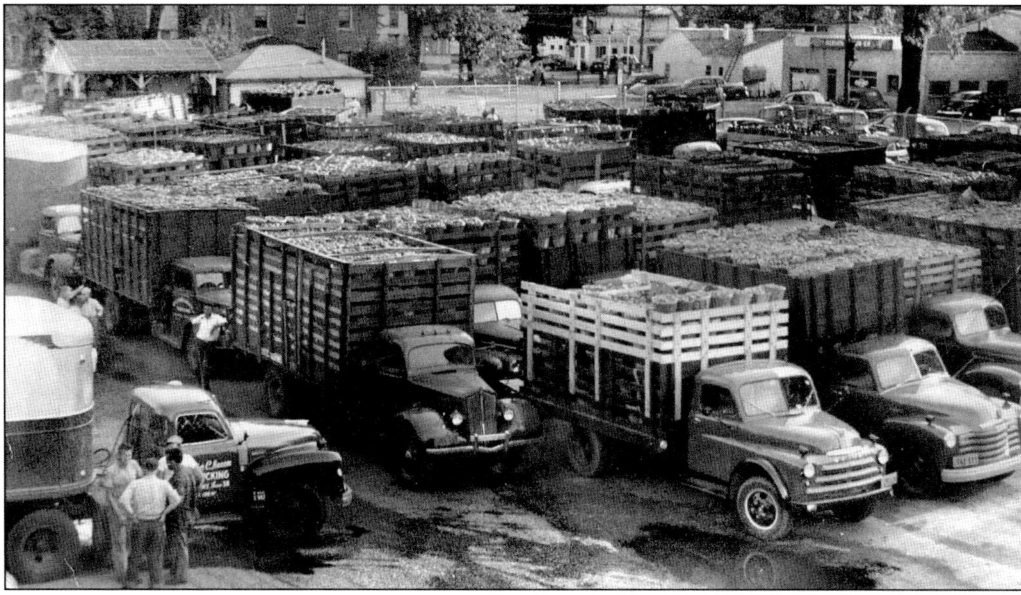

OUTSIDE THE CANNING FACTORY. There are too many hampers to count in this 1950 photograph of tomatoes waiting to be taken inside the canning factory for processing. (Courtesy of Orleans County Department of History.)

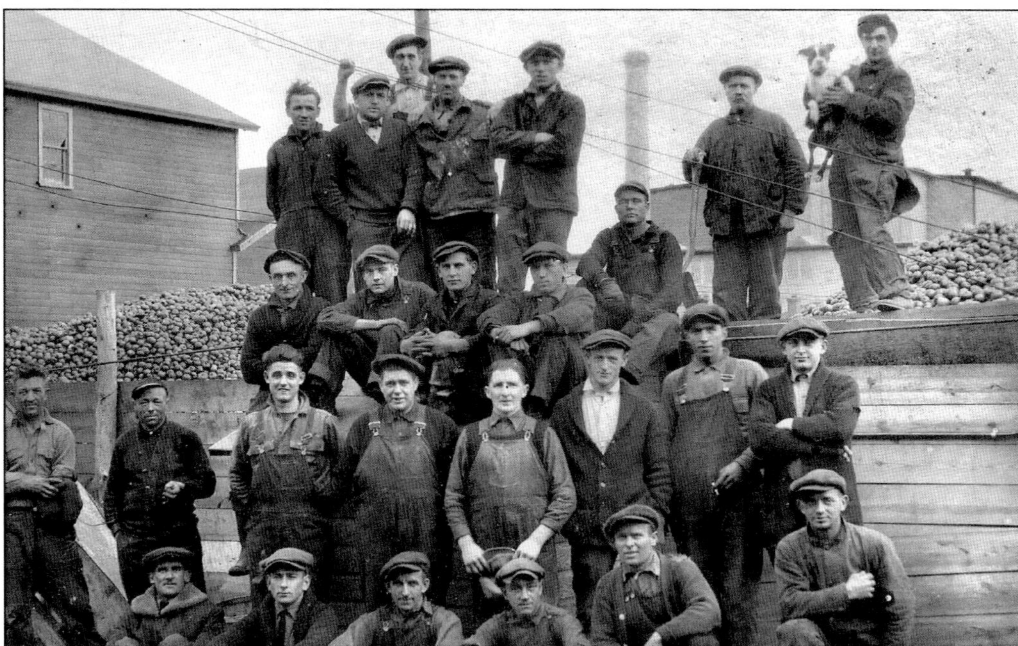

VINEGAR WORKERS. Employees of the Albion Vinegar Works around 1920 are, from left to right, as follows: (first row) J. Crane, unidentified, L. Daniels, L. Loreck, E. Luczak, and J. Rice; (second row) three unidentified persons, C. Day, unidentified, J. Rice, L. Omanski, and unidentified; (third row) S. Telga, J. Eicsielski, F. Bloom, P. Bruski, and unidentified; (fourth row) V. Marks, J. Rise, J. Sadowski, B. Holland, and three unidentified persons. (Courtesy of Orleans County Department of History.)

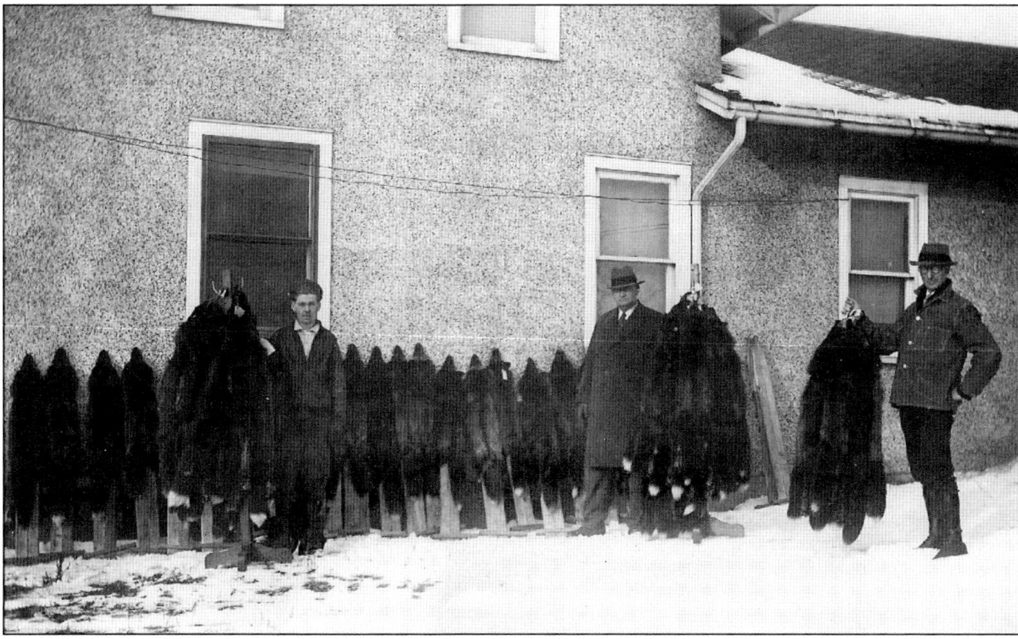

SILVER FOX FARM. Fox pelts are stretched on boards next to the farmhouse on Route 31 that raised silver foxes to be used for fur coats. Holding finished coats are, from left to right, a worker and owners Irving Weet and Ross Wilson. This business was popular with the furring trade during the 1920s and 1930s. (Courtesy of Orleans County Department of History.)

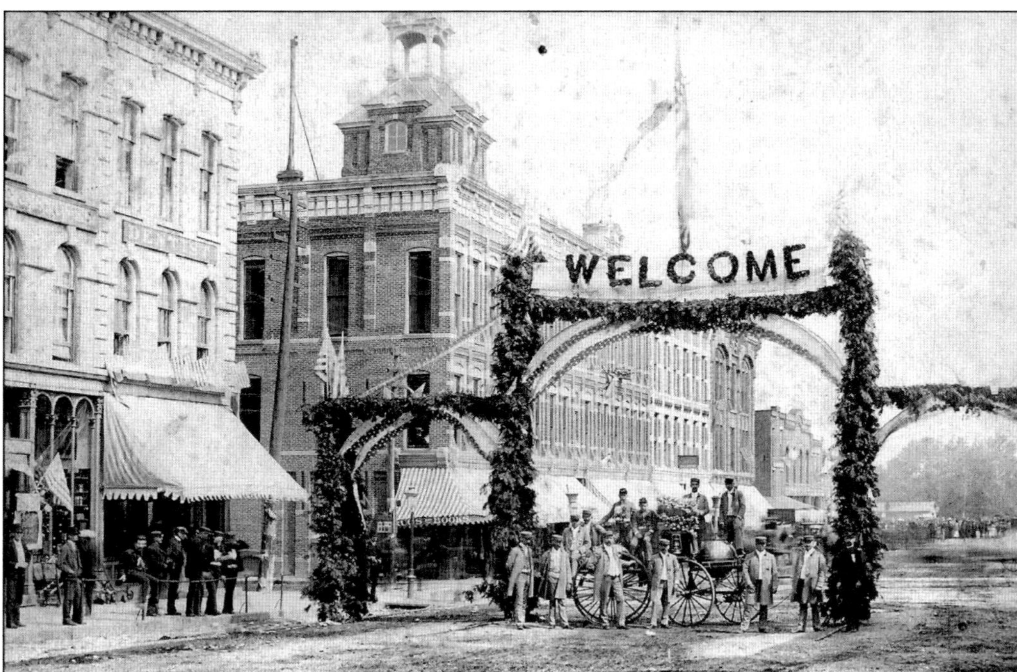

WELCOME TO ALBION. The welcome sign is out on Main Street around 1890 for a Western New York Firemen's convention. (Courtesy of Orleans County Department of History.)

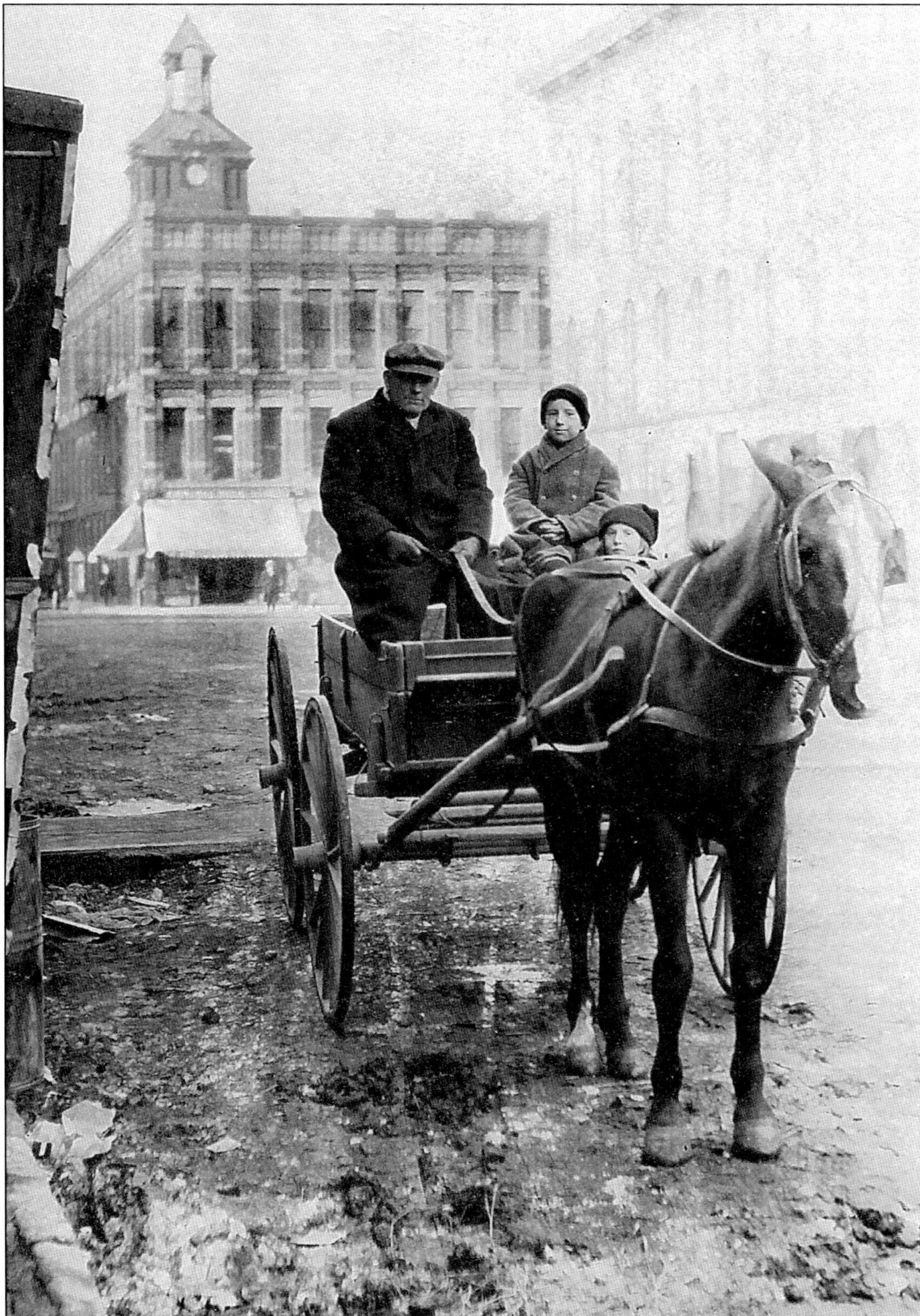

A Trip Downtown. A family takes a trip into downtown Albion on a rainy fall day around 1905. The Swan Block is in the background. (Courtesy of Orleans County Department of History.)

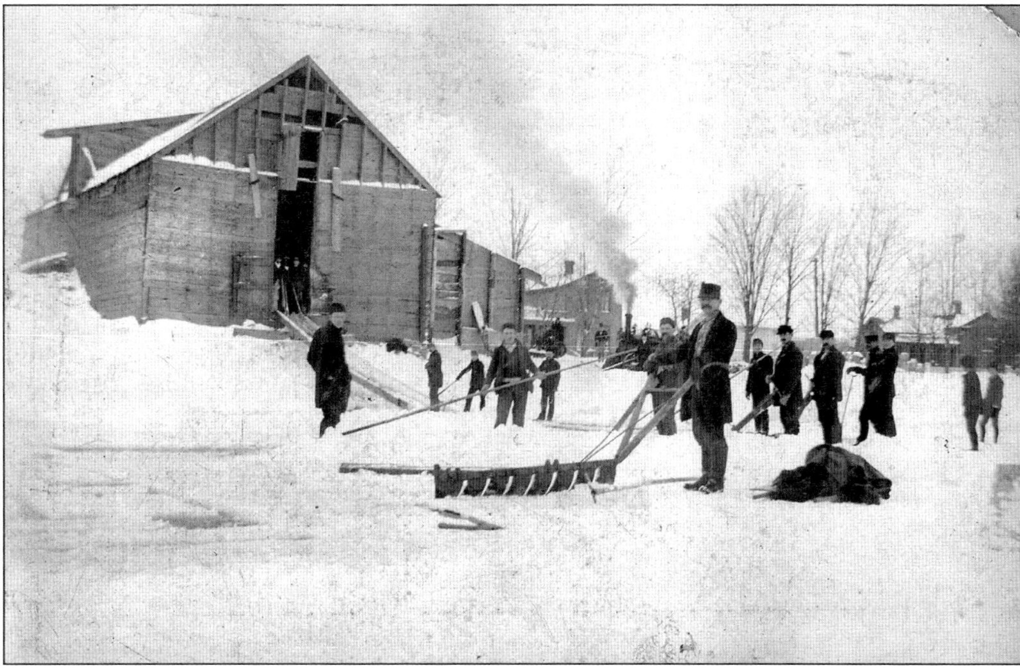

CUTTING ICE. Shourds Icehouse provided ice during the summer for many Albion residents. George Shourds (left) poses with his workers on the old millpond, located off East State Street, on a blustery January day in 1895. (Courtesy of Orleans County Department of History.)

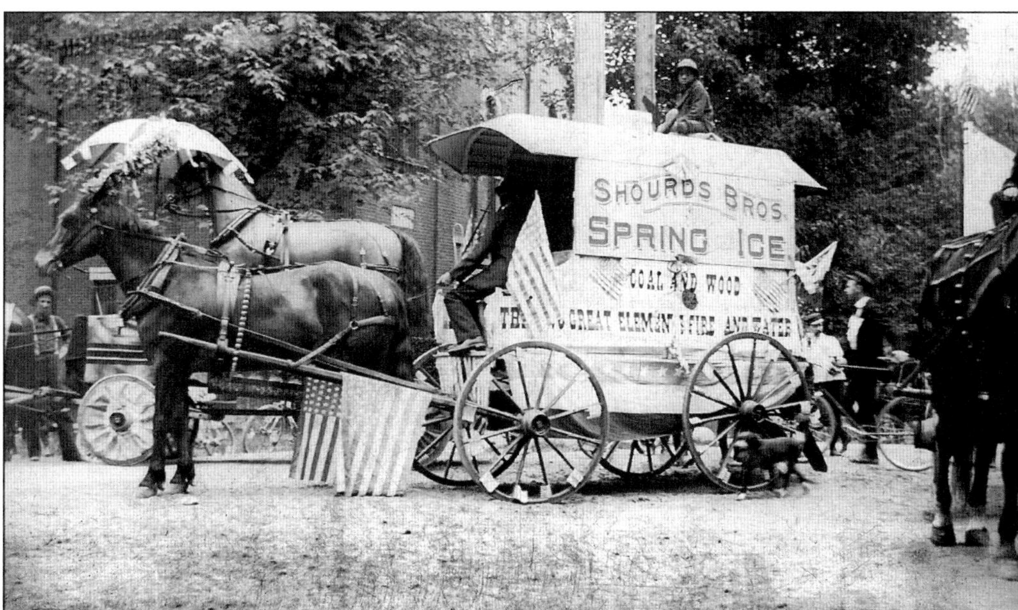

ICE WAGON. After the ice sits in the icehouse all winter, packed in sawdust to keep it from melting, Shourds Brothers delivery wagon distributes it to residents during the warm months. The wagon advertises "Shourds Bros. spring ice. Coal and wood. The world's great element is fire and water." This wagon was on display during a summer parade. Note the umbrella over the horse's head. (Courtesy of Orleans County Department of History.)

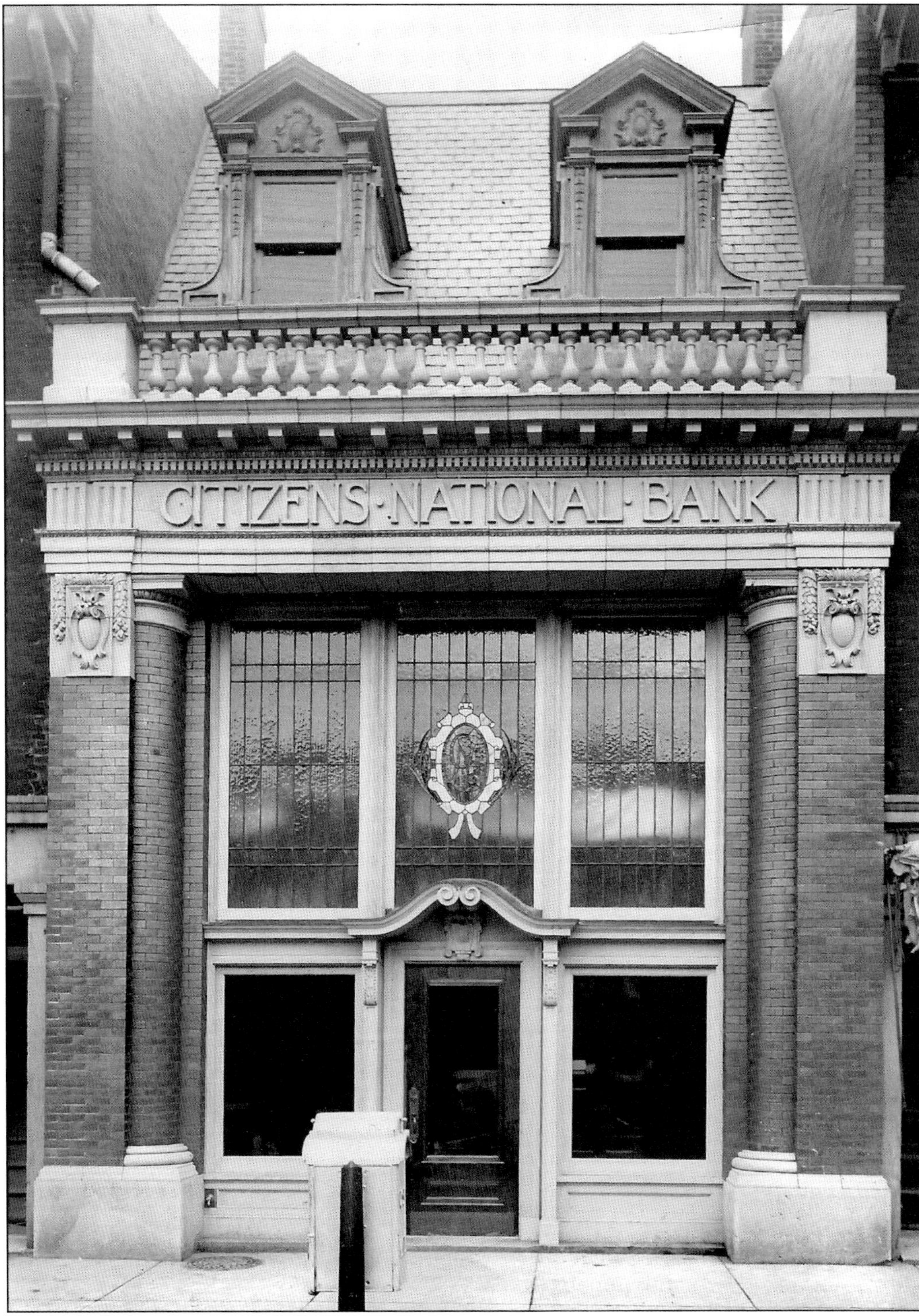

CITIZENS NATIONAL BANK. The Citizens National Bank was established in 1884, enlarged in 1923, and closed in 1931. This photograph was taken in 1919. (Courtesy of Orleans County Department of History.)

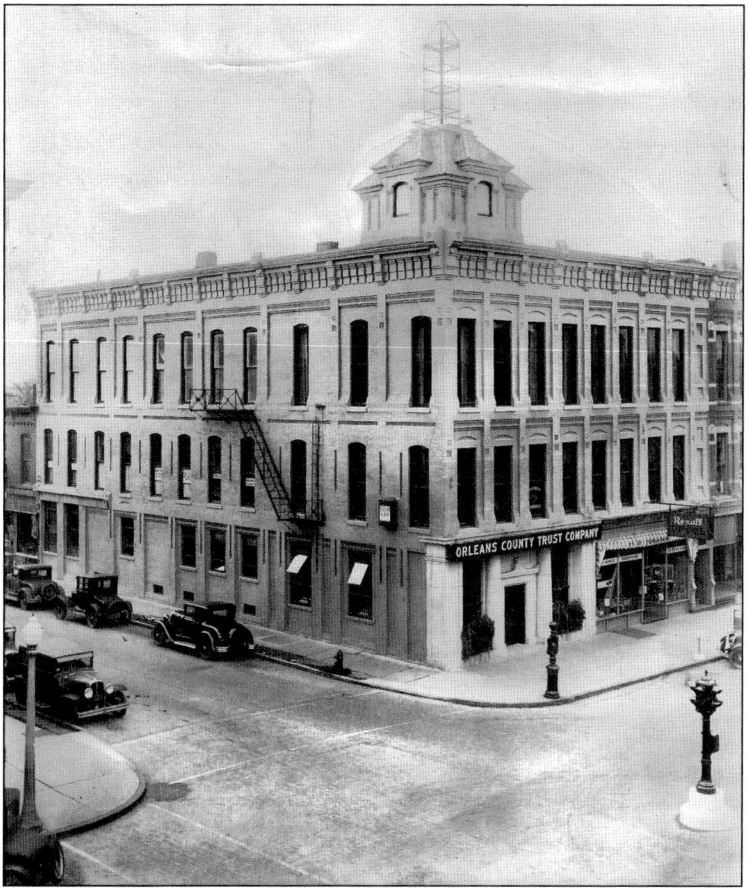

ORLEANS COUNTY TRUST COMPANY. The bank moved to this location in 1920. The tower was removed in the 1950s. (Courtesy of Orleans County Department of History.)

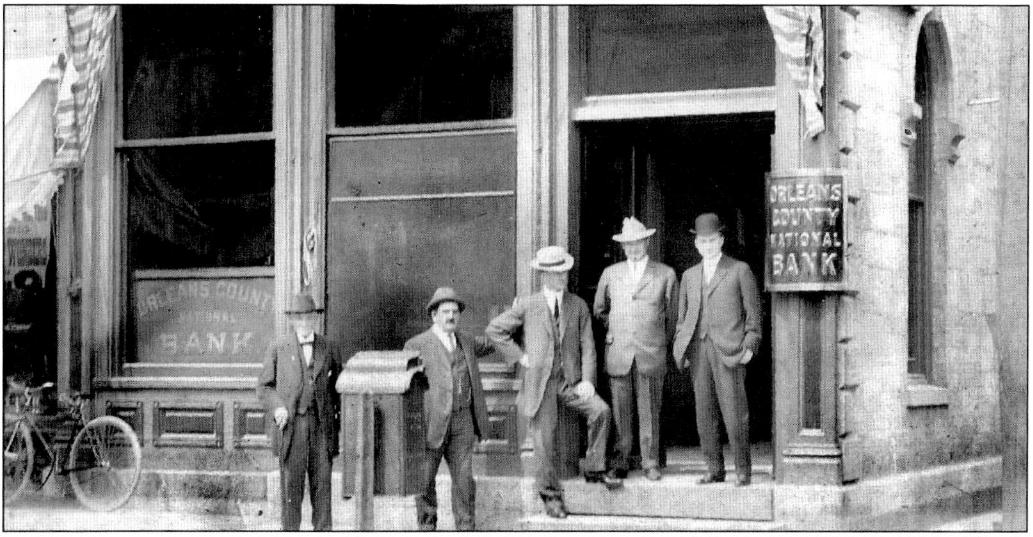

ORLEANS COUNTY NATIONAL BANK. This was the forerunner of the Orleans County Trust Company. It stood on the southwest corner of West Bank Street and Main Street. It was the site of the first bank in Albion, known as the Bank of Orleans. These men were associated with the bank. (Courtesy of Orleans County Department of History.)

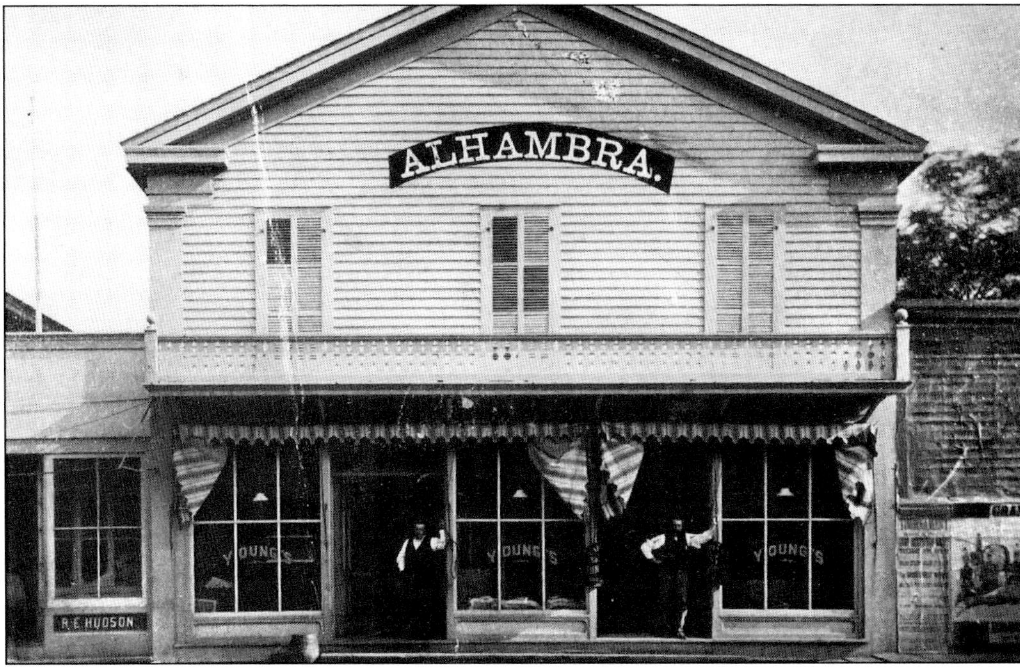

ALHAMBRA. Young's Hotel, also called Alhambra, stands on the north side of East Bank Street around 1875. The hotel was replaced in 1878 by a brick building constructed of materials taken from the old Orleans County Clerk's Office. In 1967, occupants of the building became Christopher's Barbershop and D'Andrea's Shoe Store. (Courtesy of Orleans County Department of History.)

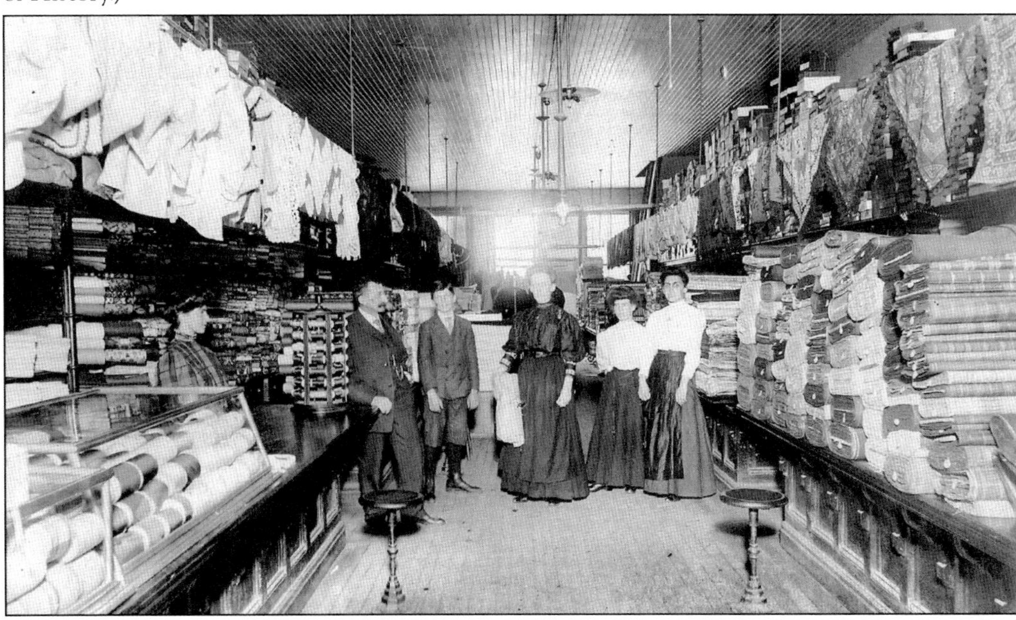

LANDAUER'S DRY GOODS STORE. Shown around 1905 is the interior of the north store, which was located on what was formerly 53–55 Main Street. From left to right are employees Ivah Chadwick, H. M. Strouse, Leo Hiesler, Florence Van Stone, Mattie Iden, and Anna Trumble. (Courtesy of Orleans County Department of History.)

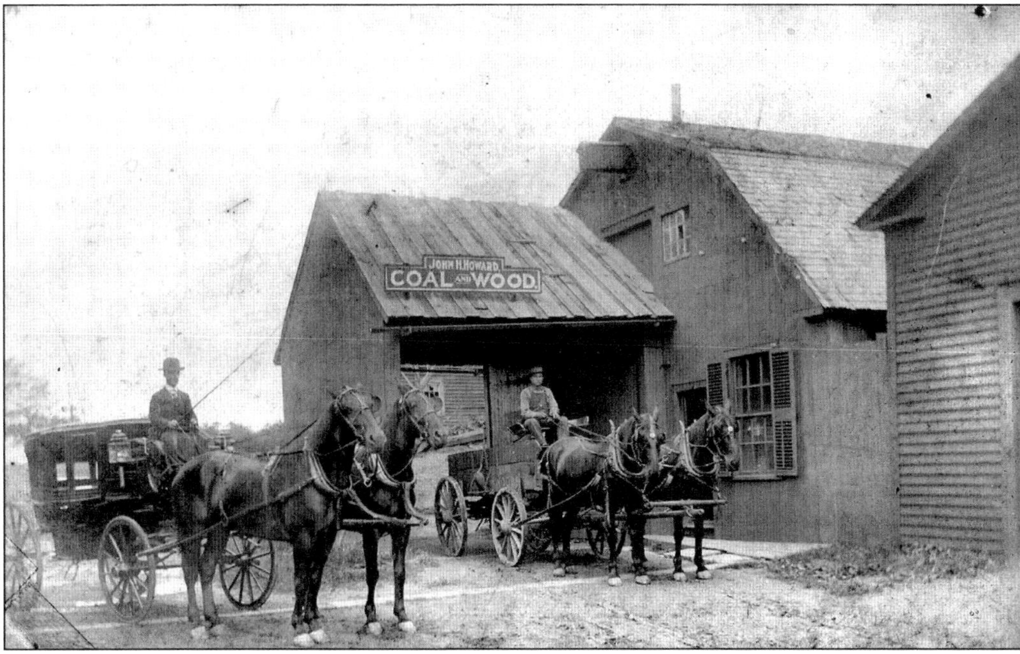

COAL AND WOOD. Businessman John Howard (left) poses in front of his coal and wood business while a worker looks on around 1900. (Courtesy of Orleans County Department of History.)

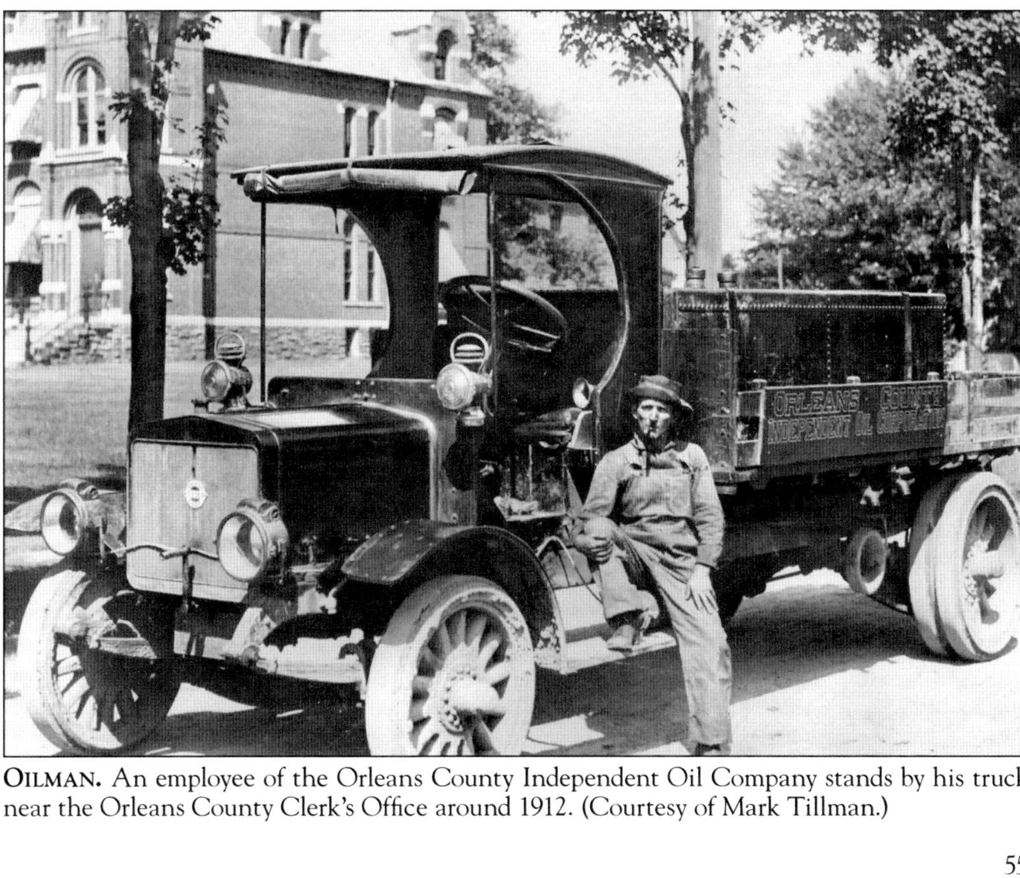

OILMAN. An employee of the Orleans County Independent Oil Company stands by his truck near the Orleans County Clerk's Office around 1912. (Courtesy of Mark Tillman.)

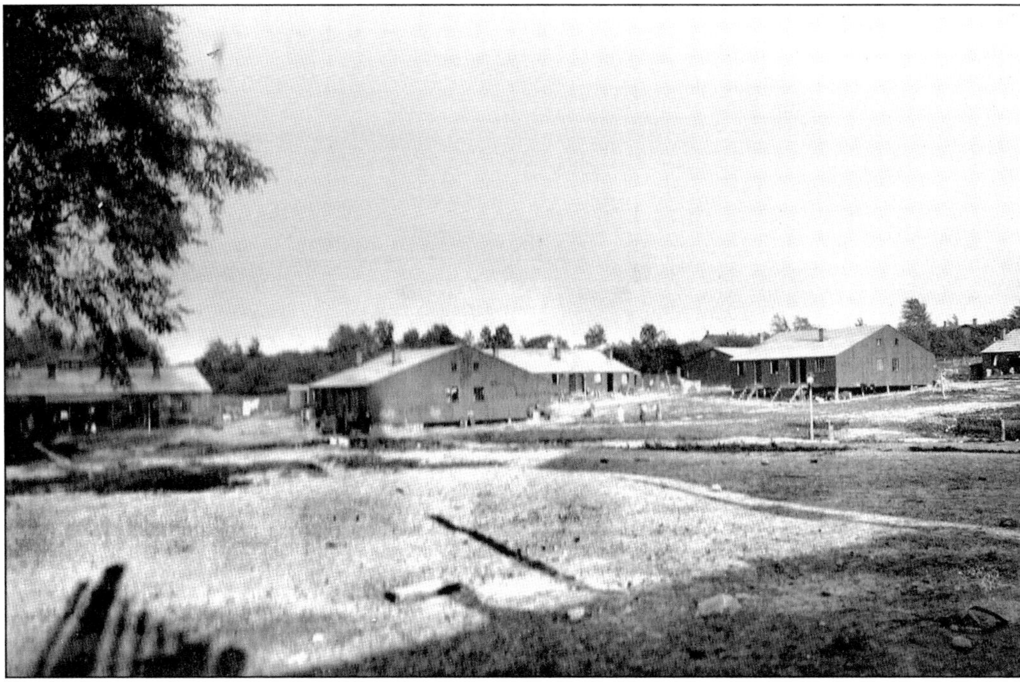

WORKERS' HOUSING. These were the accommodations that housed Italian laborers from the stone quarries. The buildings were located next to the railroad tracks west of McKinstry Street. (Courtesy of Orleans County Department of History.)

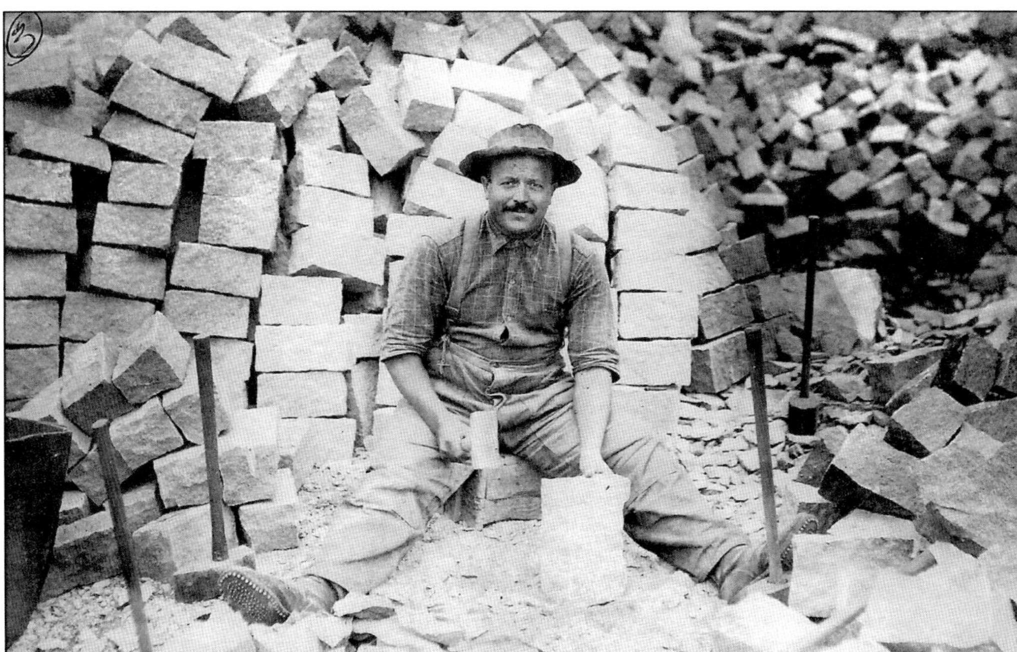

CUTTING STONE. Peter DiPalma seems to enjoy cutting stone at an Albion quarry. He was one of thousands of Italian men who came to the United States to work in the stone quarries. (Courtesy of Susan Fuller.)

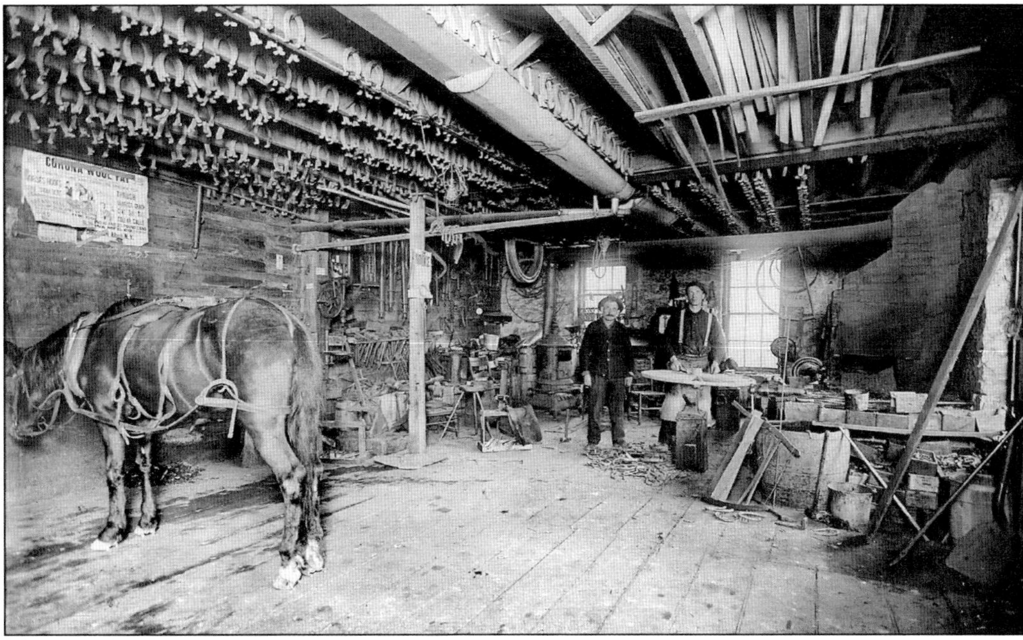

CHRISMAN'S BLACKSMITH SHOP, C. 1905. This blacksmith shop was located off West Bank Street where the Hong Kong Shanghai Bank of China drive-in teller is located now. (Courtesy of Orleans County Department of History.)

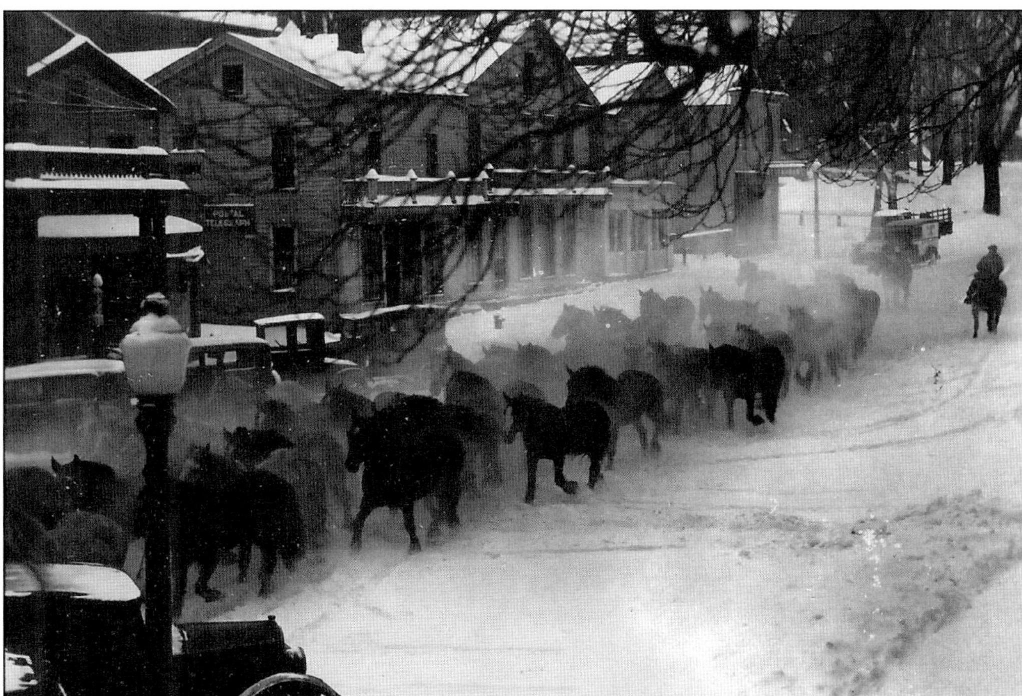

WILD HORSES. A wrangler drives a herd of horses down Main Street around 1935, destined to the Harry Nesbitt farm on the Peter Smith Road. (Courtesy of Orleans County Department of History.)

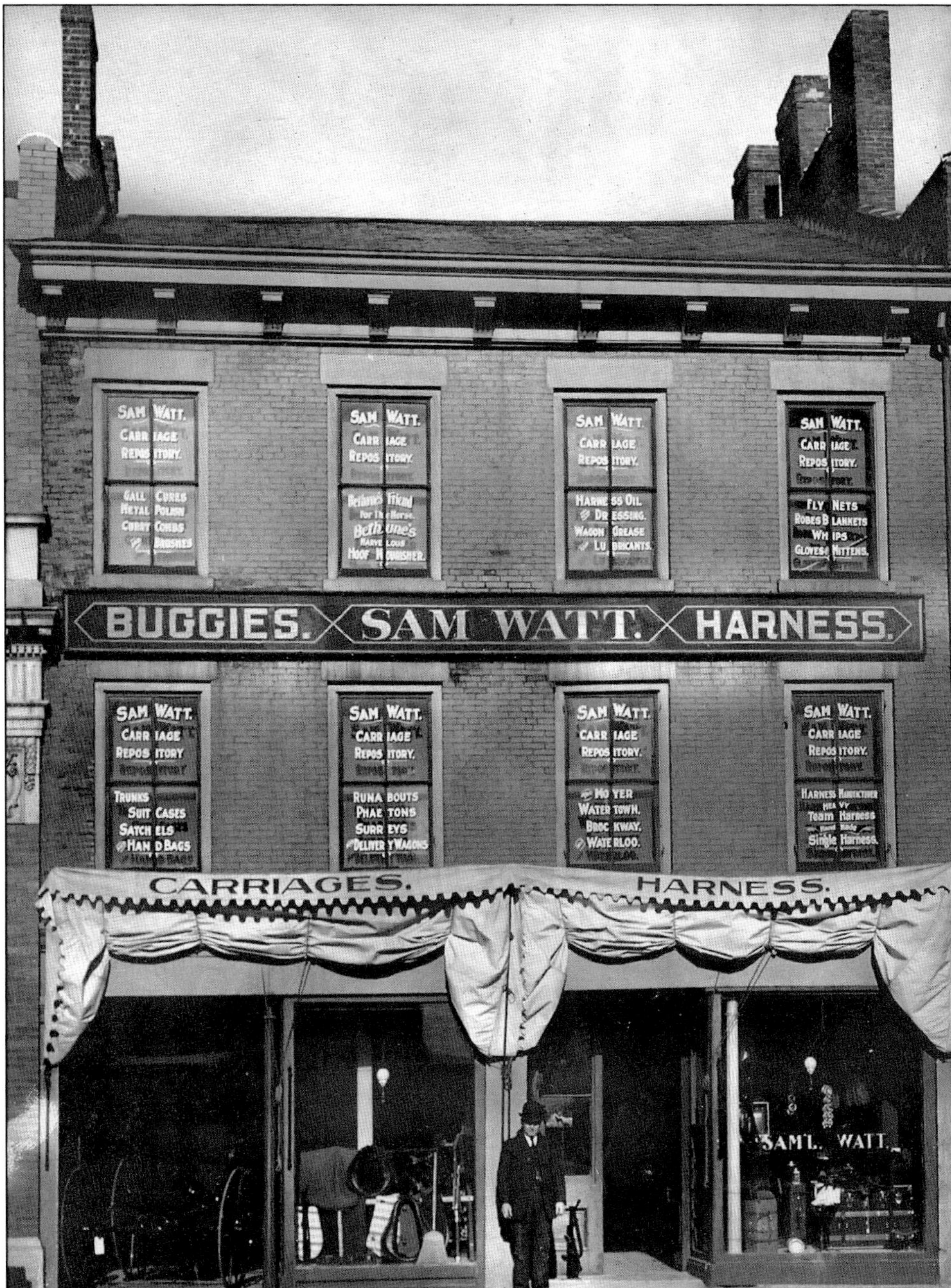

SAM WATT'S HARNESS STORE. Sam Watt poses in front of his buggy and harness shop in downtown Albion around 1900. The upper half of each window advertises "Sam Watt Carriage Repository." In the lower half of some Watt's windows are advertisements for a range of different products, including gall cures, metal polish, curry combs and brushes, Bethune's hoof nourisher, harness oil and dressing, wagon grease and lubricants, suitcases, satchels, handbags, runabouts, phaetons, surreys, delivery wagons, fly nets, robes, blankets, whips, gloves, and mittens. (Courtesy of Orleans County Department of History.)

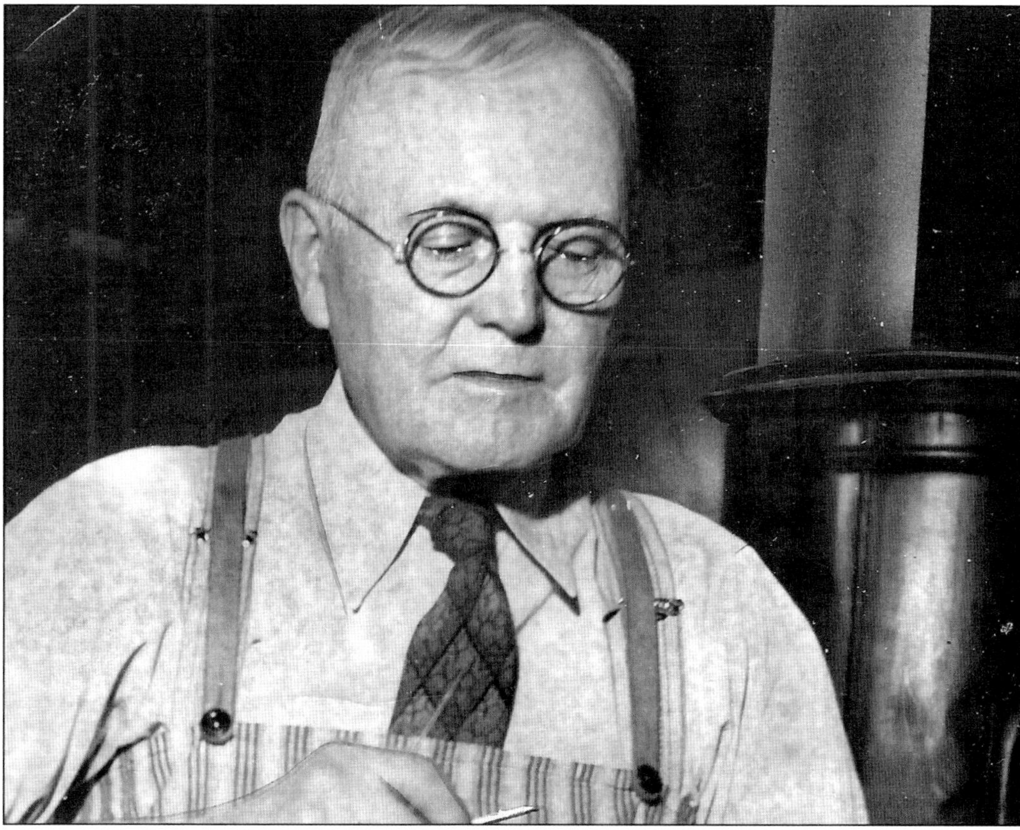

Making Harness. Sam Watt sews on a piece of leather in his shop on September 10, 1937. He was hands-on in his harness business, working daily at his store, putting out the best product he could. He (Courtesy of Orleans County Department of History.)

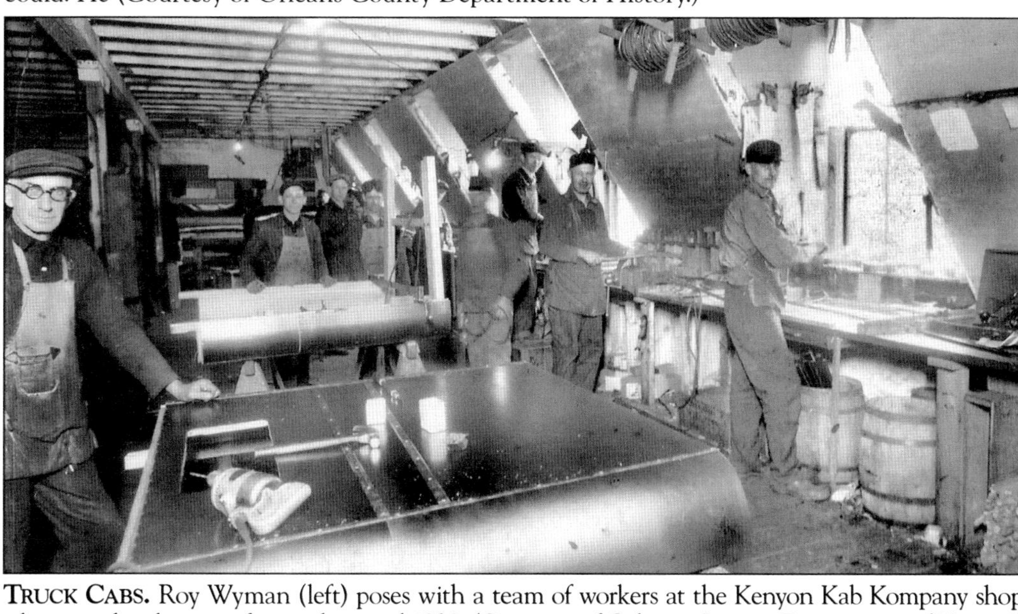

Truck Cabs. Roy Wyman (left) poses with a team of workers at the Kenyon Kab Kompany shop, where truck cabs manufactured around 1930. (Courtesy of Orleans County Department of History.)

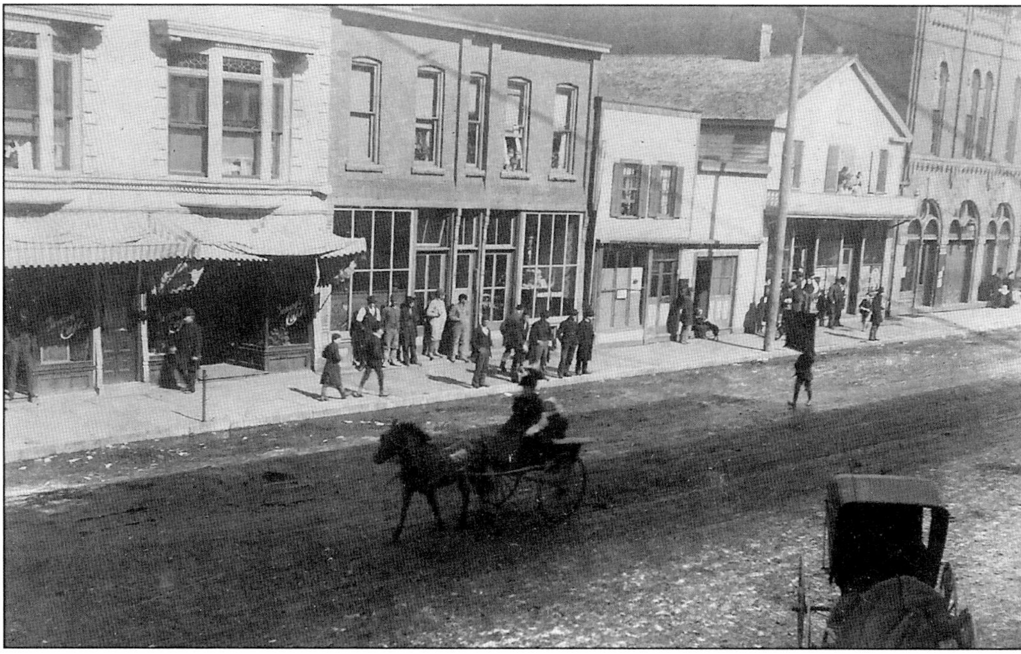

EAST BANK STREET. Albion was a thriving community in the late 19th century, with people walking along the sidewalks and horses and buggies clip-clopping down the street. In the foreground, a buggy is parked, and in the street, a pony pulls a cart along the thoroughfare in 1898. (Courtesy of Orleans County Department of History.)

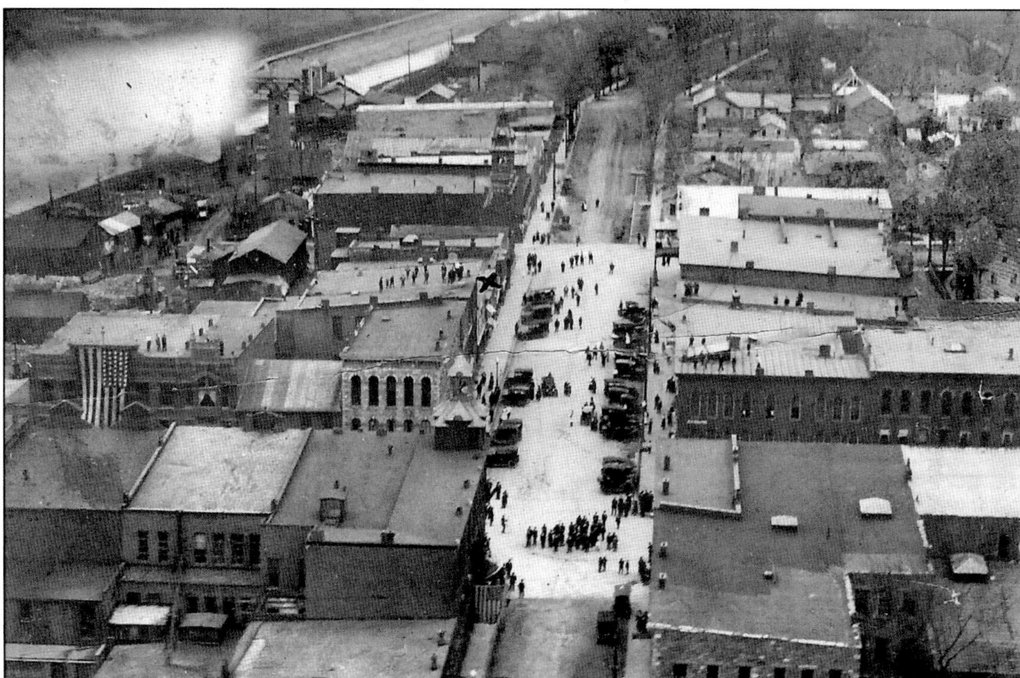

EAST BANK STREET. This is an aerial view of East Bank Street prior to 1920. (Courtesy of Orleans County Department of History.)

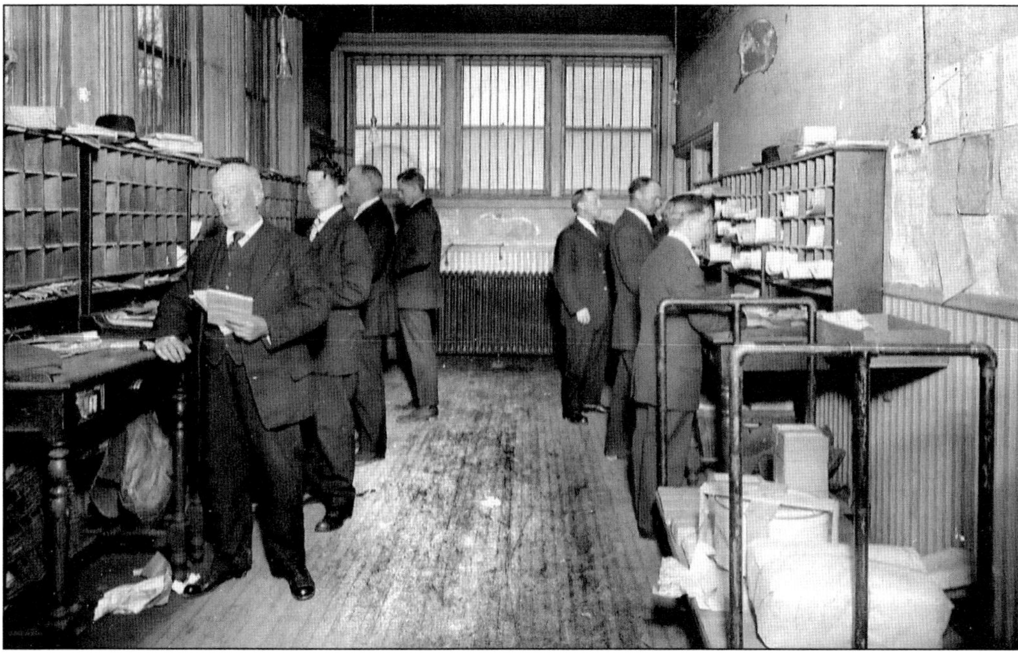

SORTING THE MAIL. Postal employees sort mail in the East Bank Street post office around 1915. (Courtesy of Orleans County Department of History.)

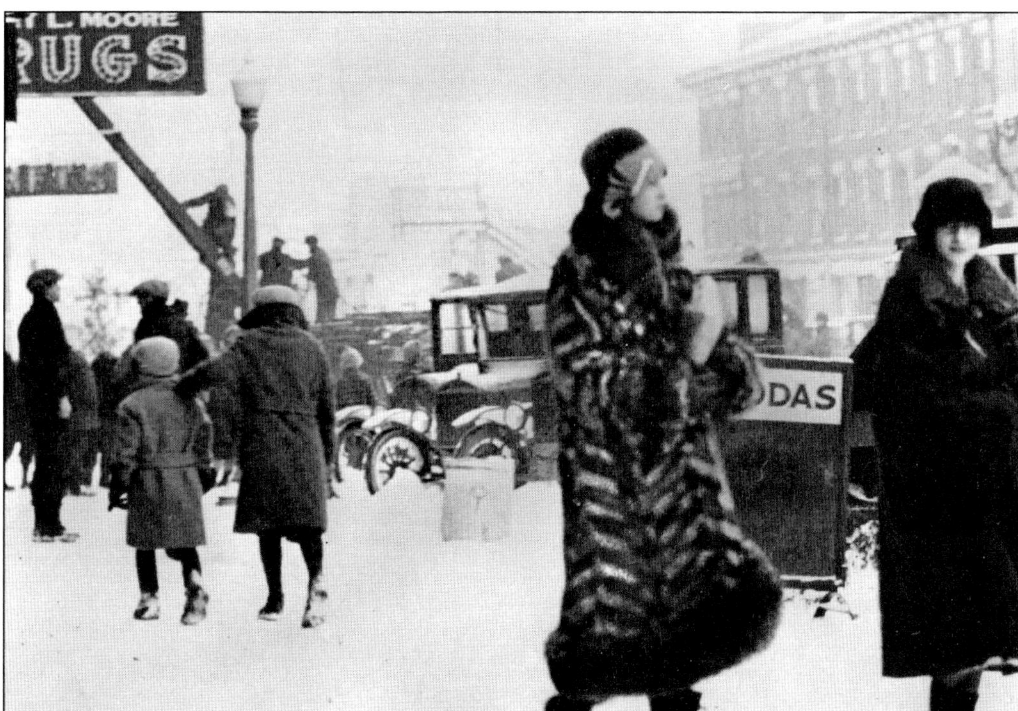

ALBION WINTER. Folks enjoy walking in the snow in downtown Albion around 1925. Note the buildings on the other side of the road, almost totally obliterated by a light snow. (Courtesy of Mark Tillman.)

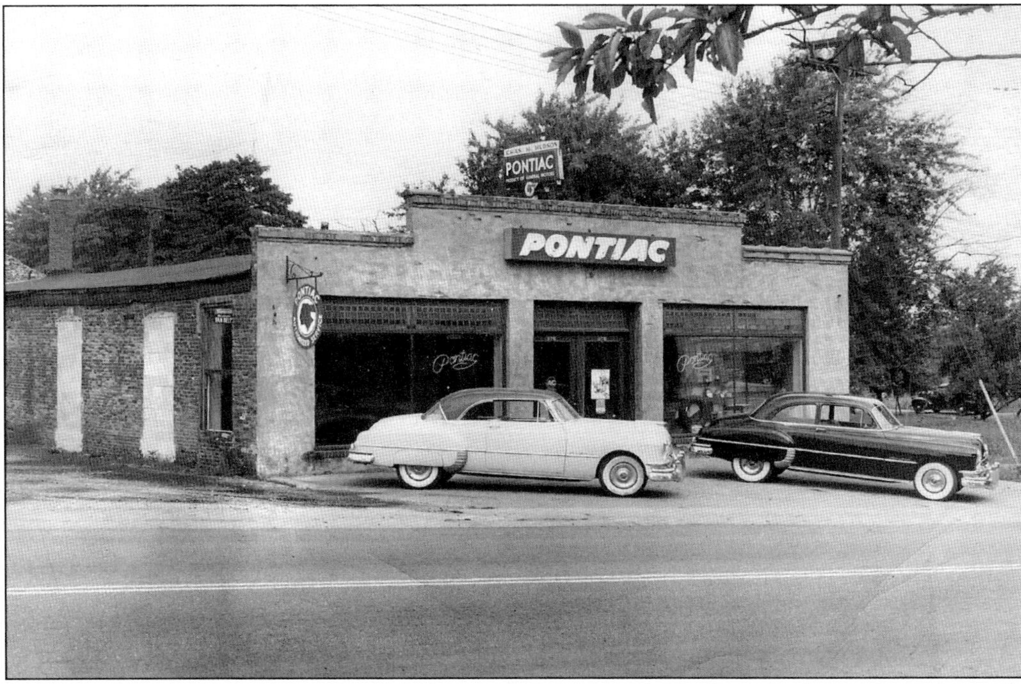

PONTIAC DEALERSHIP. This picture shows the Pontiac dealership in the early 1950s. The building now houses the Lake Country Pennysaver. (Courtesy of Orleans County Department of History.)

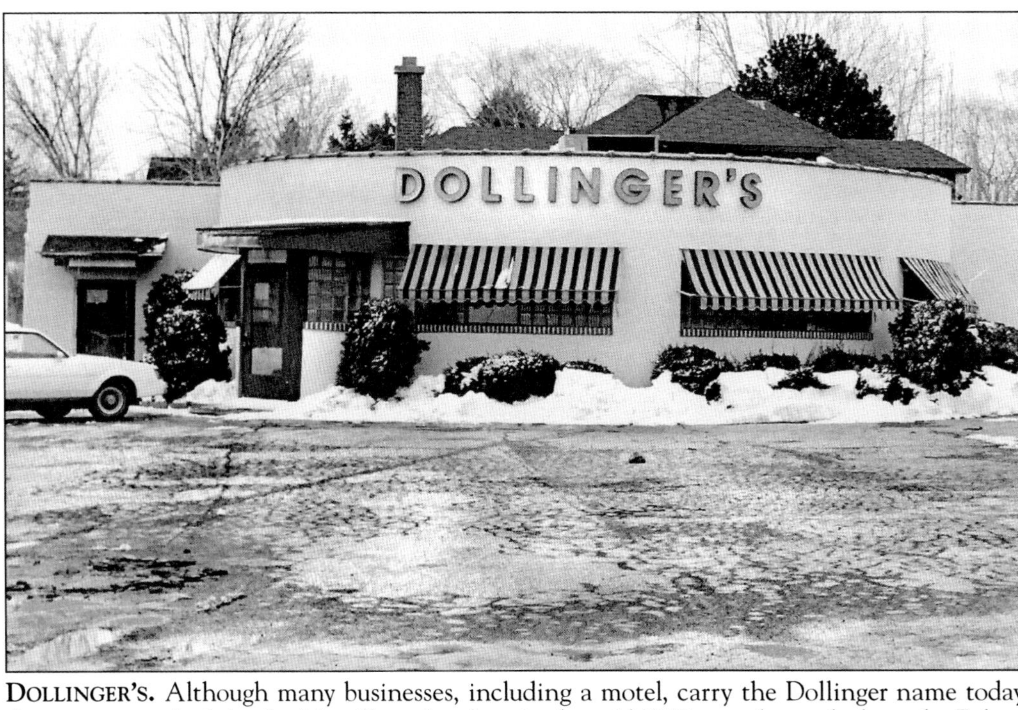

DOLLINGER'S. Although many businesses, including a motel, carry the Dollinger name today, this restaurant, built by the Martillotta brothers in the mid-1940s, was located where the Eckerd Drugstore stands today. (Courtesy of Orleans County Department of History.)

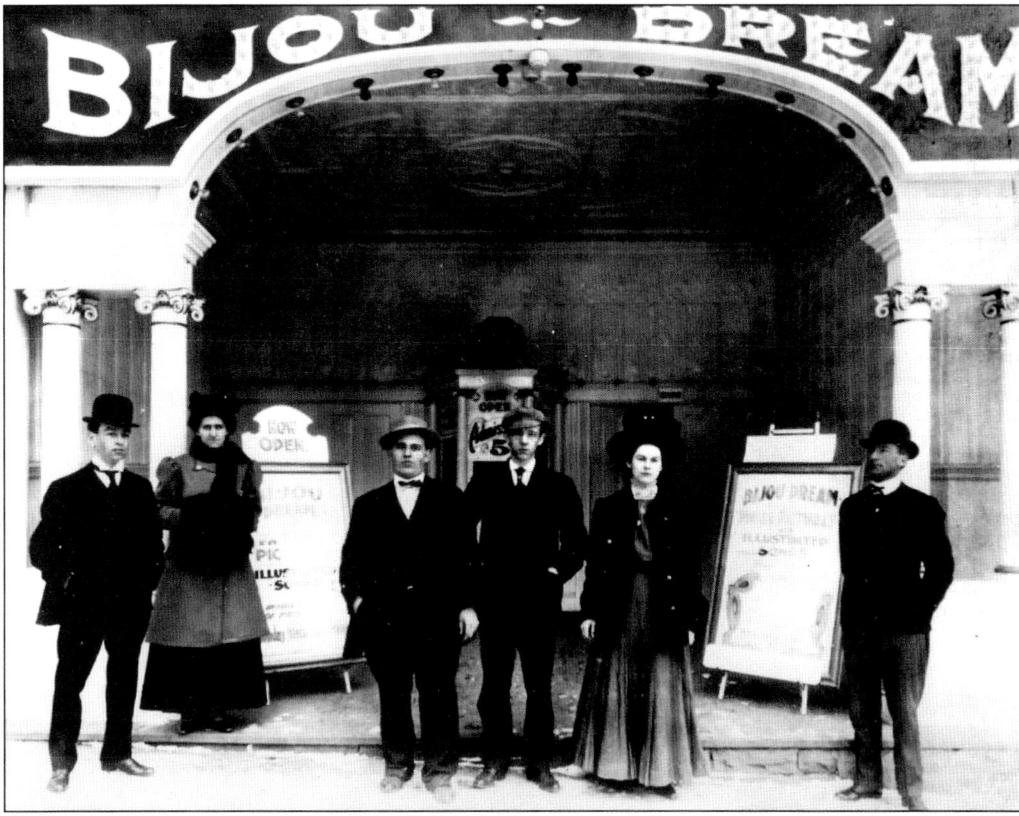

THE BIJOU DREAM. The Bijou Dream was one of Albion's first movie theaters, located near the Swan Library. Admission was 5¢ in 1908. (Courtesy of Mark Tillman.)

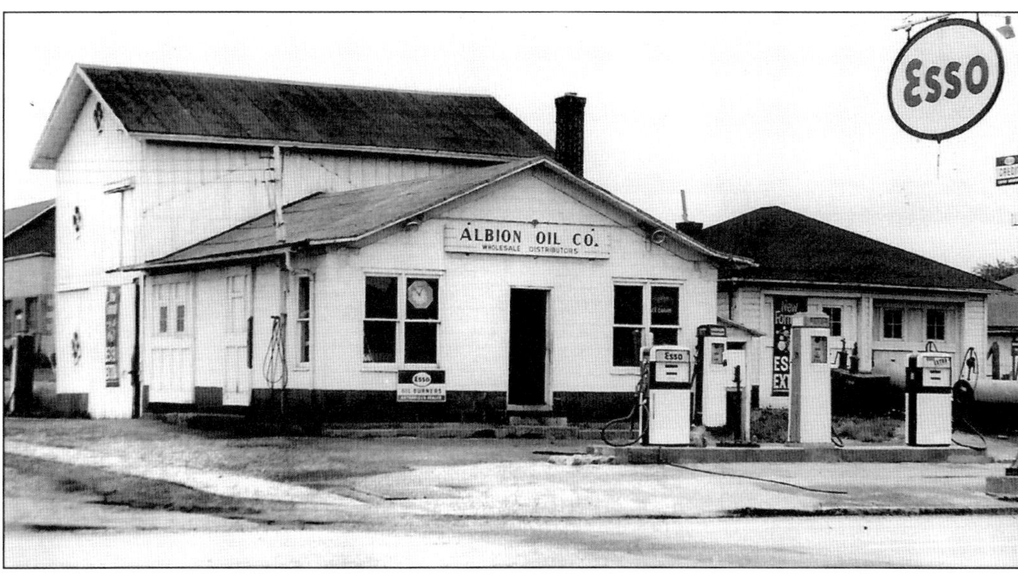

ESSO STATION. The Albion Oil Company owned the Esso station on the southwest corner of West Academy Street and West Avenue around 1955. (Courtesy of Orleans County Department of History.)

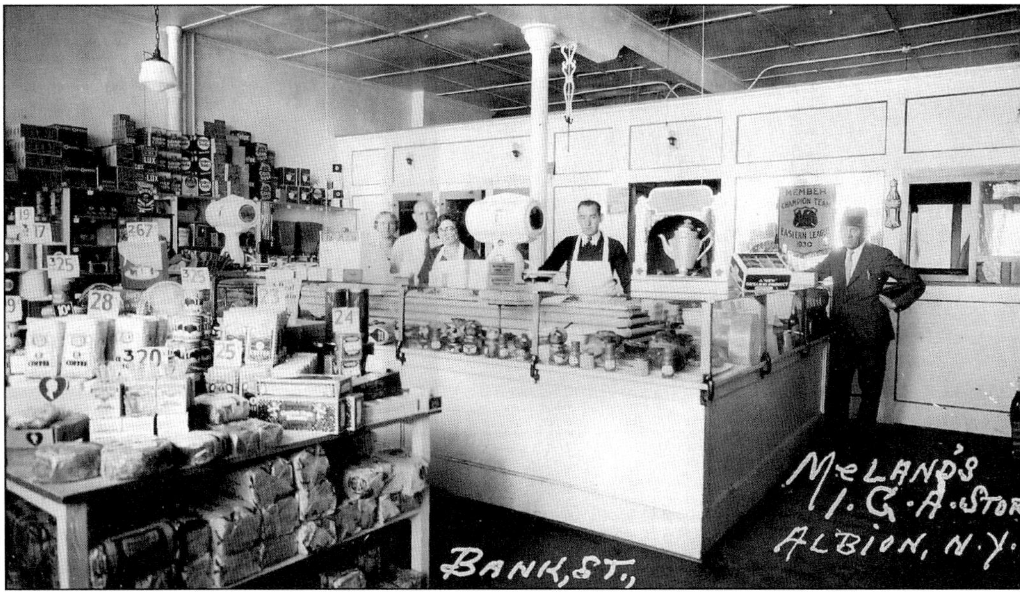

INSIDE THE IGA. Meland's IGA Store, on East Bank Street, was a popular spot in the 1920s. Rather than shelves, groceries were placed on tables and on the floor. (Courtesy of Orleans County Department of History.)

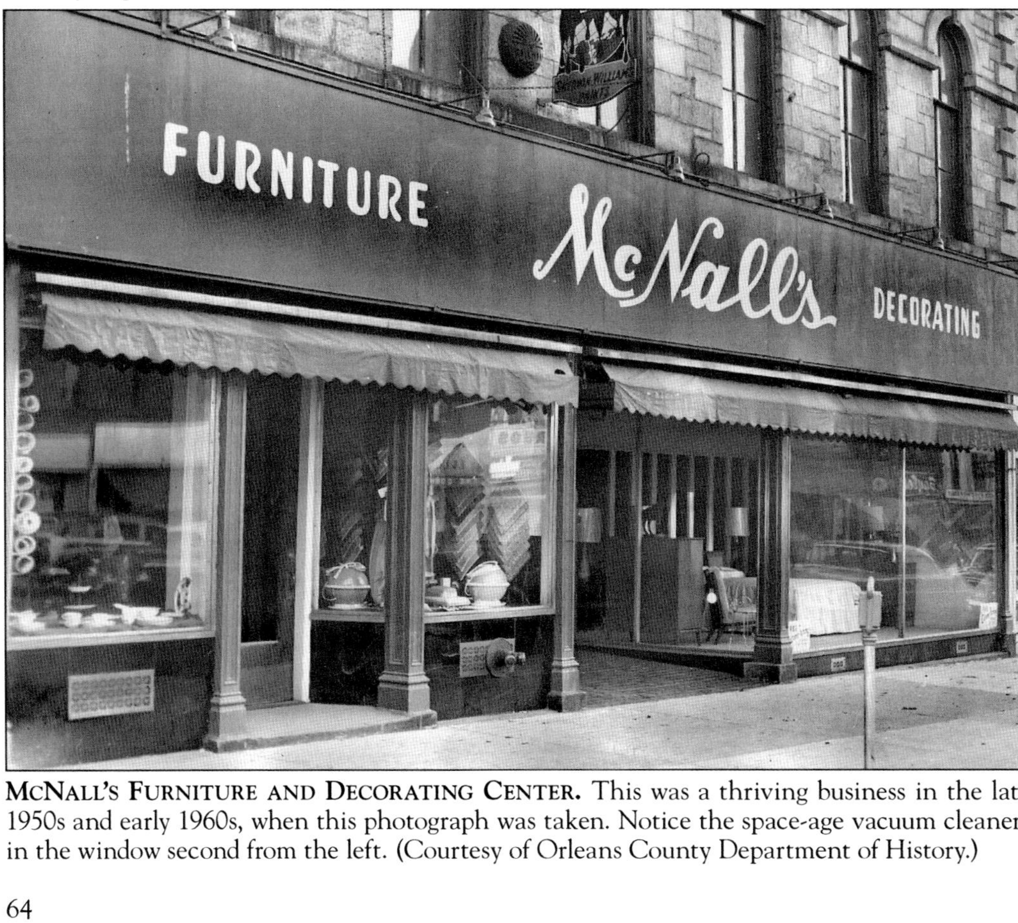

McNALL'S FURNITURE AND DECORATING CENTER. This was a thriving business in the late 1950s and early 1960s, when this photograph was taken. Notice the space-age vacuum cleaners in the window second from the left. (Courtesy of Orleans County Department of History.)

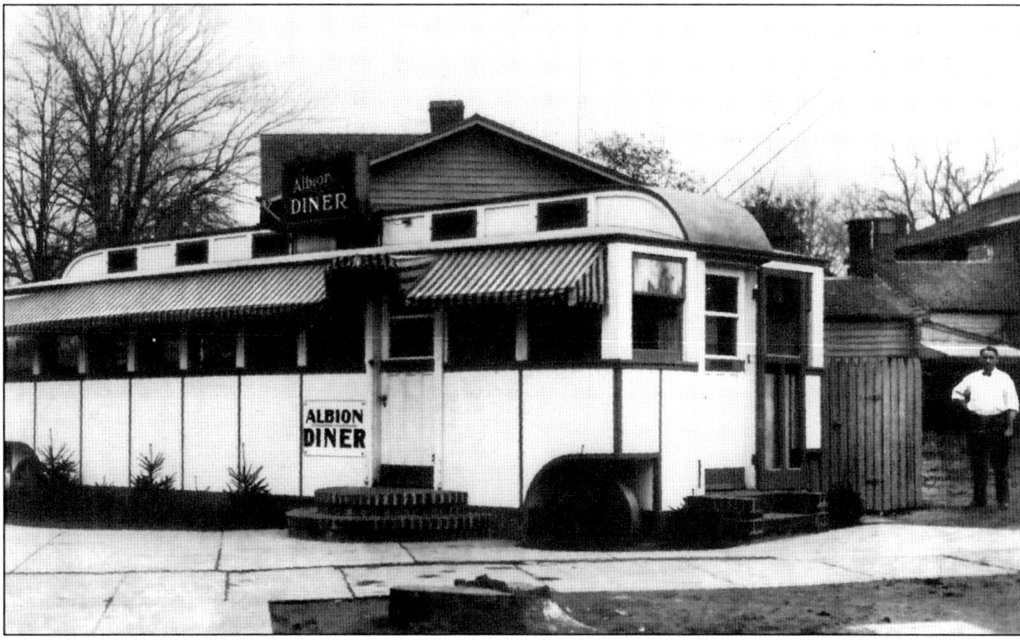

ALBION DINER. This diner was located on the corner of Platt and East Bank Streets around 1945. (Courtesy of Orleans County Department of History.)

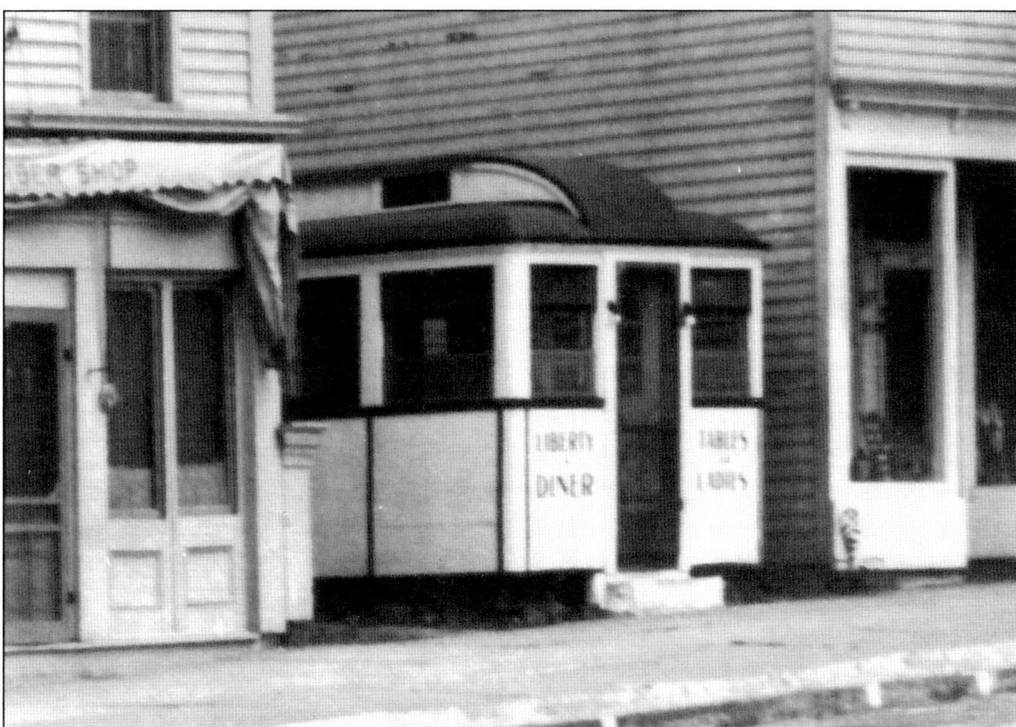

LIBERTY DINER. Although it looks like the Albion Diner, the Liberty Diner was on Main Street, wedged between two stores. (Courtesy of Orleans County Department of History.)

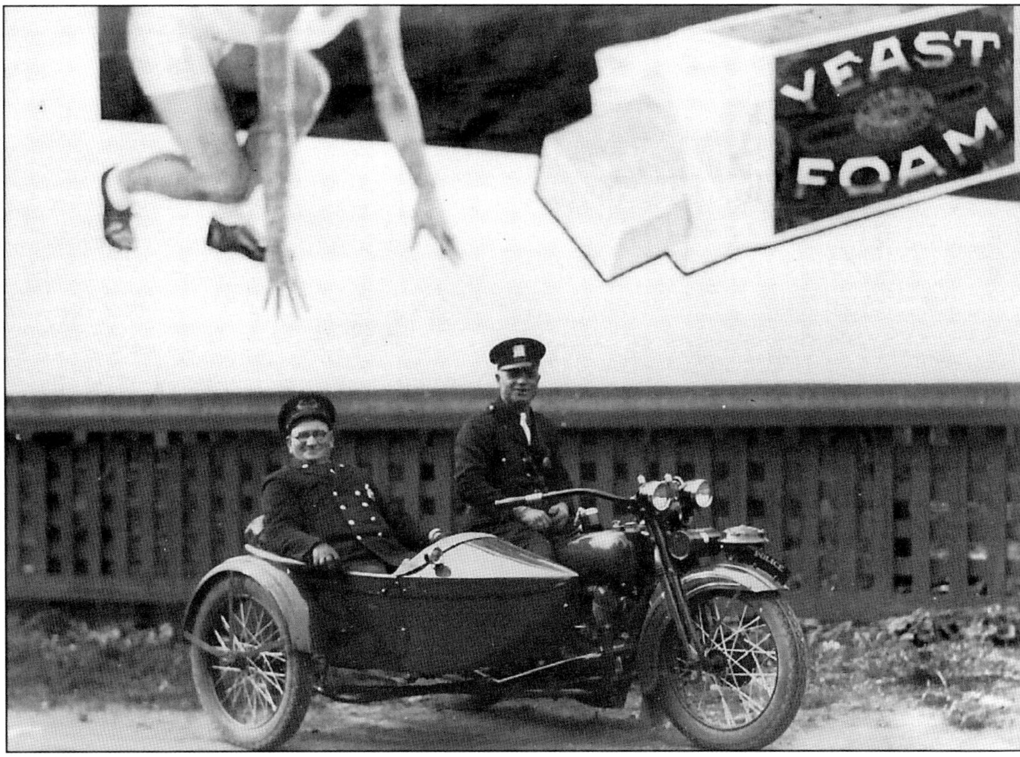

SIDECAR UNDER A BILLBOARD. Taking a break from their patrol are police chief Horace Kelsey, in the sidecar, and officer Ed Hazelbaker, on the motorcycle, around 1925. (Courtesy of Orleans County Department of History.)

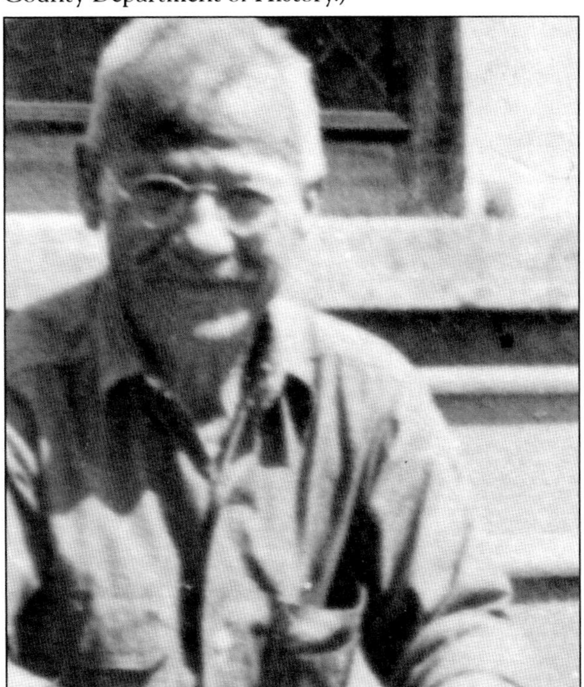

RELAXING AT HOME. Peter Monacelli enjoys sitting on his steps in the sunshine at his homestead on Hamilton Street. (Courtesy of Susan Fuller.)

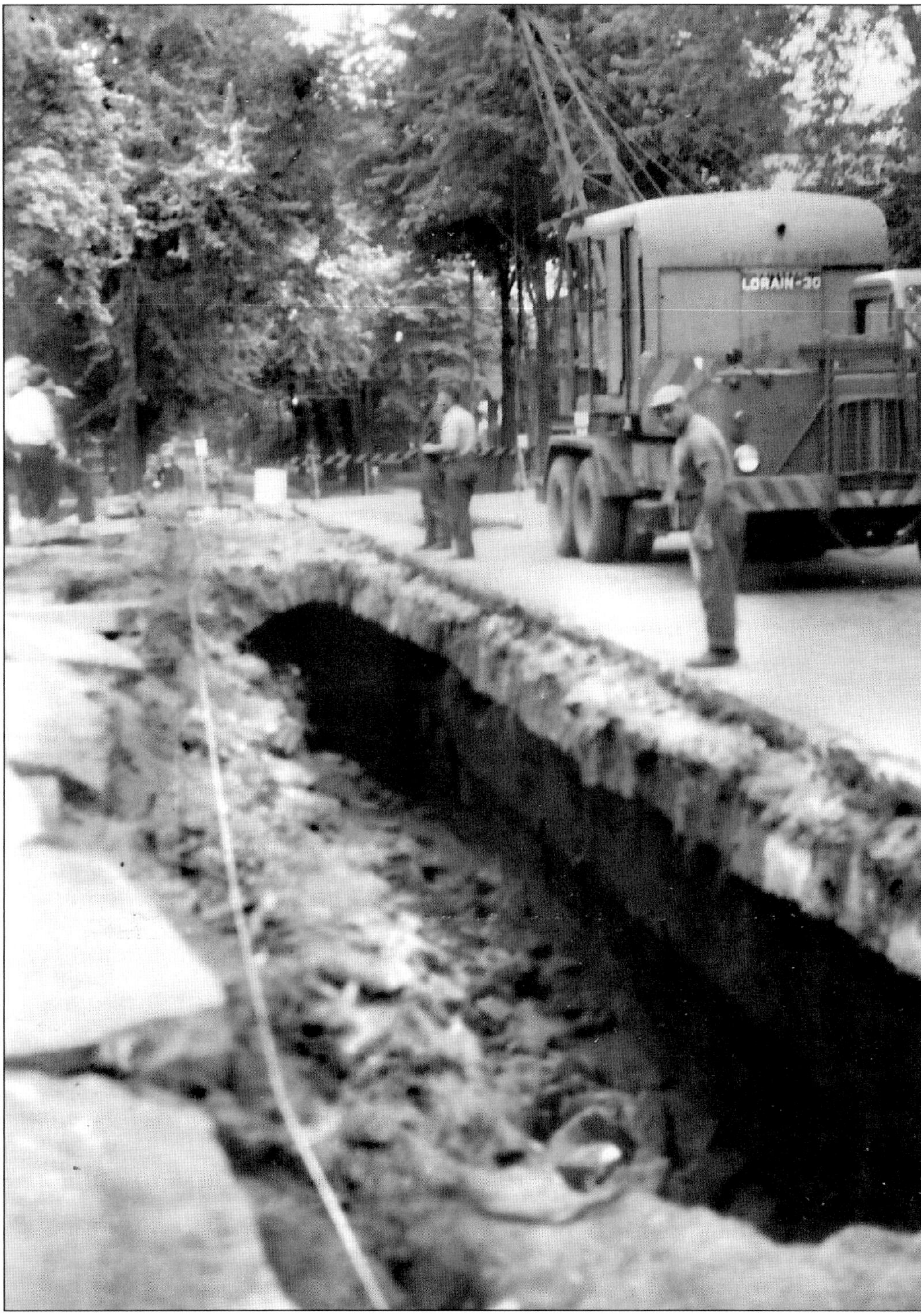

FIRE CISTERN. When Main Street was widened in 1954, an old fire cistern was discovered directly in front of the courthouse. Before fire hydrants were installed, cisterns were set below street level to store water to douse fires. (Courtesy of Orleans County Department of History.)

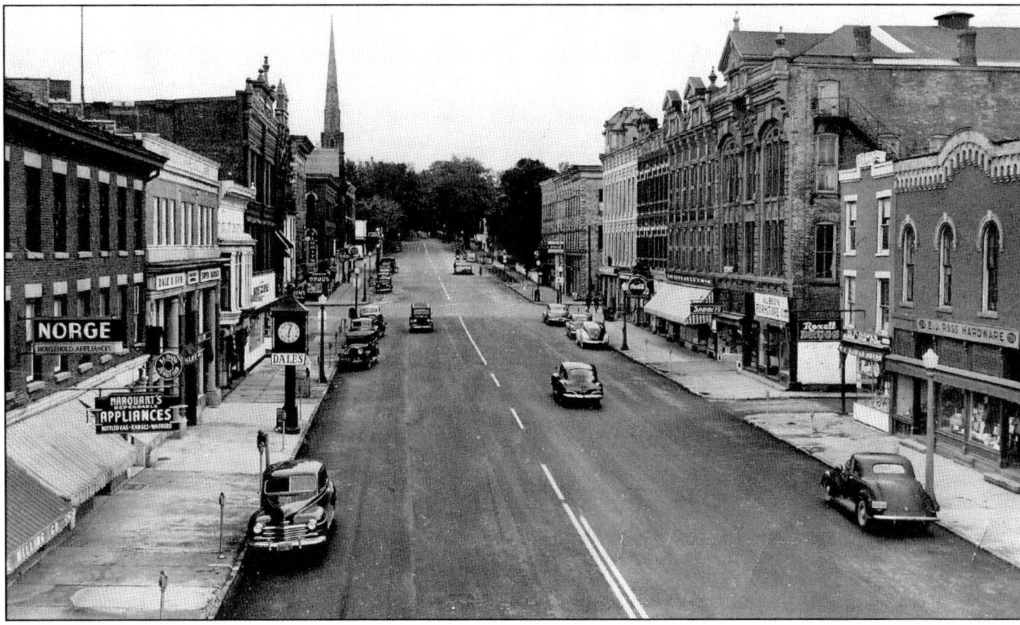

MAIN STREET. Looking south, this view is of Main Street around 1949. The large spire of the First Presbyterian Church can be seen at the left. (Courtesy of Orleans County Department of History.)

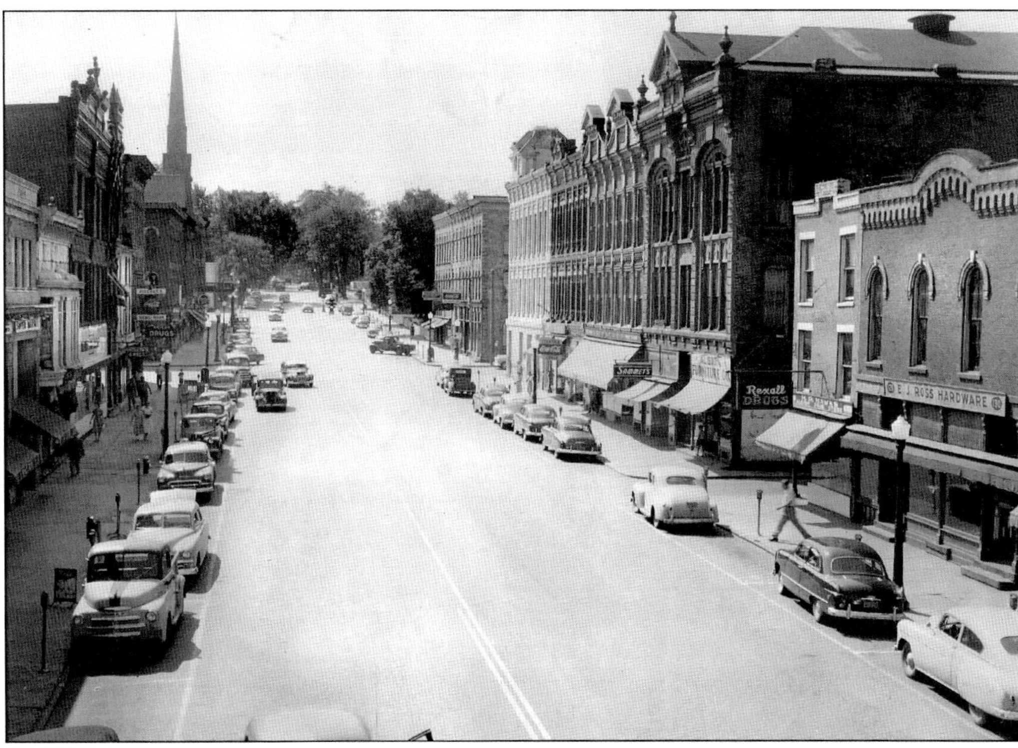

MAIN STREET. Although Albion is not a city, this 1951 view makes it look like one. The photograph was captured facing south, overlooking the business section. The steeple of the Presbyterian church looms high at the far left. (Courtesy of Orleans County Department of History.)

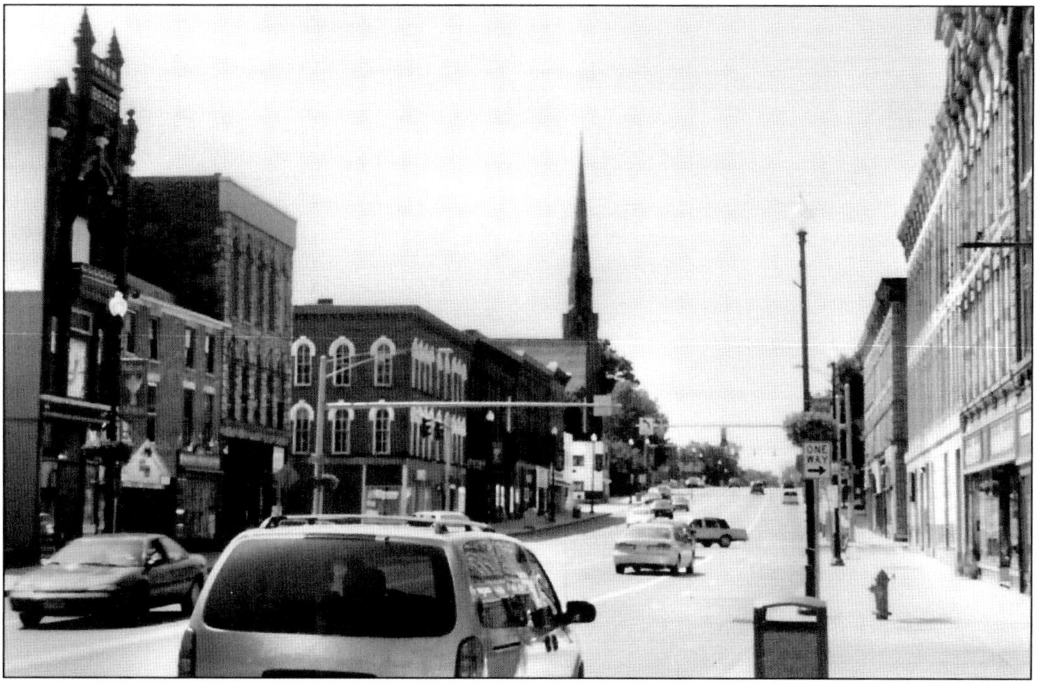

MAIN STREET TODAY. Looking south, this photograph was taken from the Erie Canal lift bridge on Main Street. The church spire looms large in the distance, and traffic is light because it is Sunday morning.

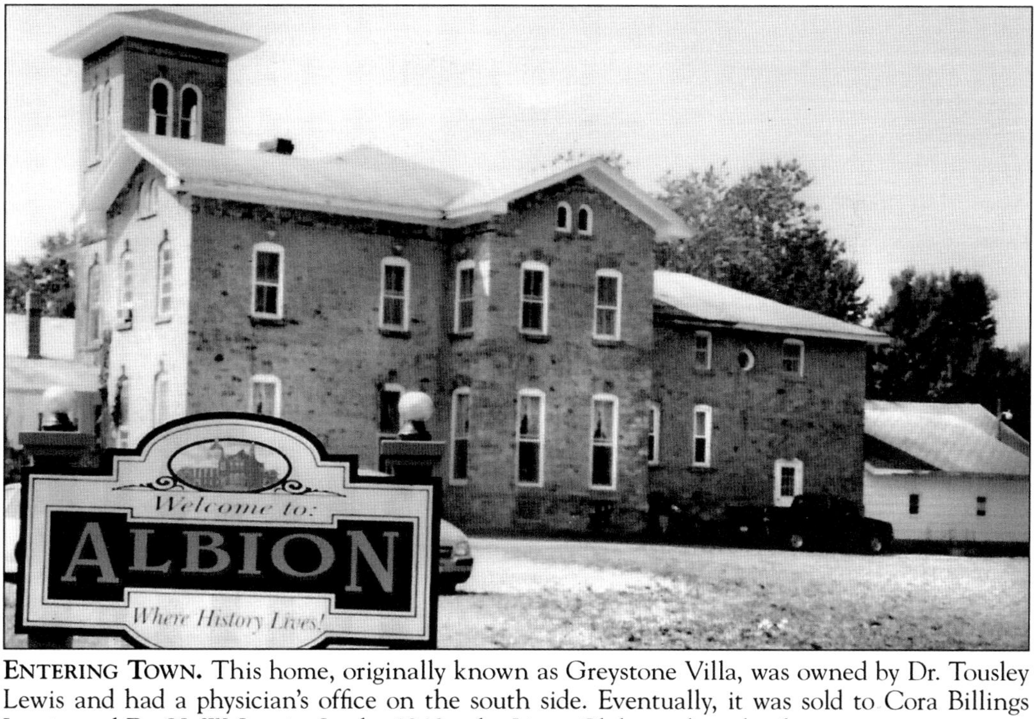

ENTERING TOWN. This home, originally known as Greystone Villa, was owned by Dr. Tousley Lewis and had a physician's office on the south side. Eventually, it was sold to Cora Billings Lattin and Dr. H. W. Lattin. In the 1940s, the Lions Club purchased it for meetings, naming it the Lion's Den. The sign informs visitors that they are entering historic Albion.

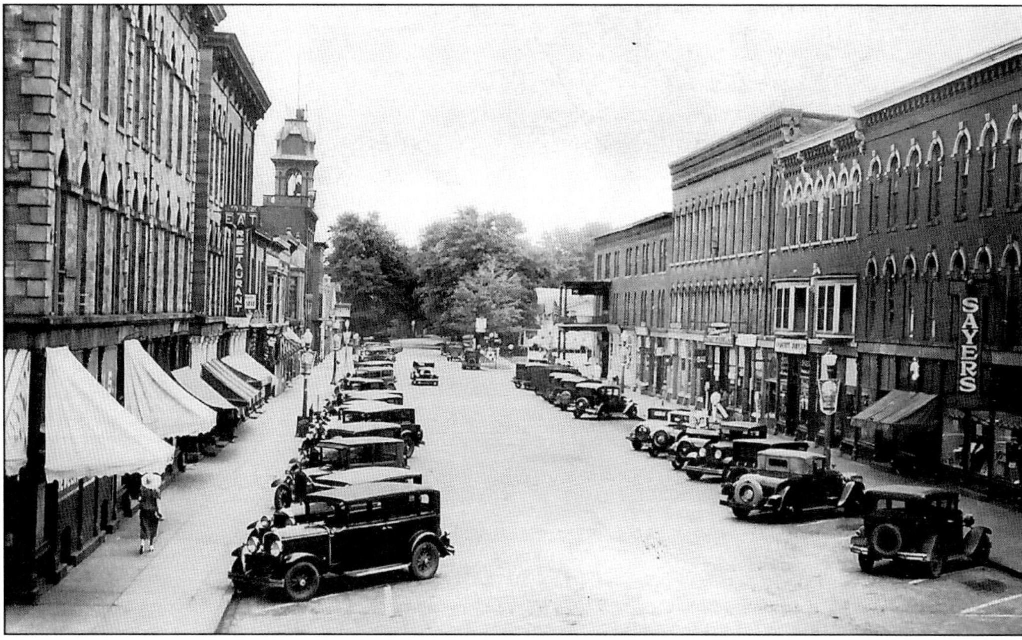

BUSY STREET. This was East Bank Street in the late 1920s. In the distance to the left is the cupola on the village hall. This was removed in the late 1950s. (Courtesy of Orleans County Department of History.)

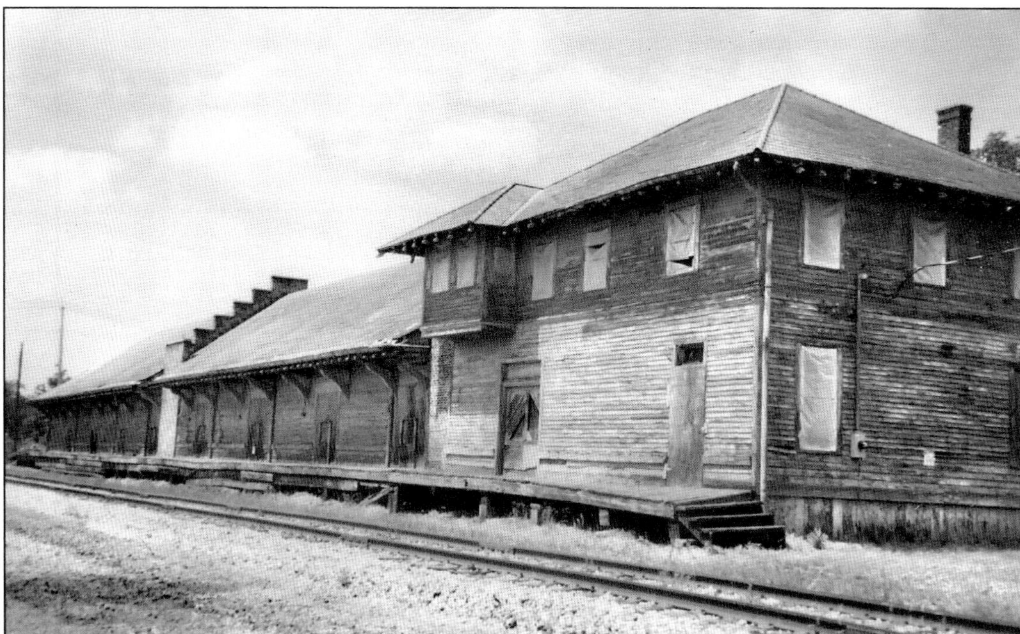

THE ORPHAN TRAIN PROJECT. During the 1920s, many orphans were sent from New York City to the West Coast, stopping along the way to find homes with families. Recently, the Orleans County Genealogical Society received a grant to restore this old freight house on the railroad tracks off Academy Street. The group plans to restore the building as a genealogical research library and museum for orphan train memorabilia.

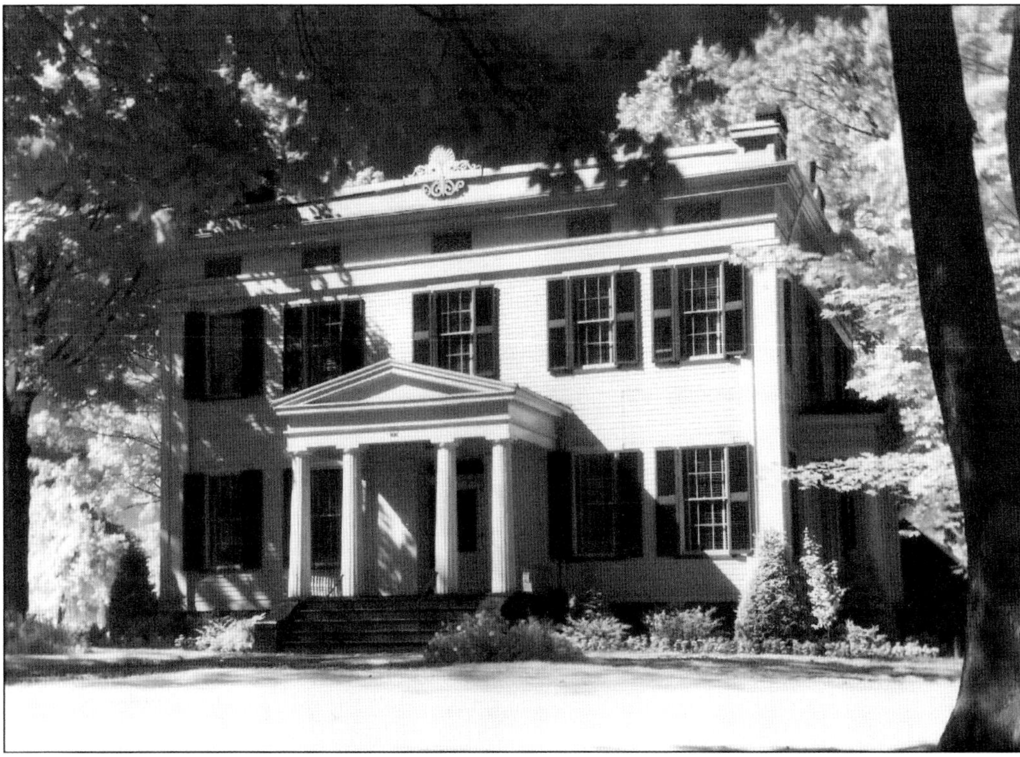

SNIDER LABORATORY. This building was located on South Main Street and was later called the Birdseye Lab. It was torn down in the early 1970s.

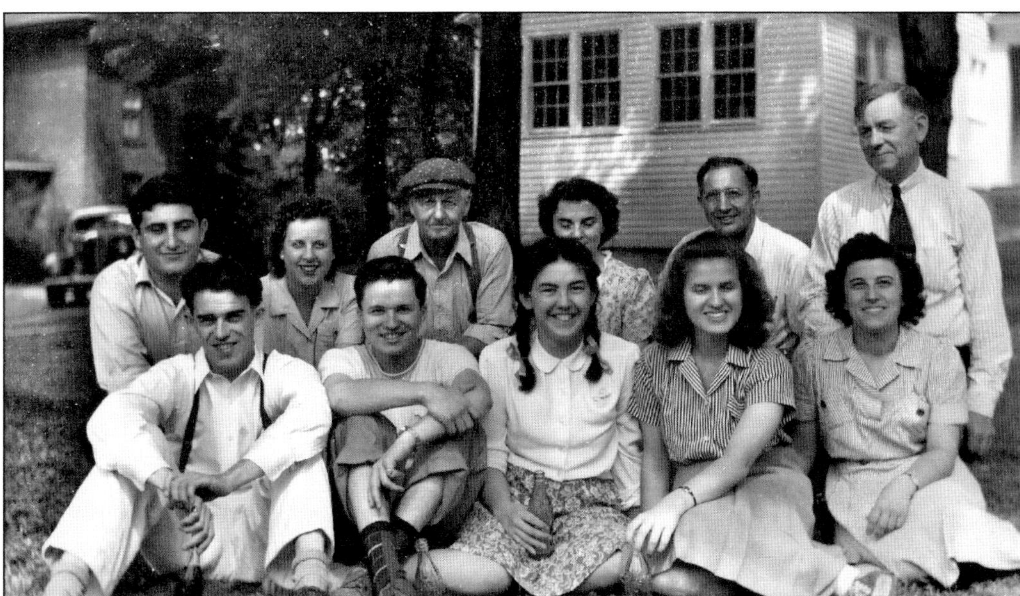

LAB WORKERS. Behind Snider Lab in 1943 are, from left to right, the following employees: (first row) Charlie Byrne, Sy Pompers, Ruth Adamy, Fern Chase, and Jessie Nenni; (second row) Hunter Cohen, Helen Collins, Bill Lee, Helen DiJuilio, W. Enzie, and John Swenholf.

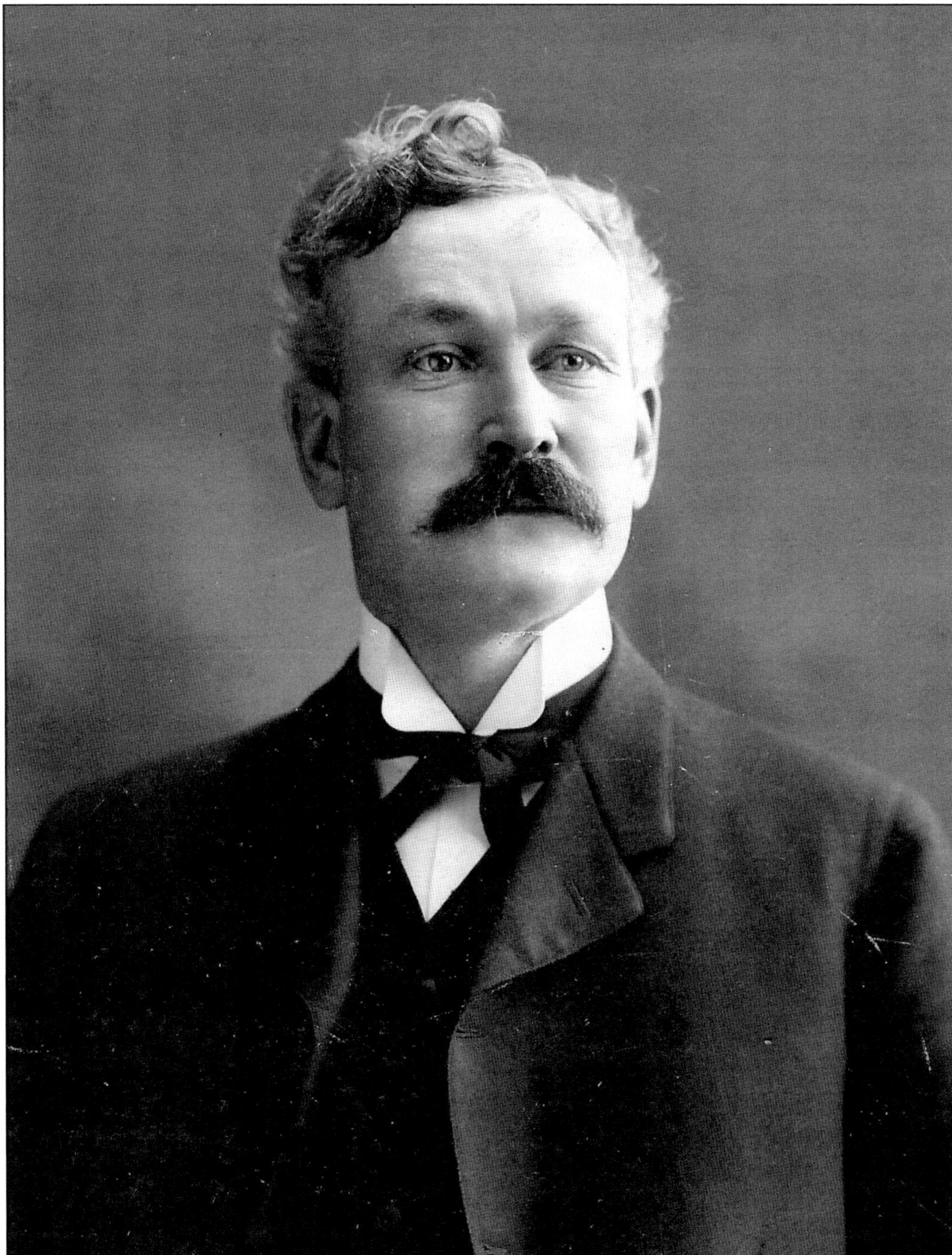

JOHN E. SUTTON. Dr. John E. Sutton was president of the Albion Board of Education in 1908 and 1909. (Courtesy of Orleans County Department of History.)

Three

SCHOOL AND SPORTS

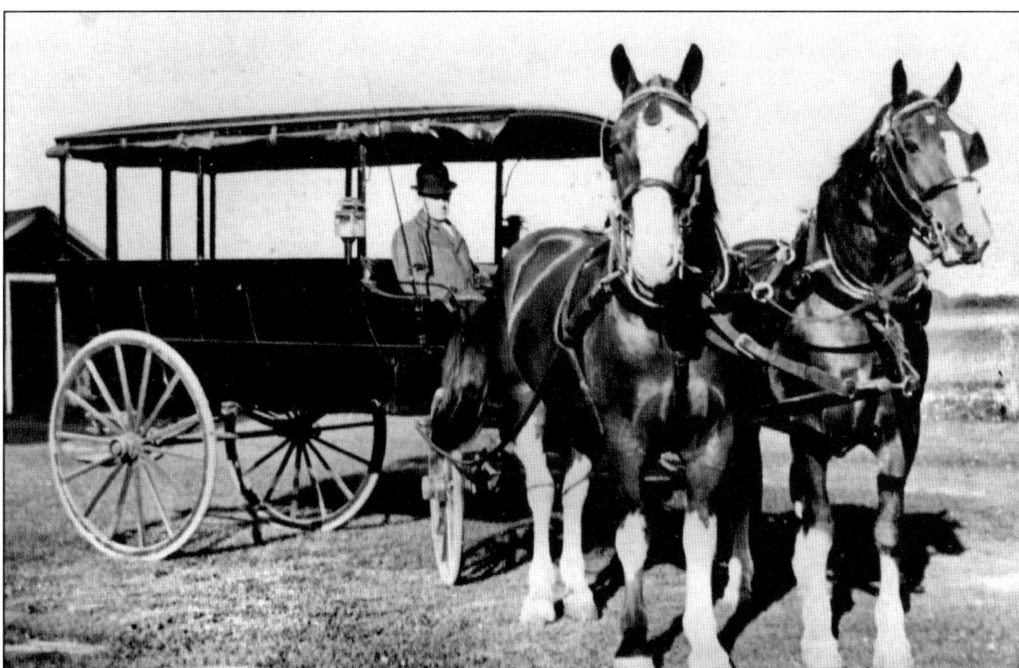

FIRST SCHOOL BUS. The Loveland School District west of Albion hired William Howard in 1908 to transport its students to Albion in this horse-drawn bus rather than hire a teacher for the one-room schoolhouse. (Courtesy of Mark Tillman.)

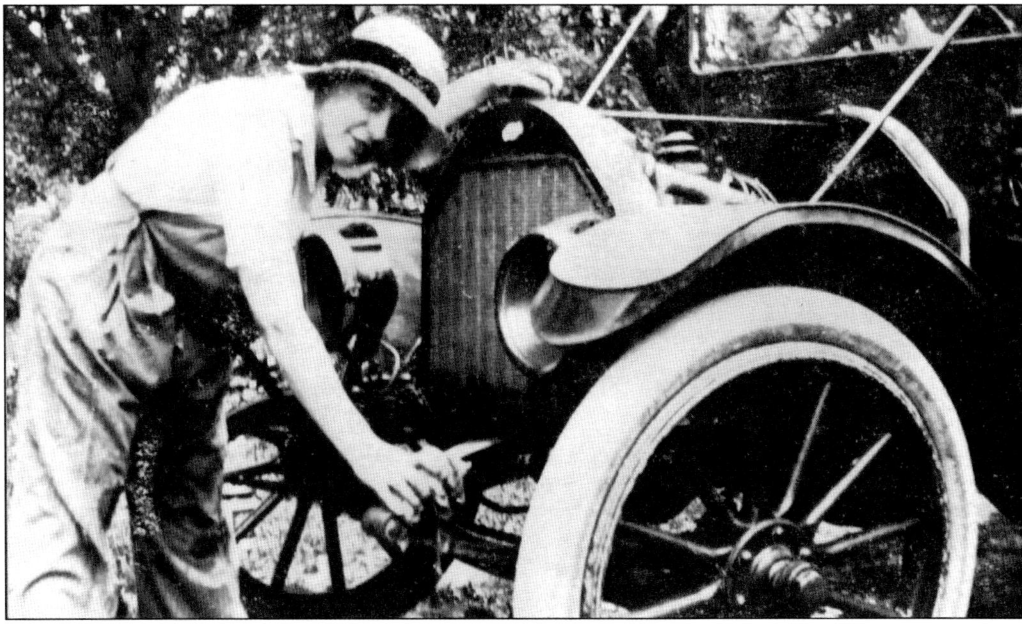

DRIVING TO SCHOOL. Clara Cliff, shown in 1916, was the first student to drive to Albion High School. She even learned how to work the crank to start it up. Her parents bought her a car rather than have her board with another family during the school year, as was the norm in those days. They wanted her home each night. (Courtesy of Tillman's Village Inn.)

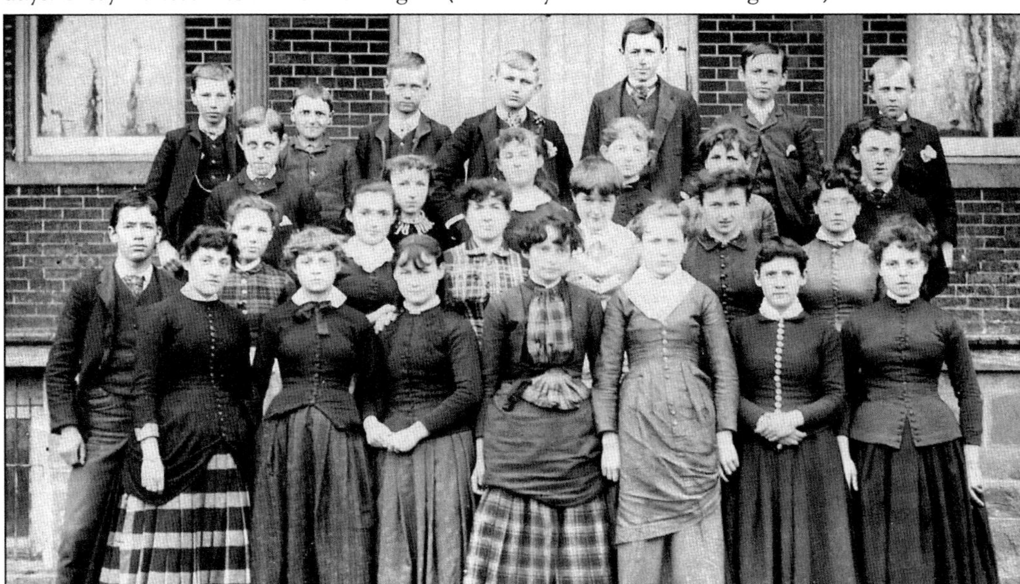

ALBION STUDENTS. This photograph dates from 1889. Students are, from left to right, as follows: (first row) Mable Young, Belle Higgerson, Carrie Brown, Minnie Smith, Mamie Dowd, Gurtha Bushnell, and unidentified; (second row) George Harris, Grace Robbins, Lily Howard, Minnie Grinnell, Ella Love, May Eddy, and Alice Bushnell; (third row) Don Stimson, Lillian Achilles, Florence Rogers, Jennie Smith, Kitty Gaskill, and Bert Day; (fourth row) Charles Mack, ? Buck, Robert Osburn, F. M. Thompson, Louis Spaulding, Bert Hunt, and Frank Brown. (Courtesy of Orleans County Department of History.)

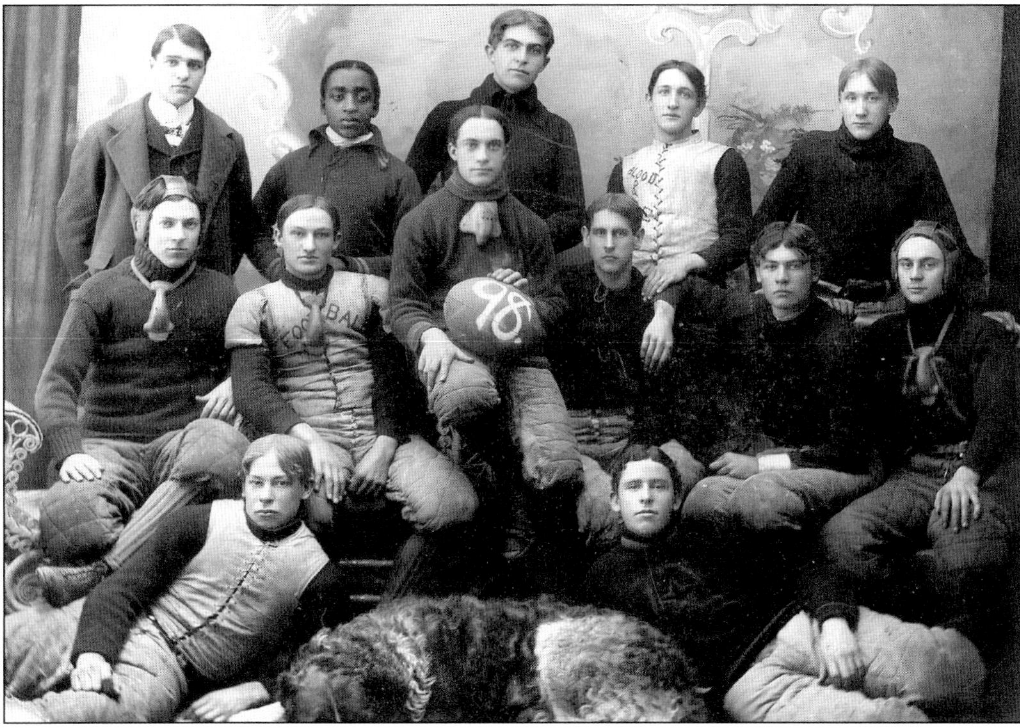

FOOTBALL TEAM, 1898. Members of the Albion High School football team pose in 1898 with the game ball and their large, fluffy canine mascot. From left to right are the following: (first row) Murray Hardenbrook, Bower the mascot, and Guyler Leslie; (second row) Fred Hillspaugh, Pete Galarneau, Billy Rose, Bert Squire, George Sullivan, and Bob Clark; (third row) John Wilson, Frank Mason, Gene Barnum, Clayton Blood, and George Wall. (Courtesy of Mark Tillman.)

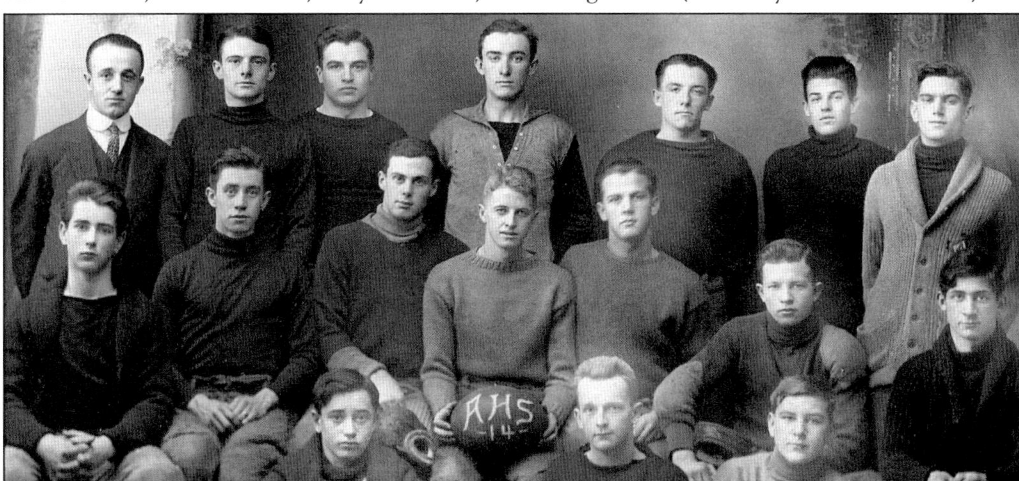

FOOTBALL TEAM, 1914. This is the Albion High School football team in 1914. From left to right are the following: (first row) T. Donahue, F. Storeis, and T. Kast; (second row) Bob Crull, Harold Pickett, Fred Thom, Scott Clark, E. Stillman, C. Burrows, and L Humphrey; (third row) coach Francis Sturgis, I. Osbourne, L. C. Mew, A. Kirby, L. Bliss, E. Ryan, J. Ryan, and A. Elleston. (Courtesy of Orleans County Department of History.)

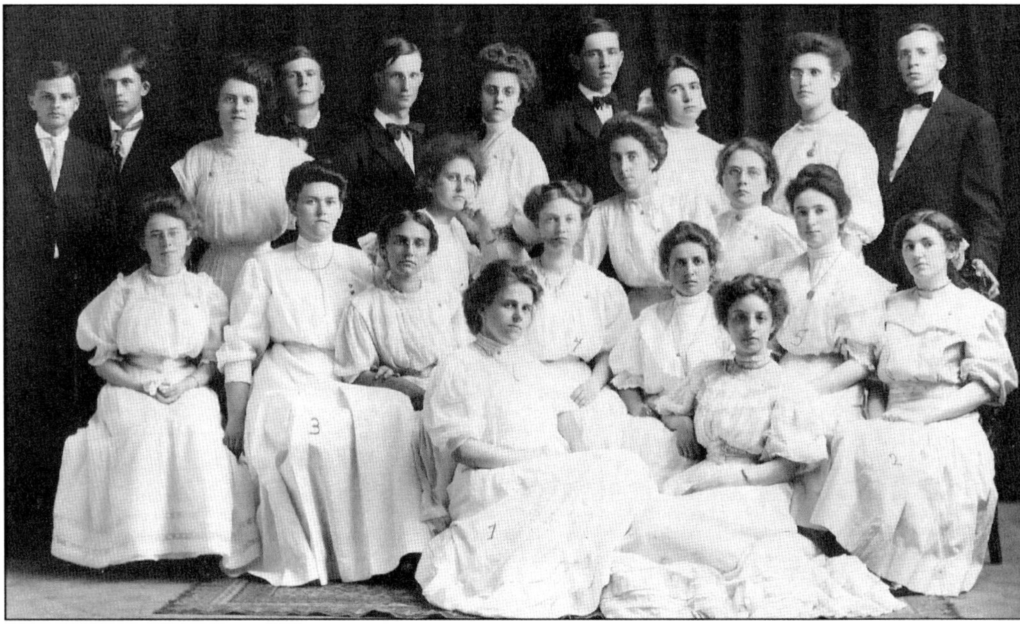

CLASS OF 1908. The girls in this class wore beautiful white dresses to celebrate their graduation. The identified girls are Velma Harding (front row, left), Mary Hyde (seated, second from the left), Ethel Mattison (fourth from the left), Florence Bates (second from the right), and Sadie Britton (far right). The identified boys are Mort Vick (back row, far right) and Tim O'Donnell (fourth from the right). (Courtesy of Orleans County Department of History.)

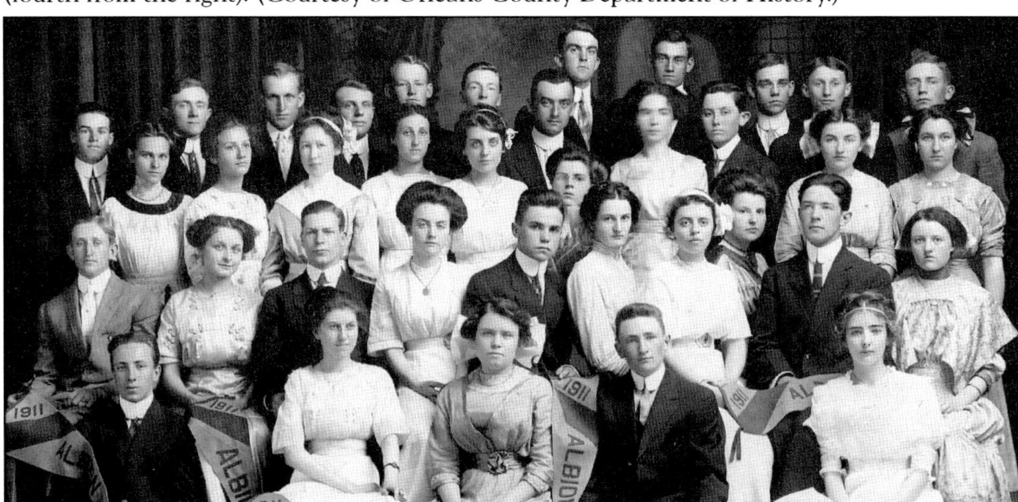

CLASS OF 1911. This was the graduating class of 1911. From left to right are the following: (first row) Harvey Waffle, Gladys Beckwith, Clara Peters, Timothy O'Brien, and ? Drew; (second row) Willis Gregaory, Florence Hubbard, Henry Clark, Lucy Porter, Hartwell Tompkins, Jessie Bennett, Maybelle Howard, Georgia Posson, Francis Maloney, and Nettie Palmer; (third row) Elizabeth Chadwick, Helen Sanford, Eunice Richardson, Jane Botsford, May Canham, Blanche Parsons, Olive Clark, John Parker, Kate Vanderpool, and Emma Delaney; (fourth row) Clinton Blowers, J. Howard Pratt, Carl Parker, Edwin Phillips, John Sutton, Harold Allen, Leo Woodside, Vernon Wood, M. Blowers, Myron Babbit, Arthur Holt, and Franklin Whitwell. (Courtesy of Orleans County Department of History.)

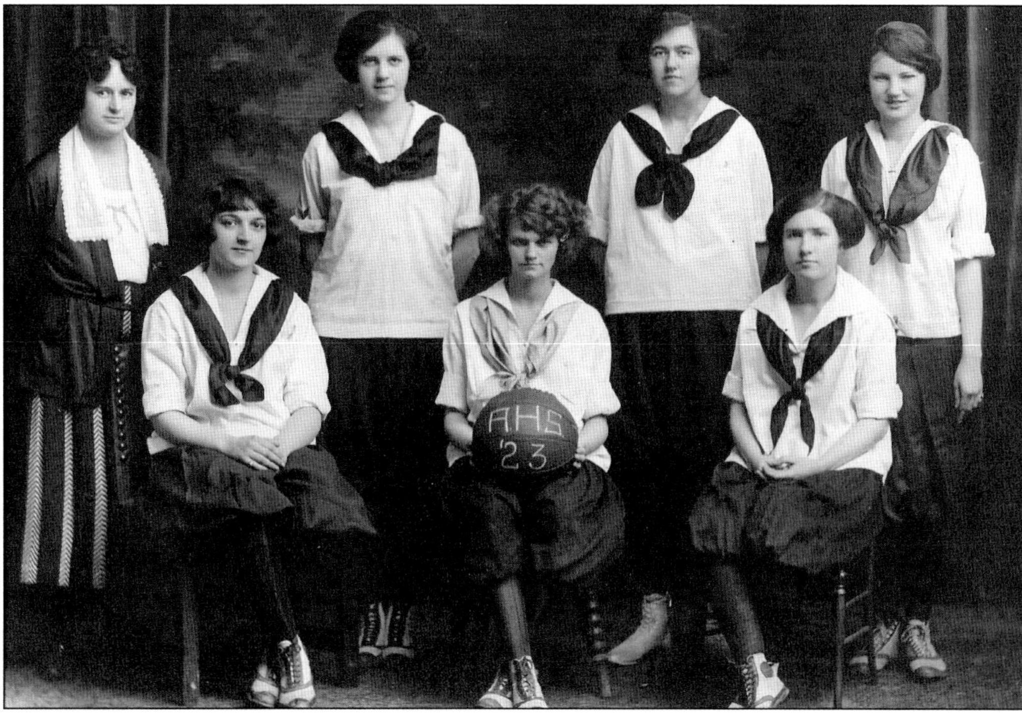

GIRLS' BASKETBALL. The Albion girls' basketball team poses with its game ball in 1923. From left to right are as follows: (first row) ? Spalla, Mildred Sayers, and Melva Vagg; (second row) unidentified coach, Elizabeth Karns, ? McNall, and unidentified. (Courtesy of Orleans County Department of History.)

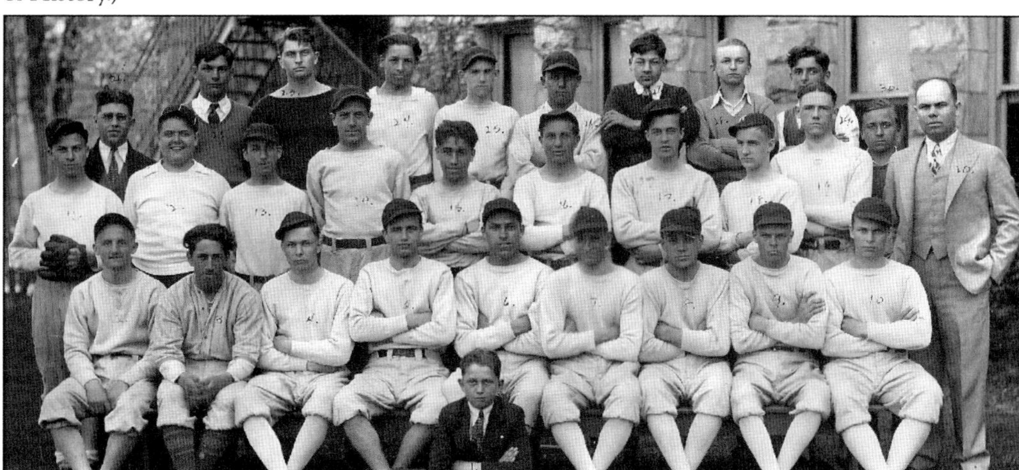

BASEBALL. The Albion High School baseball team of 1933 had lots of members. From left to right are the following: (first row) batboy Richard Foster; (second row) Pat Monacelli, Anthony "Coke" Ross, Philbrook Vick, Nellio DiGuilio, Amady "Cal" Colonna, Edmond Biordi, Louis Hollenbeck, Clyde Furness, and Robert Bloom; (third row) Peter DeLuca, Craig Campbell, Sam Juliana, Sam Martillotta, Louis "Pooch" Massaro, John Pusselli, Jack Newmon, Ralph Tiffany, Robert Wood, Henry Dragon, and ? Spierdowis (coach); (fourth row) Angelo Bell (manager), Mike Christopher, Tad "Bear" DiLaura, Steve Adams, Bruce Farnsworth, Dominic Delodavico, Frank "Pete" Morrow, George Dragon, and Joe Christopher. (Courtesy of Orleans County Department of History.)

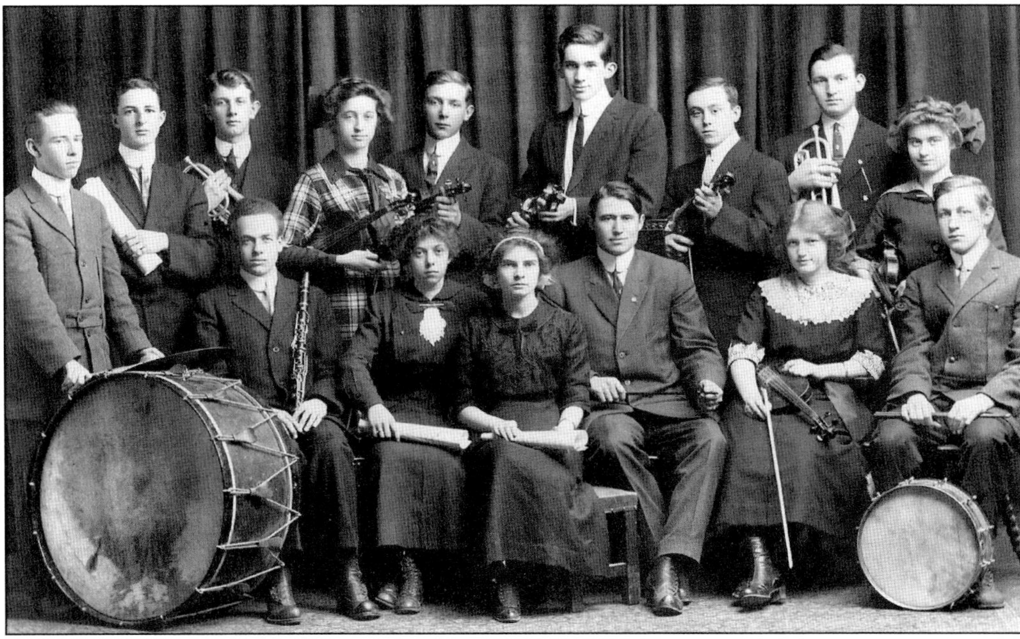

Albion High School Orchestra. These well-dressed musical students of 1913 are, from left to right, the following: (first row) C. Nelson, Marion Waldron, unidentified, Forrest Reese (director), Naomi Parker, and Albert Smith; (second row) Herbert Hudson, Earl Daum, Charles Clark, Elsie Eddy, William Trolley, Earl Harding, unidentified, Curtis Parker, and Gladys Watt. (Courtesy of Orleans County Department of History.)

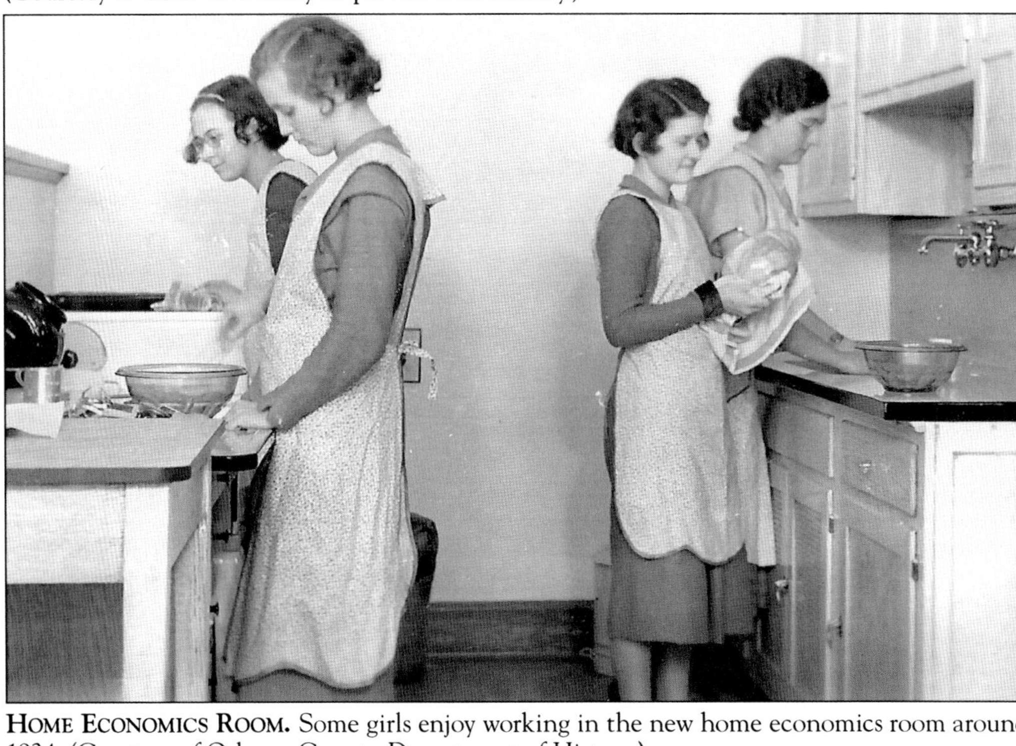

Home Economics Room. Some girls enjoy working in the new home economics room around 1934. (Courtesy of Orleans County Department of History.)

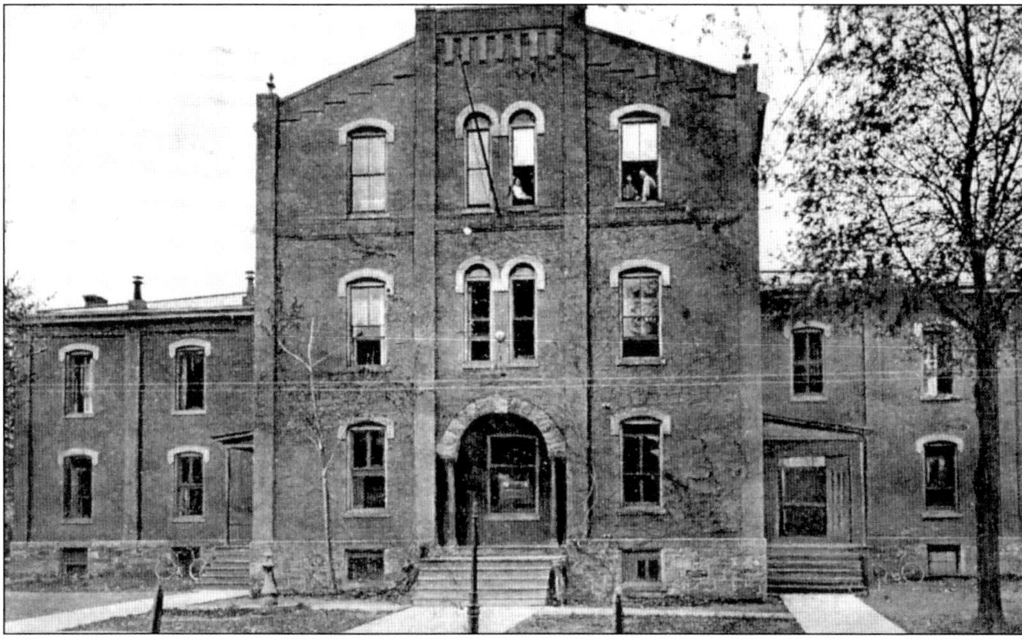

OLD HIGH SCHOOL. The old high school is pictured about 1900. (Courtesy of Orleans County Department of History.)

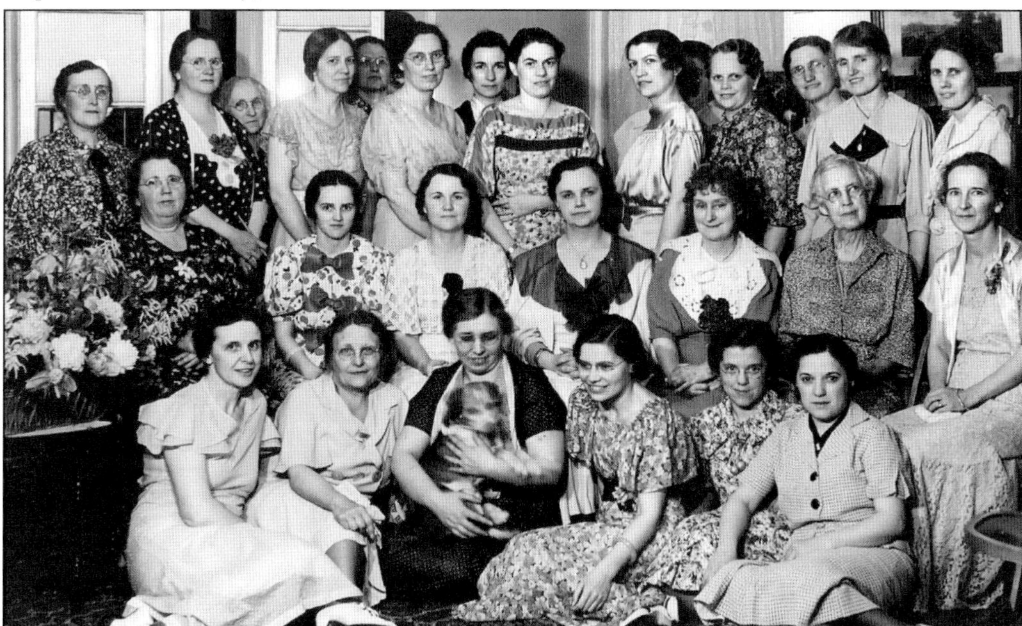

TEACHERS' GATHERING. A formal event is held at the home of superintendent Carl Bergerson around 1930. From left to right are the following: (first row) Gladys Pedler, Carrie Pratt, Hazel Bergerson (with her dog), Hazel Ganiard D'Amico, unidentified, and Mrs. Charles D'Amico; (second row) two unidentified persons, Mrs. Adams, Iva Wright-Smith, Jesse Valnia, Ida Larwood, and Irene Harrigan; (third row) Mrs. Stevens, Julia McGuire, unidentified, Christine Filkins, unidentified, Mary Trumble, Doris Spierdowis, Sadie Britton, and Doreen Sundell; (fourth row) Lillian Achilles, three unidentified persons, and Helena Hogan.

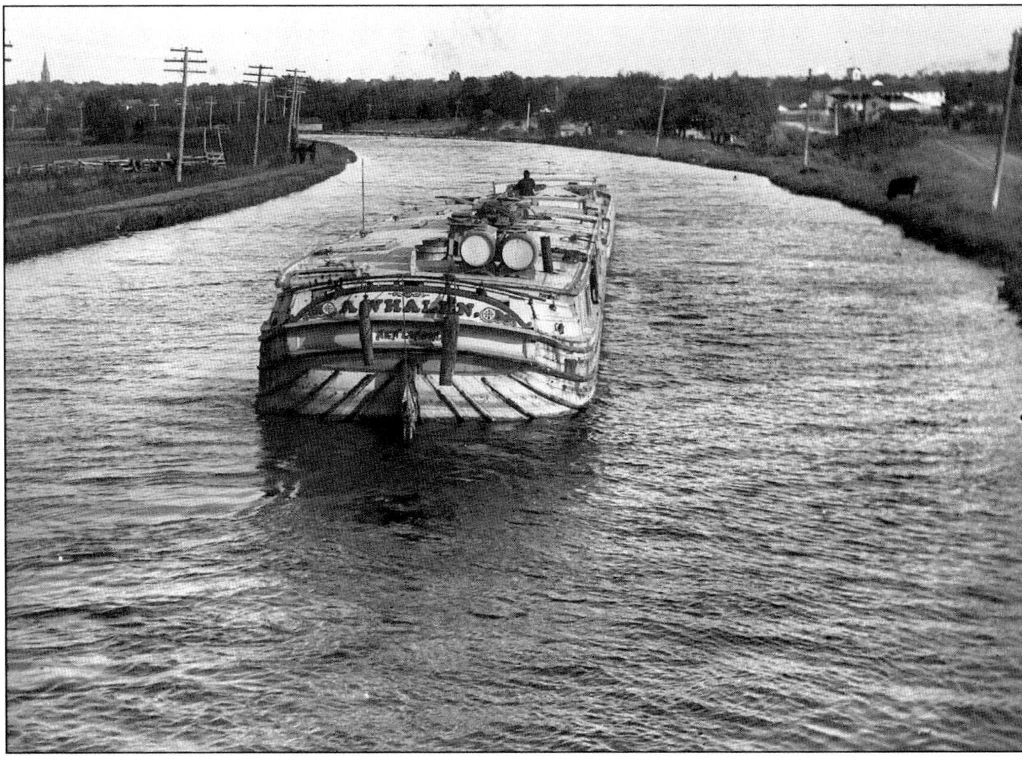

EAGLE HARBOR. A packet boat makes its way down the Erie Canal from the Eagle Harbor area of Gaines. This photograph, taken about 1895, shows the Albion Baptist Church spire at left and the fairgrounds in the distance at top right. (Courtesy of Orleans County Department of History.)

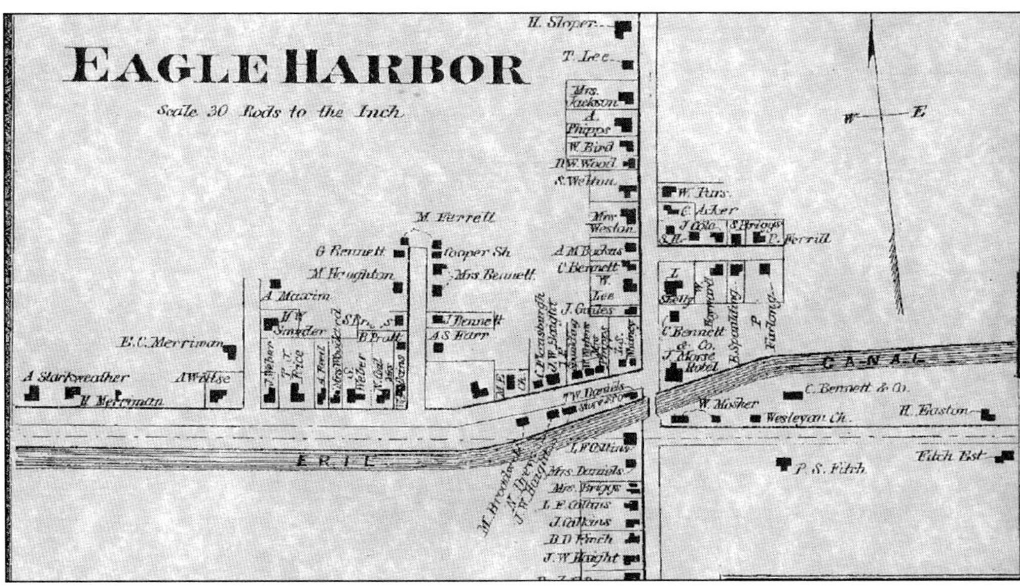

MAP OF EAGLE HARBOR. Eagle Harbor was situated along the Erie Canal just west of the village of Albion. Because of the bridge and access to boat travel, many businesses sprang up there during the canal's popular days. This map was drawn around 1875. (Courtesy of Historicaltownmaps.com.)

Four

CANAL AND WATERWAYS

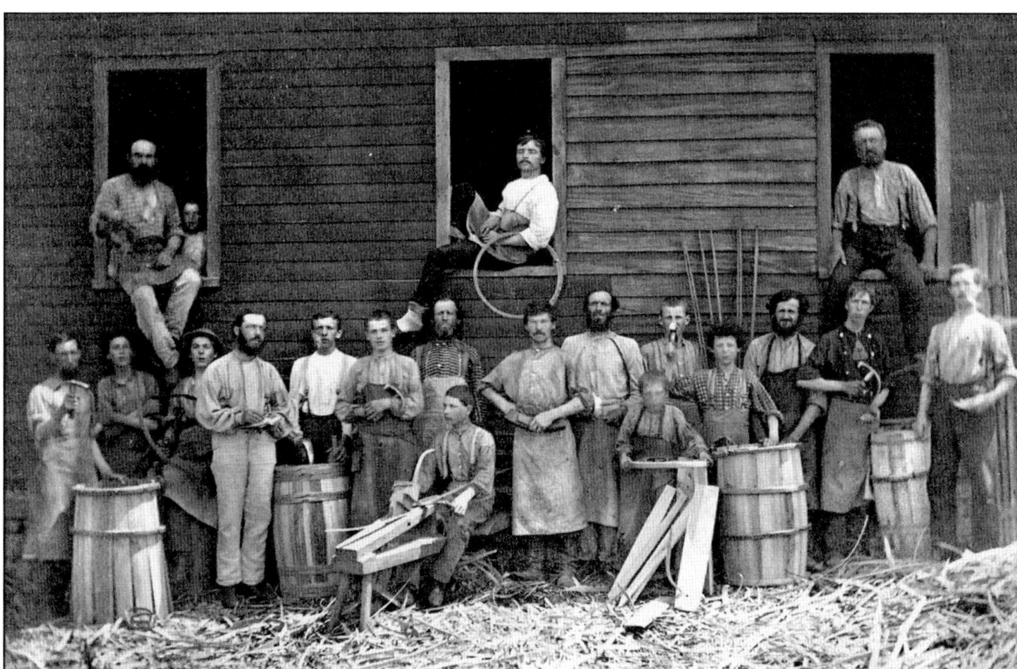

COOPER SHOP AT EAGLE HARBOR. The workers seem to be enjoying themselves at the cooper shop located on the south side of the Erie Canal at the bridge around 1880. Identified are Henry Fountain (far left), Charles Bennett (fourth from the left), and C. Bennett (in the left window). (Courtesy of Orleans County Department of History.)

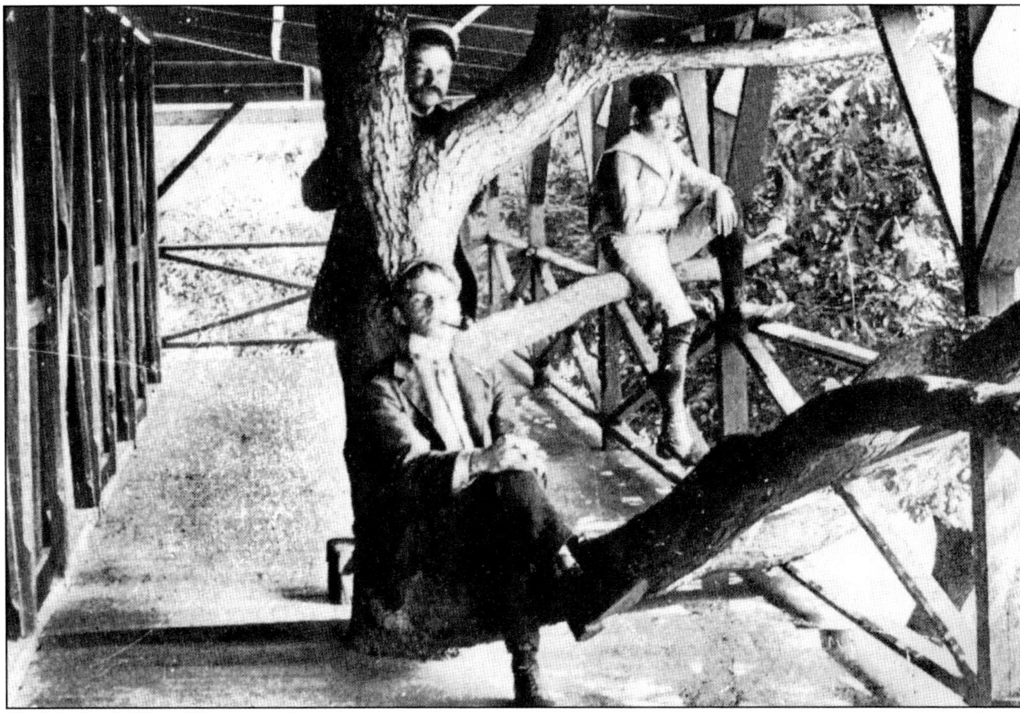

A Tree Grows through It. Some folks relax on the veranda of the Lakeside Hotel around 1895, utilizing the tree branches growing up through the flooring as seats. The hotel was located on Lake Ontario at Lakeside Park. (Courtesy of Tillman's Village Inn.)

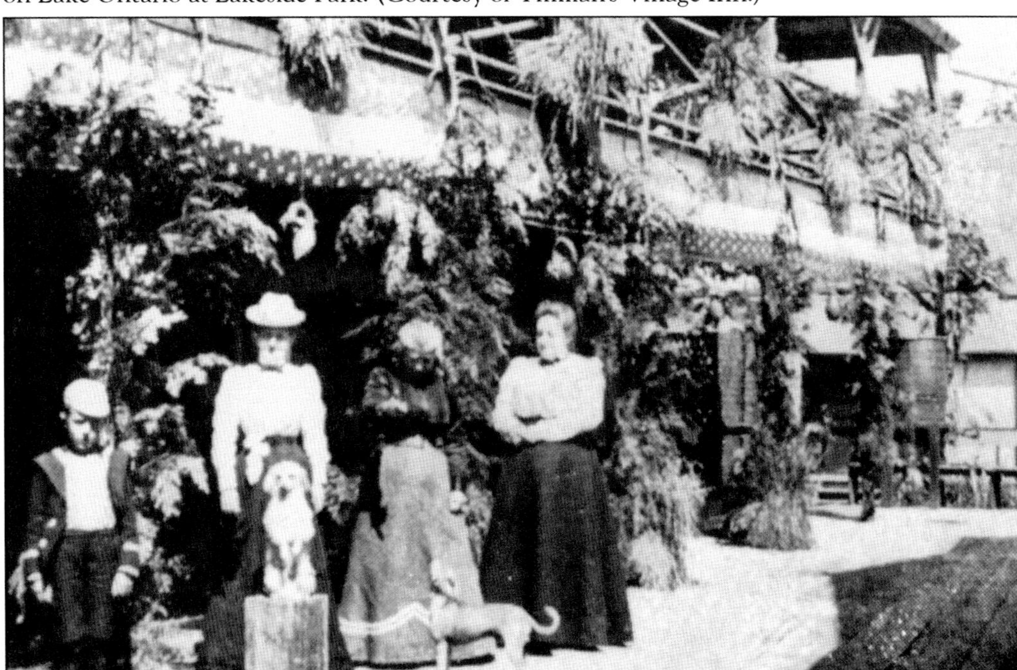

Puttin' on the Dog. Some women and a boy pose for the camera in 1890 in front of the Lakeside Hotel, decorated here with fall foliage. (Courtesy of Tillman's Village Inn.)

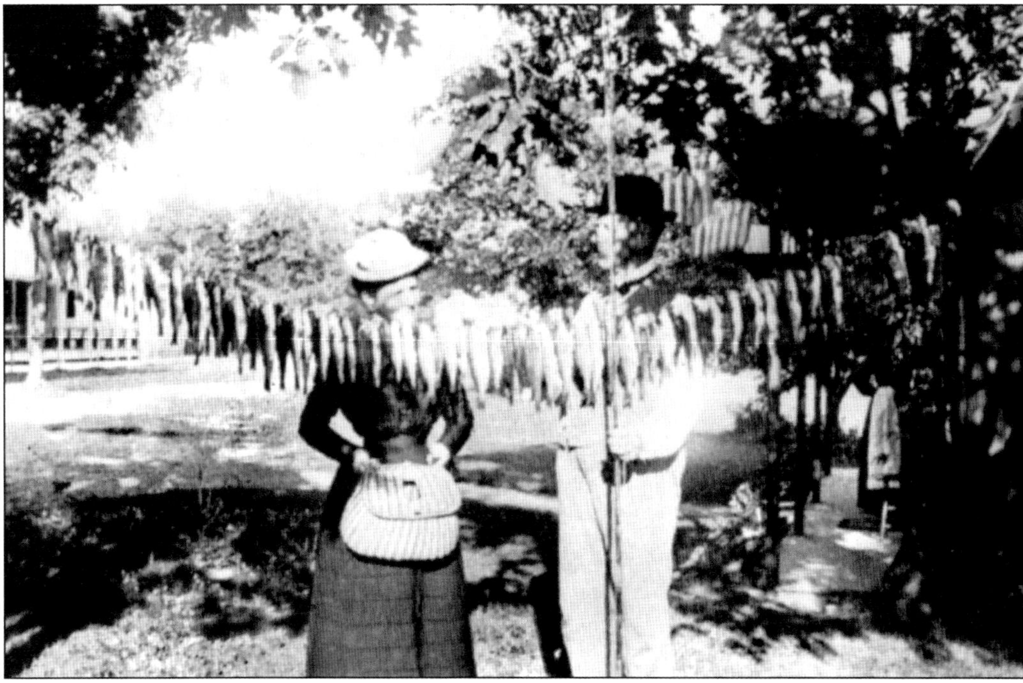

CATCH OF THE DAY. A man and woman study their catch as they vacation at Lakeside Park around 1890. (Courtesy of Tillman's Village Inn.)

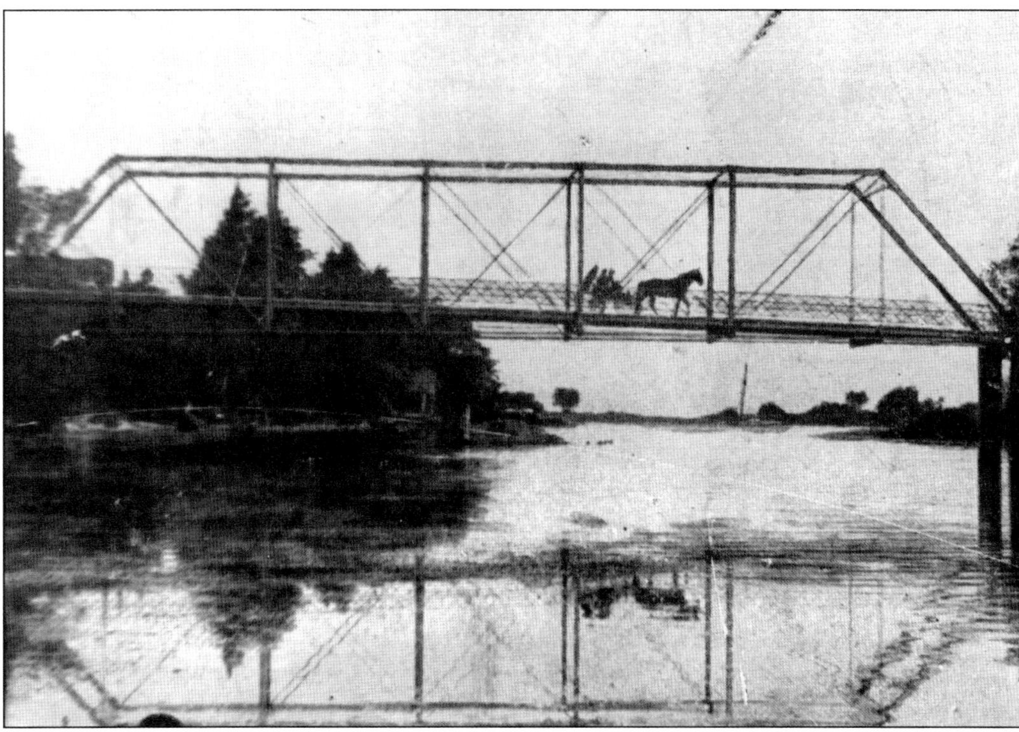

REFLECTIONS OF THE PAST. Three people enjoy a wagon ride on the bridge over Johnson Creek on their way to Lakeside Park around 1905. (Courtesy of Tillman's Village Inn.)

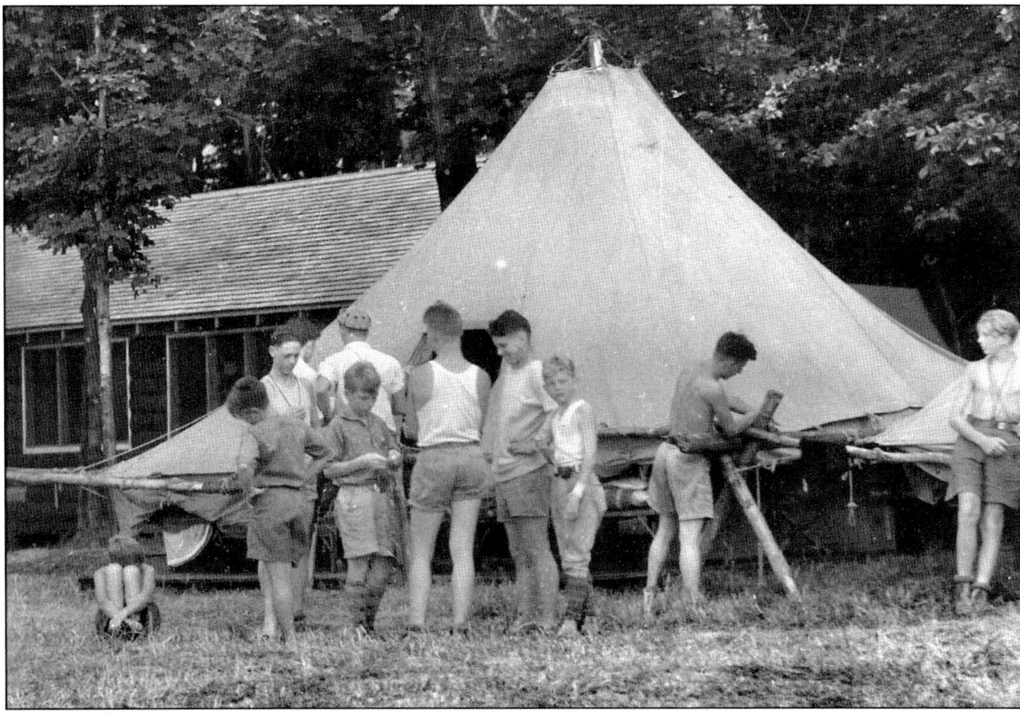

Camp Don Yonda. Camp Don Yonda (down yonder) was located in Carlton on Lake Ontario and provided boys with camping skills in the 1930s. (Courtesy of Orleans County Department of History.)

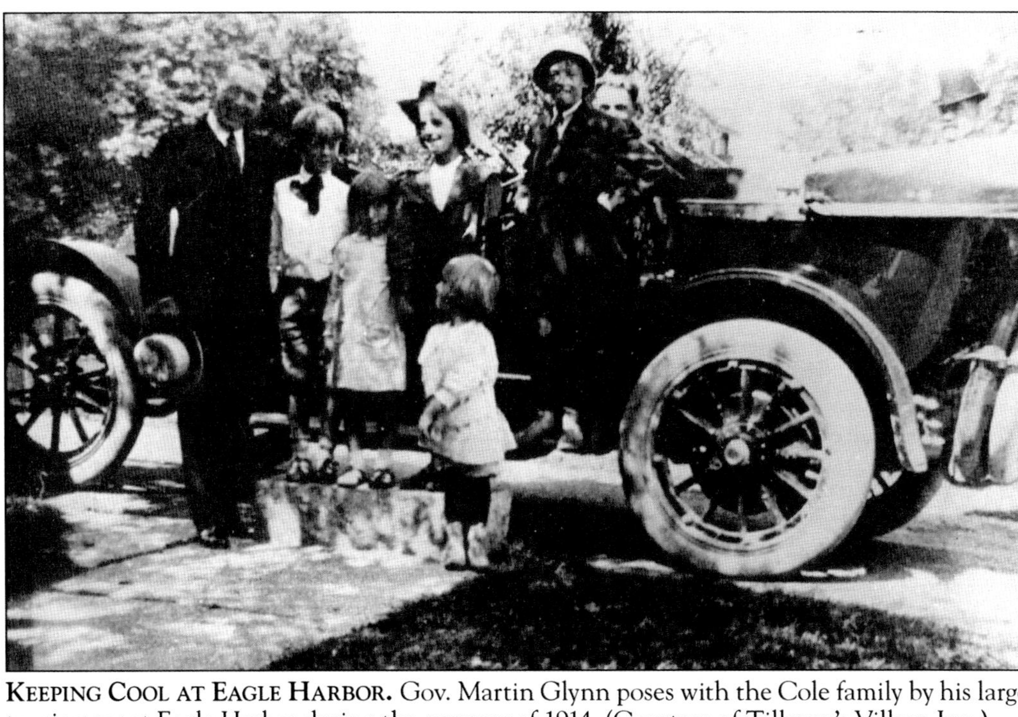

Keeping Cool at Eagle Harbor. Gov. Martin Glynn poses with the Cole family by his large touring car at Eagle Harbor during the summer of 1914. (Courtesy of Tillman's Village Inn.)

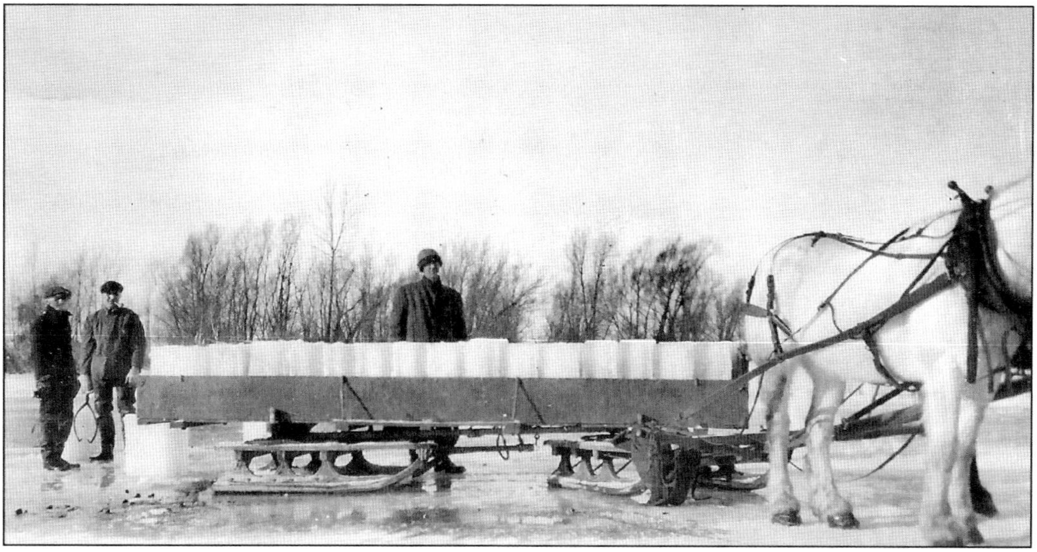

HAULING ICE. Men and a team of horses prepare to pull blocks of ice off the Oak Orchard Harbor to be stored at the icehouse for warm weather. The ice was packed in sawdust so that it would remain frozen through the summer. (Courtesy of Orleans County Department of History.)

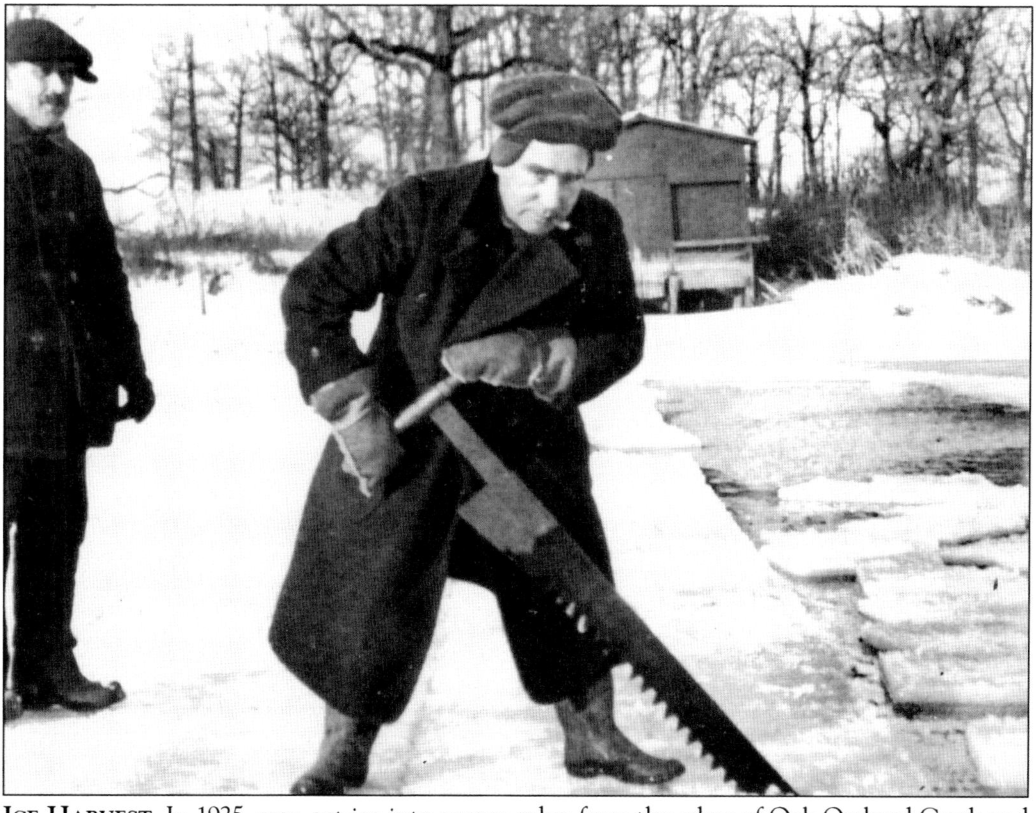

ICE HARVEST. In 1925, men cut ice into square cakes from the edges of Oak Orchard Creek and stored them in icehouses. Each block of ice was packed in sawdust, which kept the ice frozen long past spring. Joseph Achilles is seen here with the ice saw. (Courtesy of Tillman's Village Inn.)

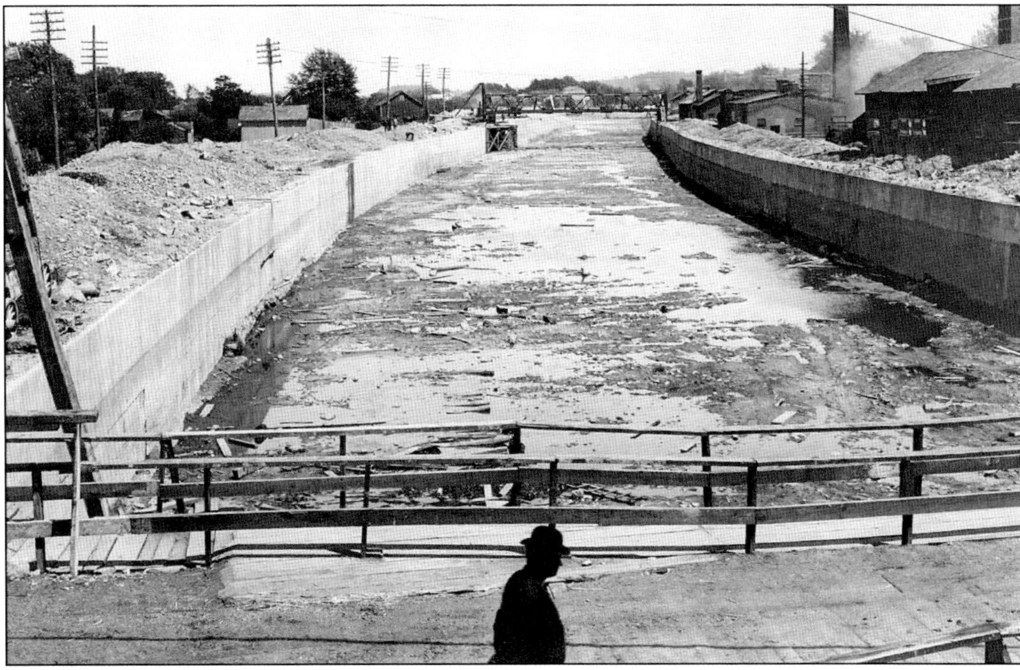

Canal Renovations. A solitary man makes his way across the Main Street bridge on May 5, 1913. The view is looking east toward Rochester. (Courtesy of Orleans County Department of History.)

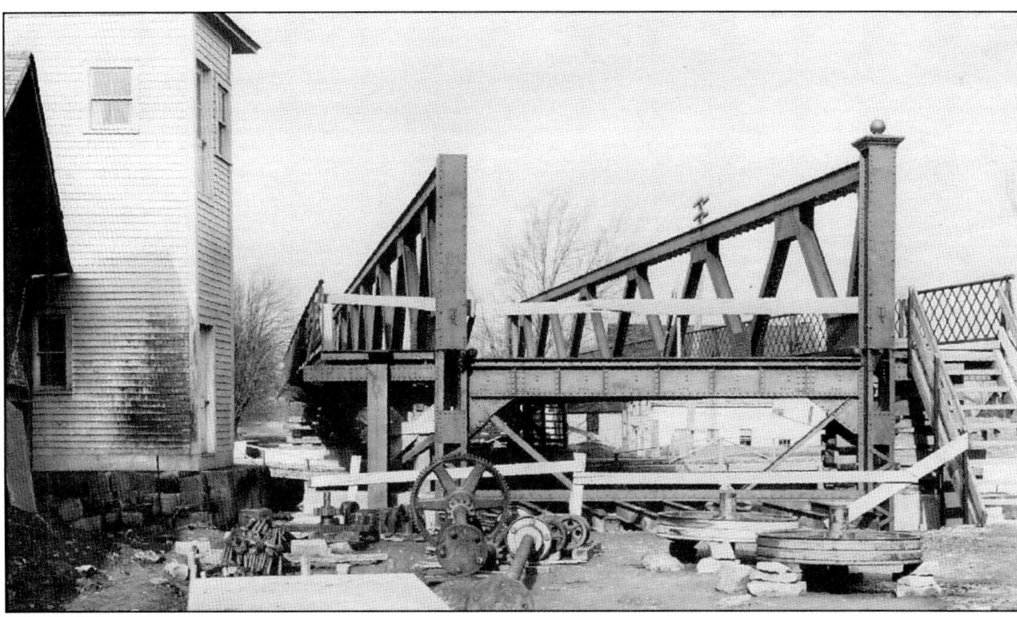

Working on the Bridge. This was the Ingersoll Street Bridge over the Erie Canal on November 21, 1913. (Courtesy of Orleans County Department of History.)

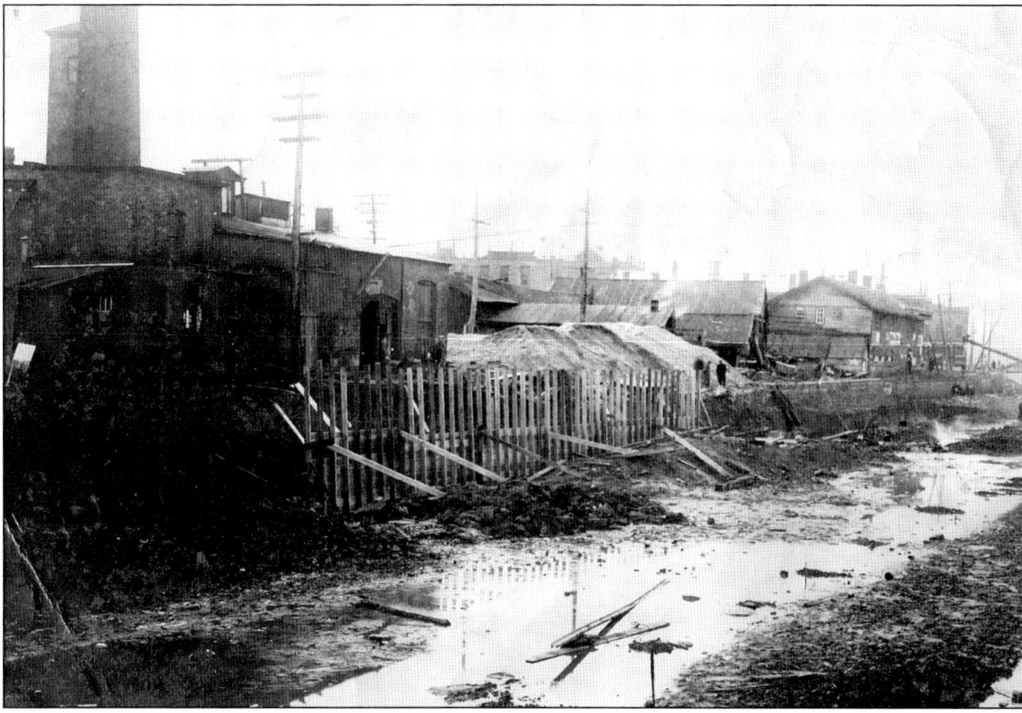

Barge Canal Construction. This photograph, taken around 1910, shows the south bank of the canal between Ingersoll Street and Main Street when it was being enlarged. Buildings to the left are part of the Albion Gas Works, established in 1858. (Courtesy of Orleans County Department of History.)

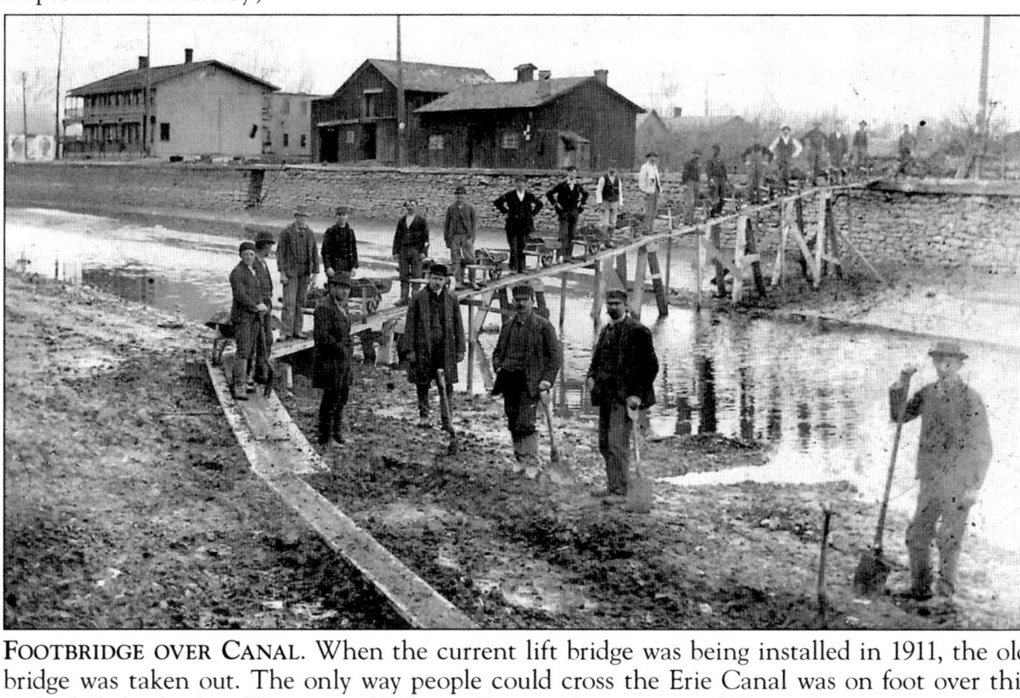

Footbridge over Canal. When the current lift bridge was being installed in 1911, the old bridge was taken out. The only way people could cross the Erie Canal was on foot over this makeshift footbridge. (Courtesy of Orleans County Department of History.)

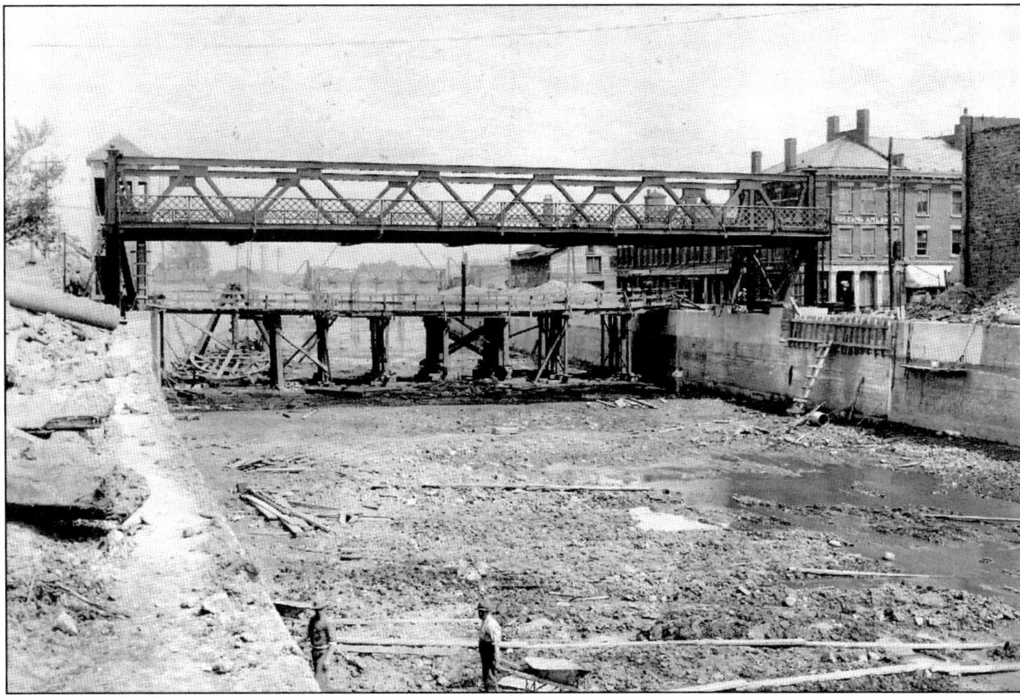

MAIN STREET BRIDGE, LOOKING EAST. The Erie Canal remained empty in Albion on May 5, 1912, as workers continued the work to widen it and install this new bridge over the span. (Courtesy of Orleans County Department of History.)

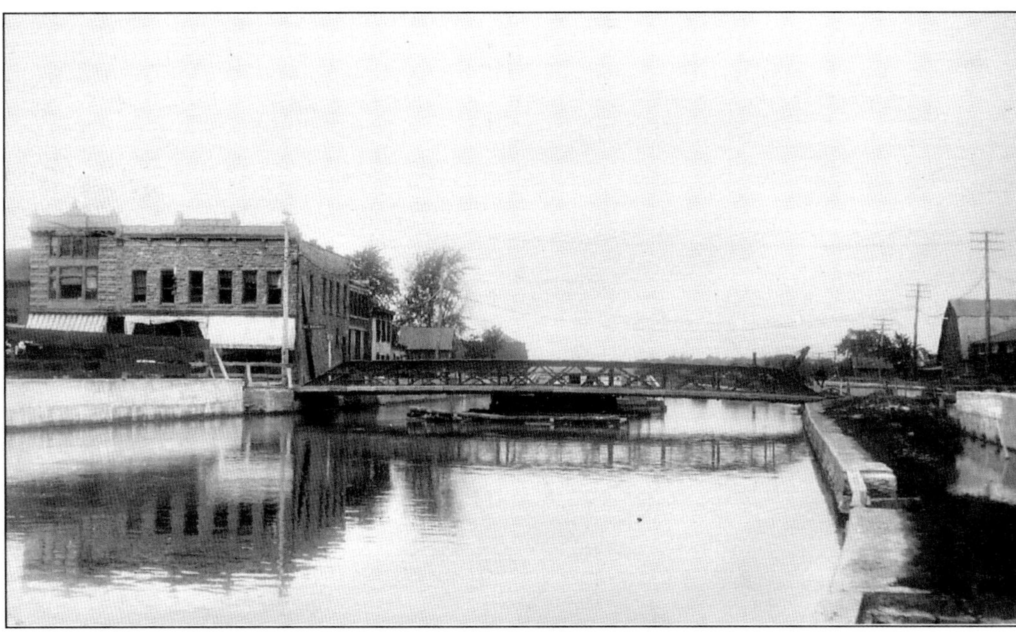

OLD SWING BRIDGE. This was the old swing bridge that spanned the Erie Canal until 1911, when a new lift bridge was installed. The canal was filled with water when this photograph was taken. The swing bridge swiveled on a pivot, allowing boats to pass. (Courtesy of Orleans County Department of History.)

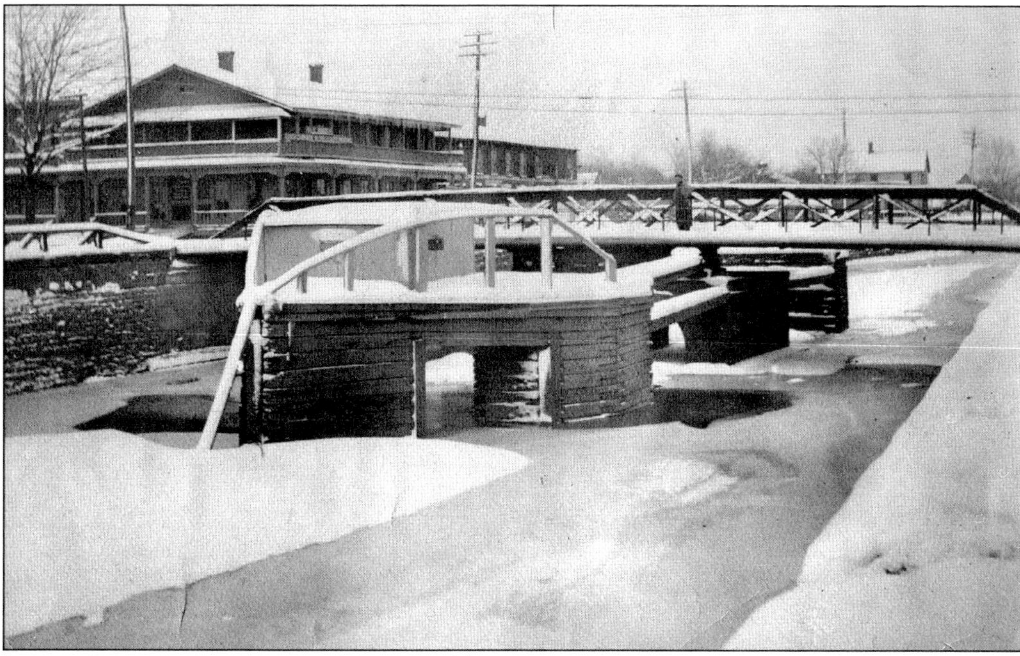

Swing Bridge in Winter. This view of the bridge, taken in the winter of 1908–1909, shows a view of the mechanism used to make the bridge pivot. (Courtesy of Orleans County Department of History.)

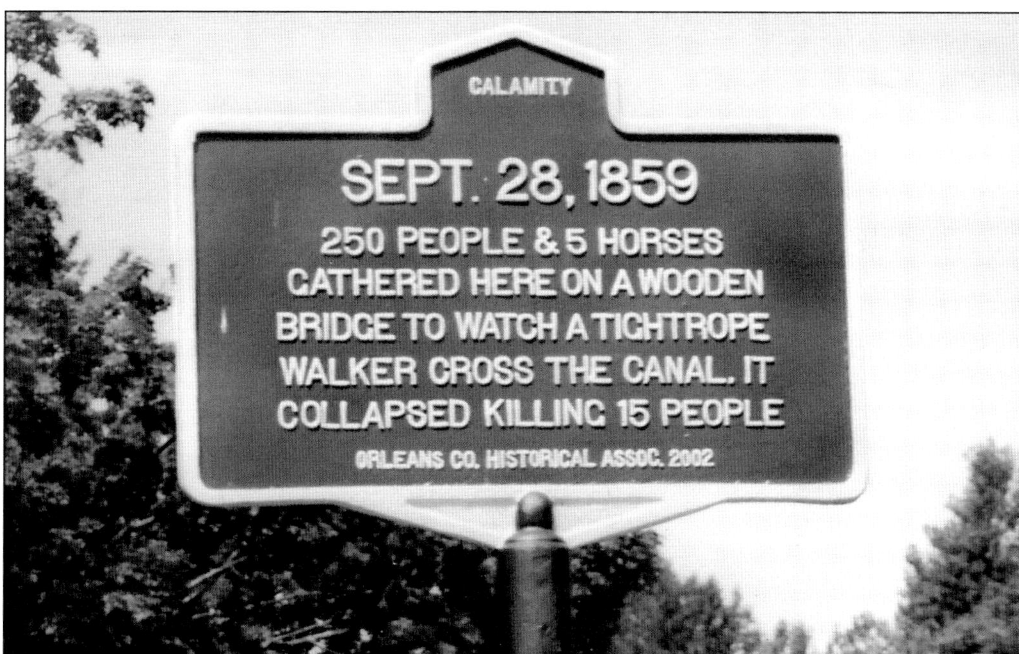

Sign Marks the Spot. In 1859, a tightrope walker crossed the canal. Several hundred people came to see him, and they all gathered on a bridge. Suddenly the bridge collapsed, and everyone fell; 15 people were killed, and many were injured. This historical marker, on the west side of the Main Street lift bridge, tells the tale.

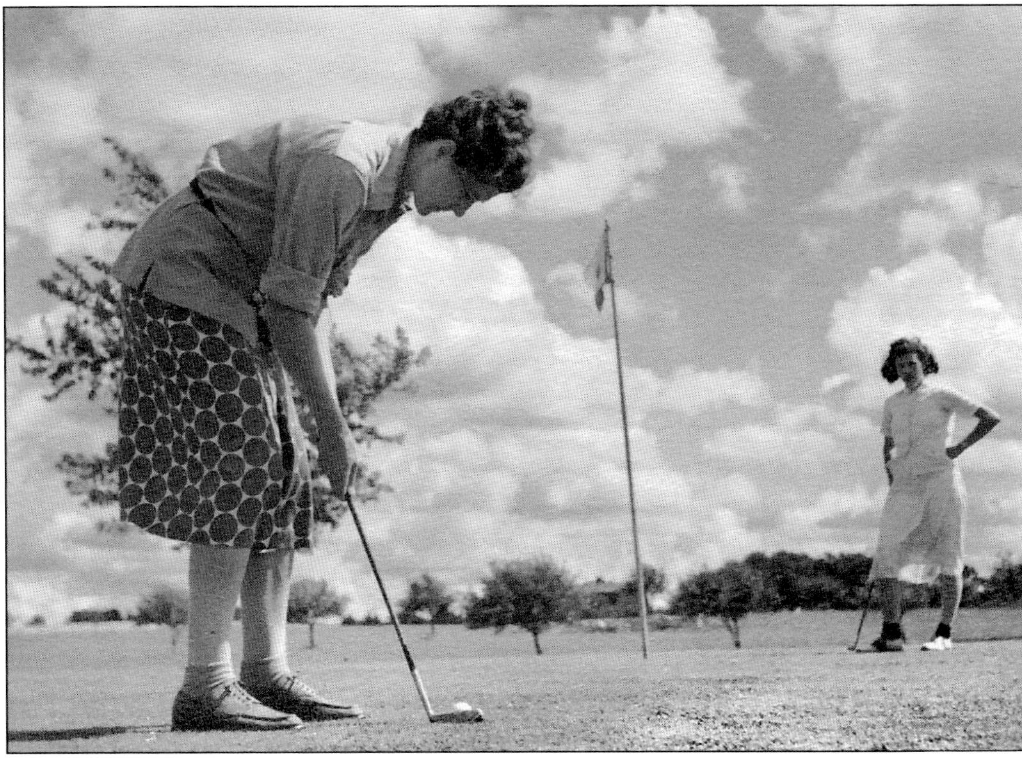

GOLFING AT EAGLE HARBOR. Two women enjoy an afternoon of golf at Eagle Harbor around 1940. (Courtesy of Orleans County Department of History.)

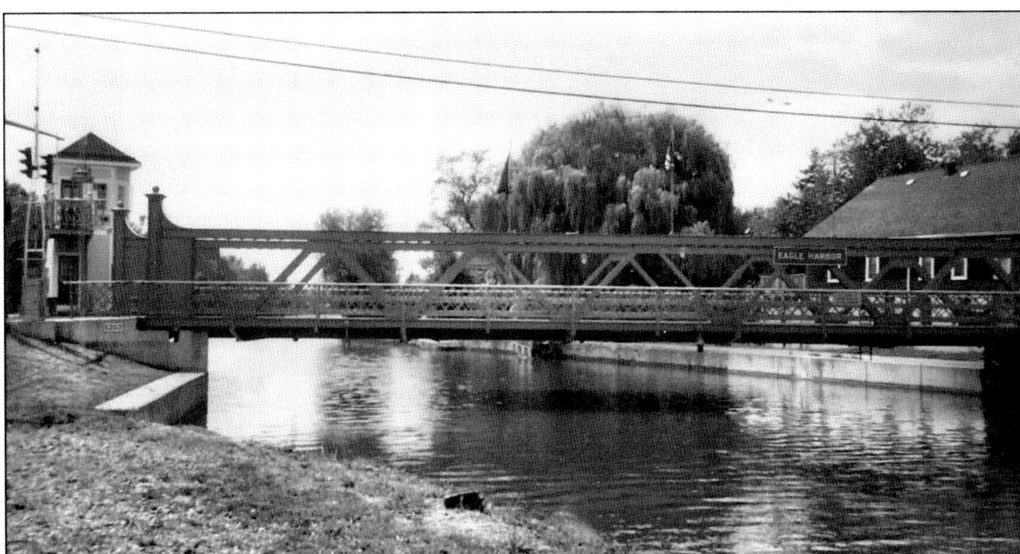

EAGLE HARBOR TODAY. Nowadays Eagle Harbor is a north-south pass-through over the Erie Canal. The bridge over the canal bears the sign "Eagle Harbor," and the towpath is available for hikers to use. This view was taken looking west. On the left is the tower where a bridge tender raises and lowers the bridge when boats pass through. To its left are signal lights to stop vehicles when boats are passing.

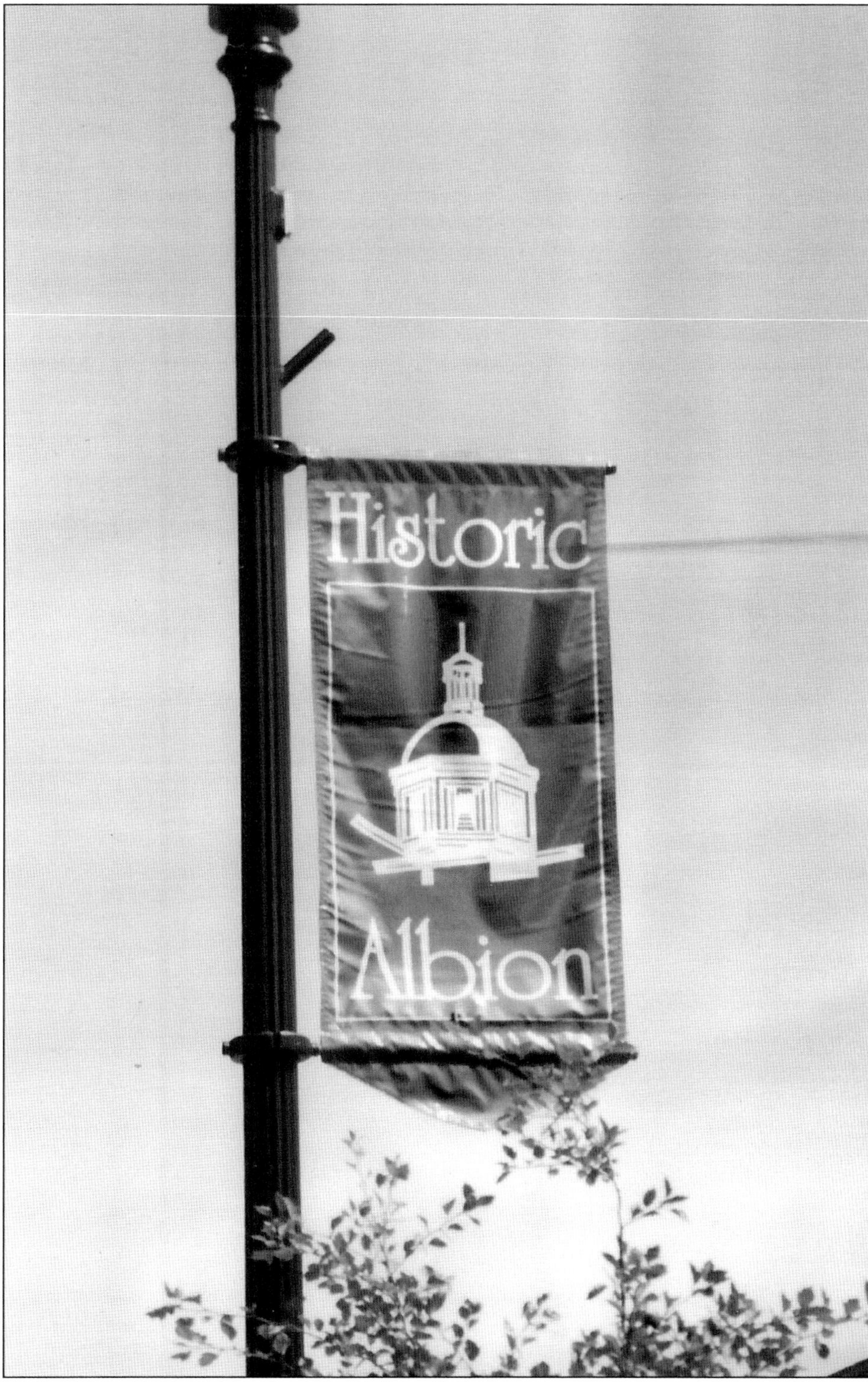

BANNERS WAVE. These banners on light poles greet visitors to Albion just across the canal. They proclaim Albion's history throughout the town.

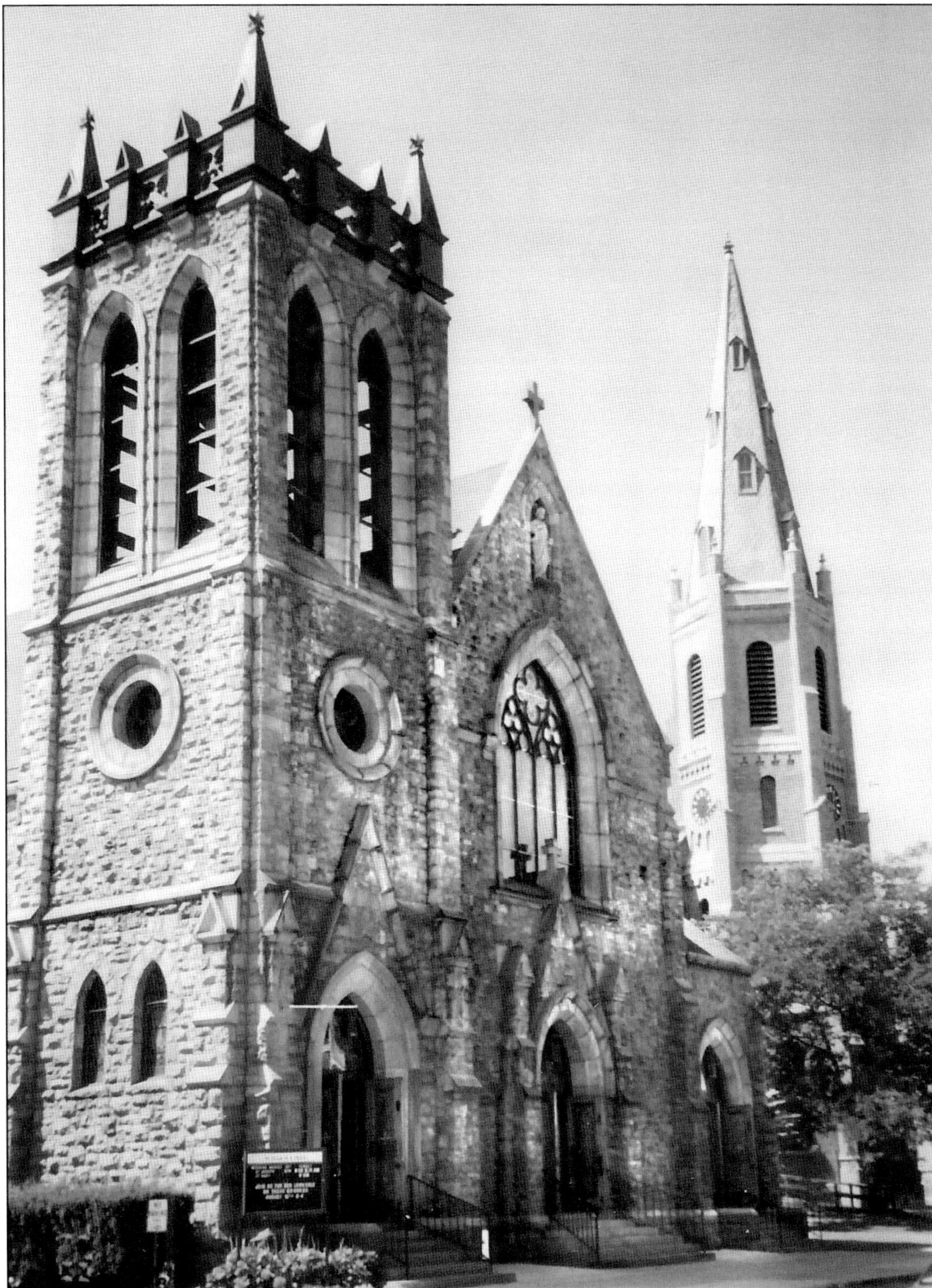

TWO CHURCHES. The spires of St. Joseph's Church (left) and the First Baptist Church vie for honors. The beauty of the churches in Albion's center is breathtaking.

Five

Churches and Mount Albion

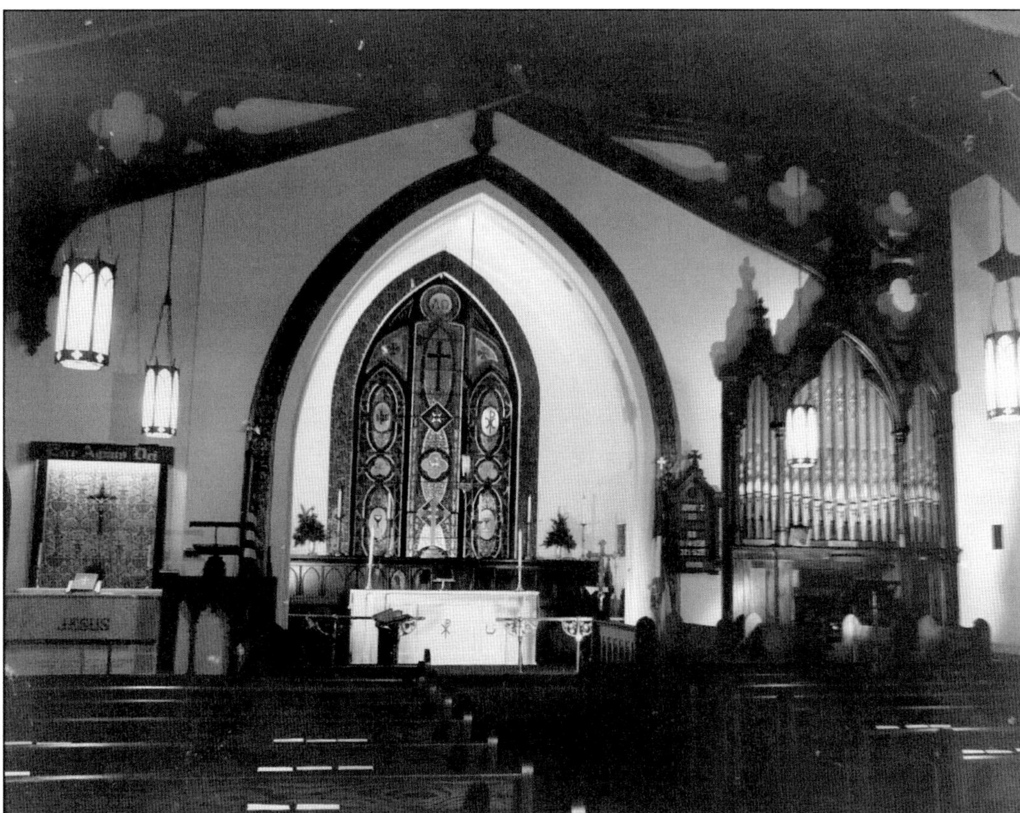

Christ Episcopal Church. Seen as it is today, this is the oldest house of worship in Orleans County, having been built in 1830. The Steer and Turner pipe organ was built in 1877 and given as a memorial to Johnathan Blott. (Courtesy of Orleans County Department of History.)

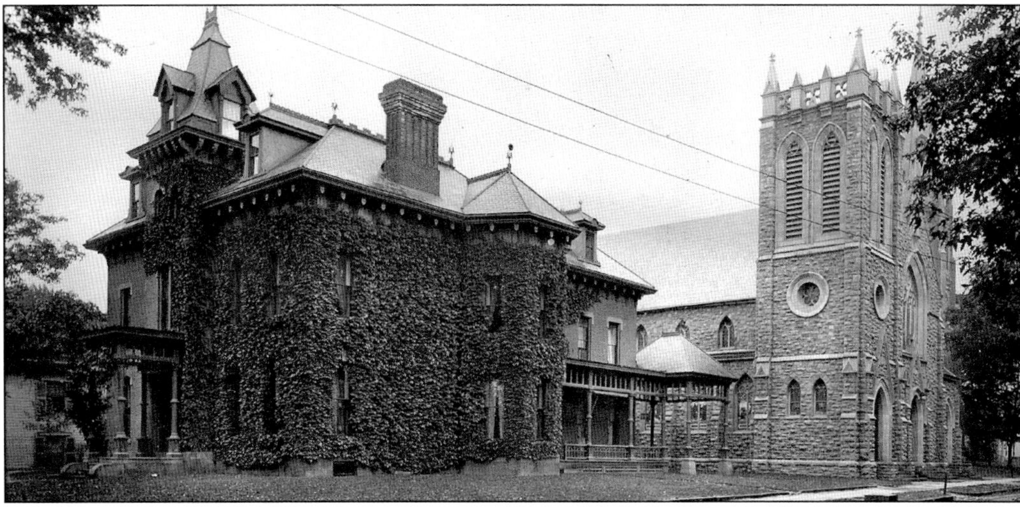

St. Joseph's Catholic Church and Rectory. In 1897, the mansion on the property was changed into a rectory and an addition was built of Medina sandstone, capable of seating 800 people. The next purchase was property south on Main Street, where a school and lyceum were built, also of Medina sandstone. This photograph was taken around 1903. (Courtesy of Orleans County Department of History.)

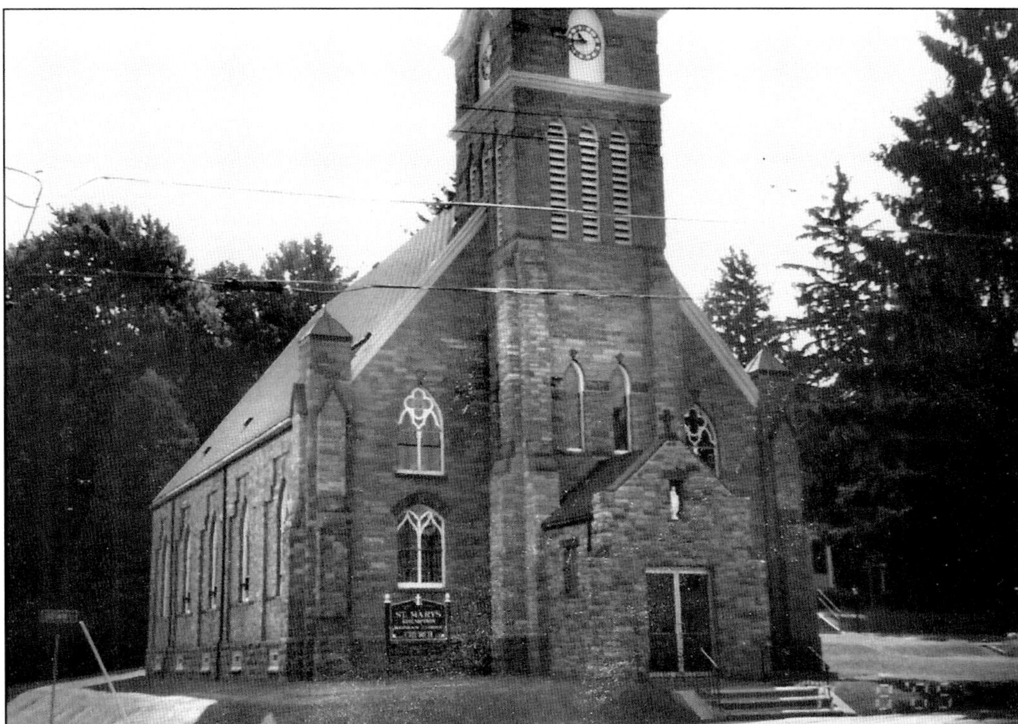

St. Mary's Assumption Church. St. Mary's was established in 1892 for the Polish residents who had settled in Albion, with property purchased on the corner of Brown and Moore Streets. When the building was dedicated in 1892, delegations from Polish parishes across New York State arrived in special trains, and bands marched and played to celebrate the new church. A rectory was added in 1912. Sacred murals on the ceiling added to the beauty of the interior.

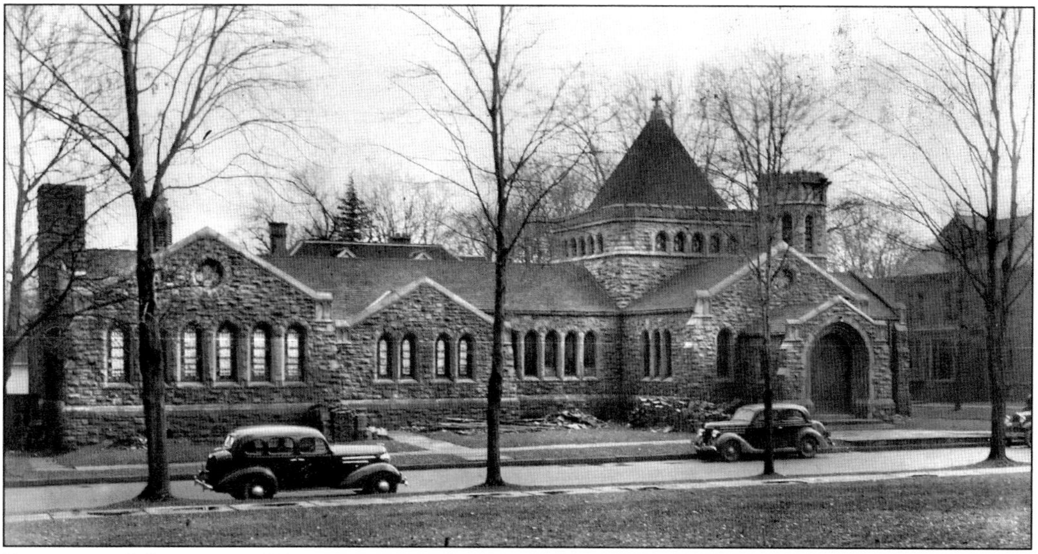

PULLMAN MEMORIAL UNIVERSALIST CHURCH. George M. Pullman of railway car fame built this church in 1894 on the corner of Main and East Park Streets as a memorial to his parents. Pullman grew up in Albion and traveled there frequently. The church's woodwork is of quartersawn golden oak. The sanctuary has 41 stained glass windows. The three windows facing Main Street are of hand-rolled glass, the largest, depicting *Christ the Consoler*, is signed by Louis Comfort Tiffany. (Courtesy of Orleans County Department of History.)

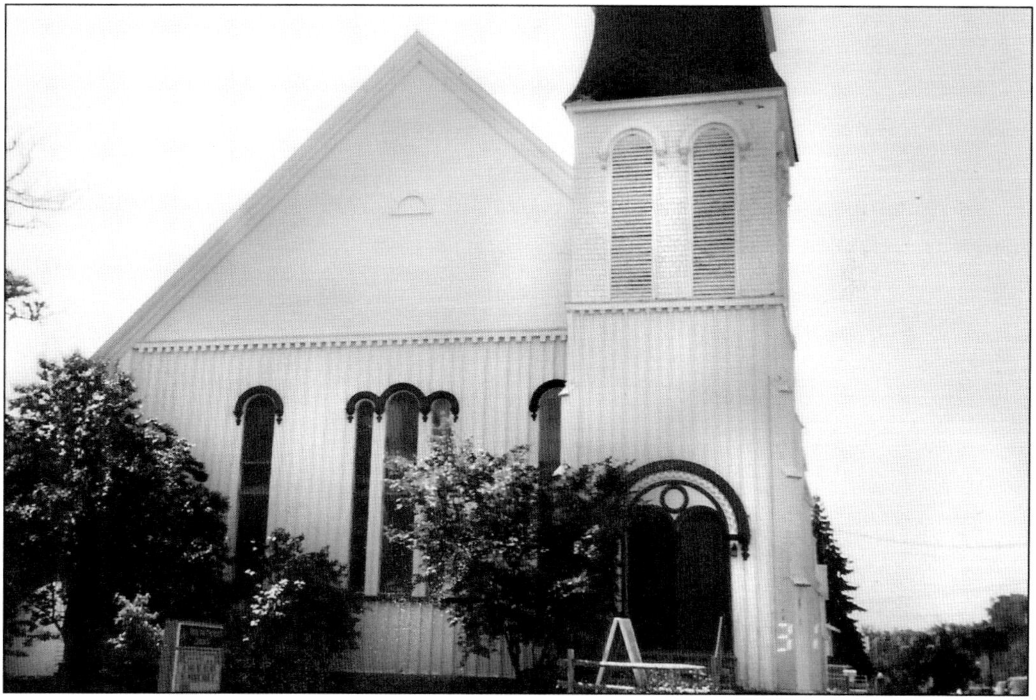

ALBION FREE METHODIST CHURCH. This congregation was organized in 1859 by the Rev. Lorin Stiles and called the Congregational Free Methodist Church. In 1866, the congregational part of the name was dropped. Remodeled in 1900, the church looks much the same today as it did then and remains the oldest Free Methodist building in the denomination.

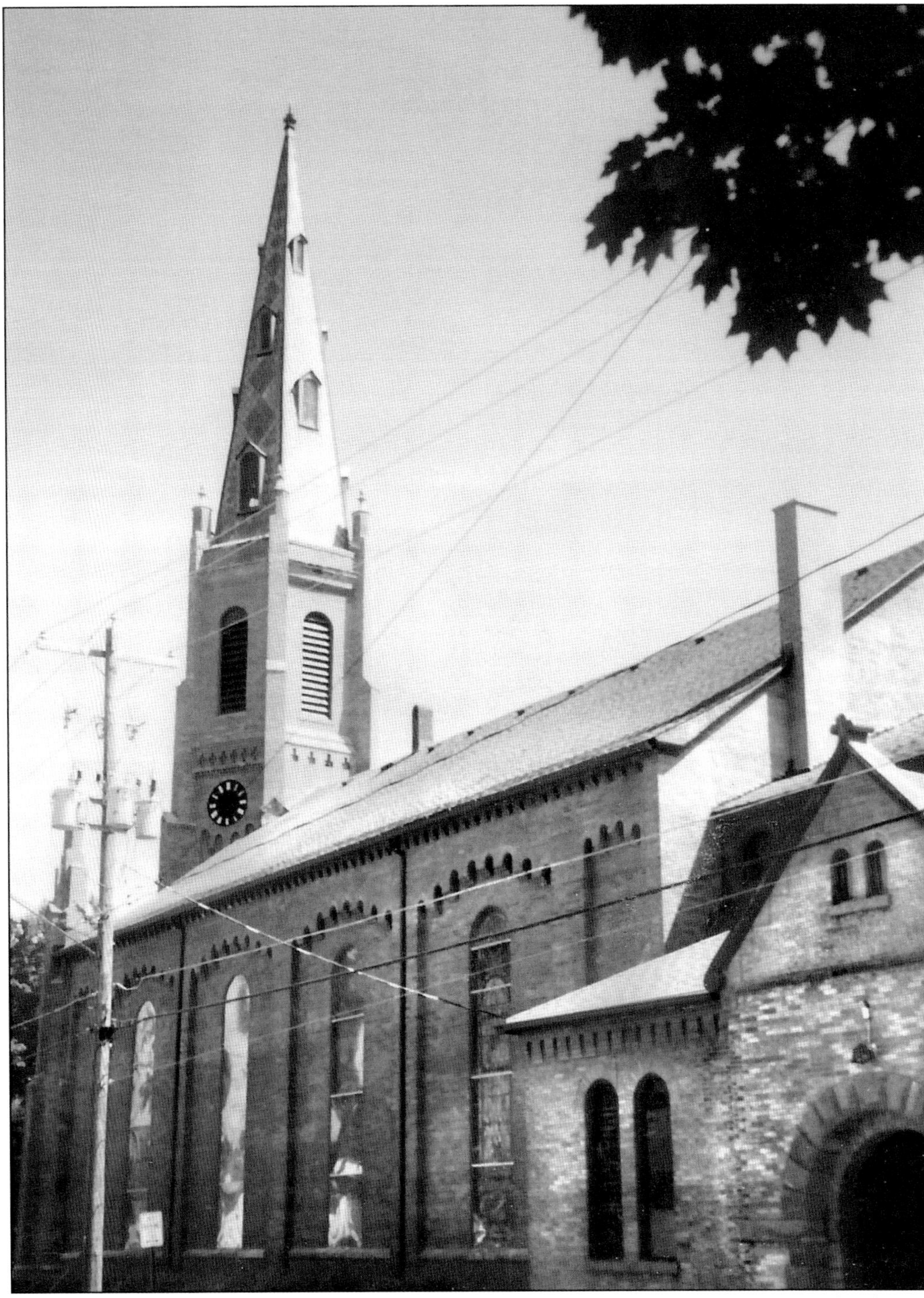

FIRST BAPTIST. The first Baptist church built in Albion was in 1832 on the west side of Main Street. In 1859, a larger church was built on the southeast corner of West Park and Liberty Streets. This is the First Baptist Church as it looks today.

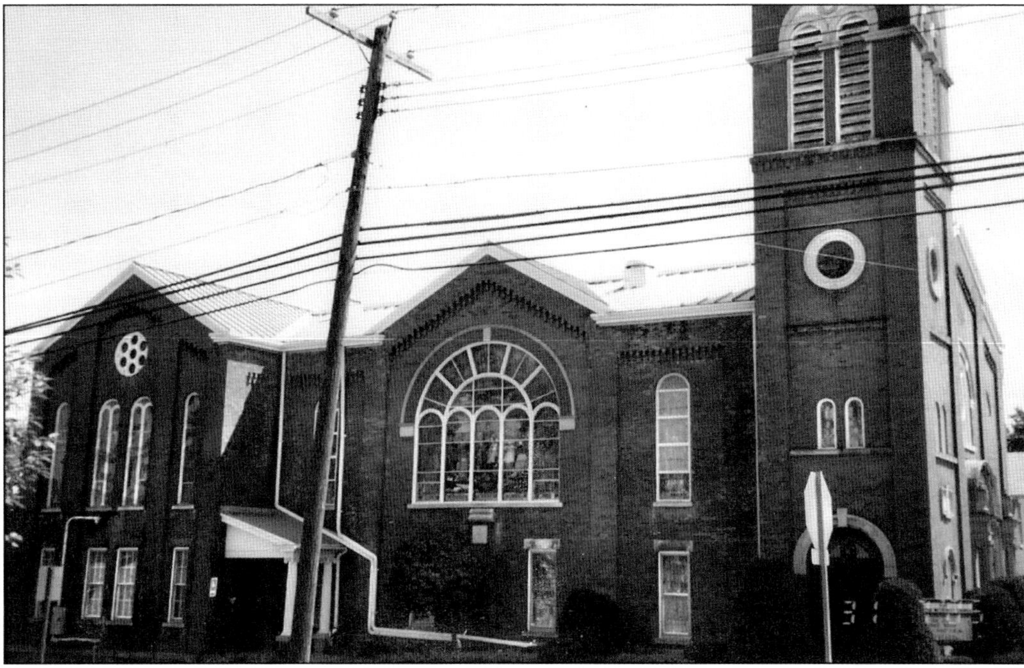

UNITED METHODIST CHURCH. The first Methodist Episcopal Society was organized about 1830. After 100 people joined, the name was changed to the First Methodist Episcopal Church of Albion, and a new church building was constructed on the corner of Platt and East State Streets. In 1859, the building was completely remodeled. Over the next 100 years, the building was remodeled several times.

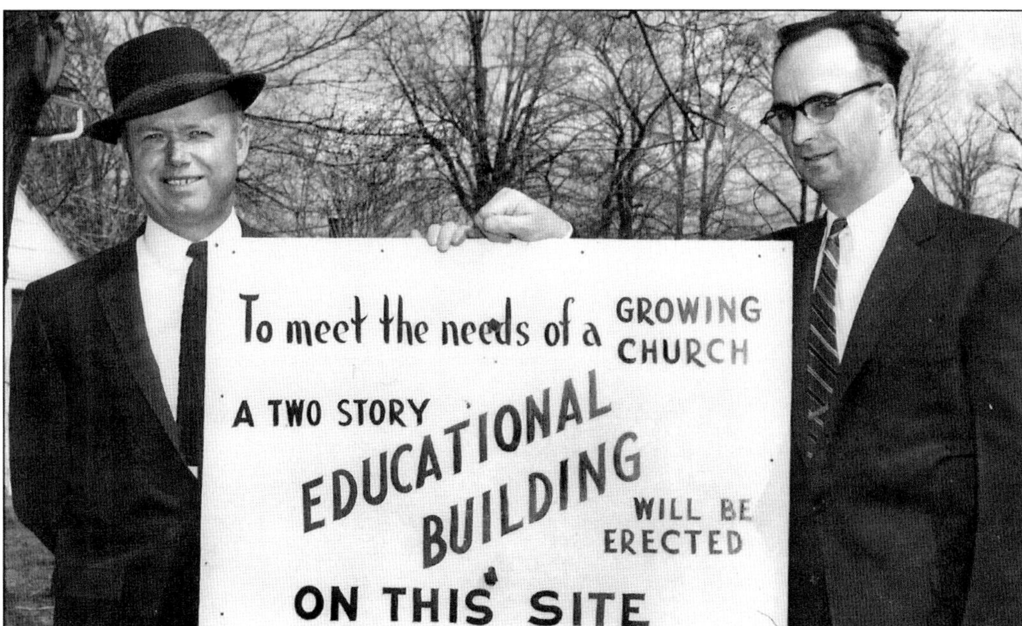

NEW BUILDING ANNOUNCEMENT. Jacob Schanals (left) and Rev. William Jessop hold up a sign declaring the construction of a new two-story educational building at the United Methodist Church. (Courtesy of Orleans County Department of History.)

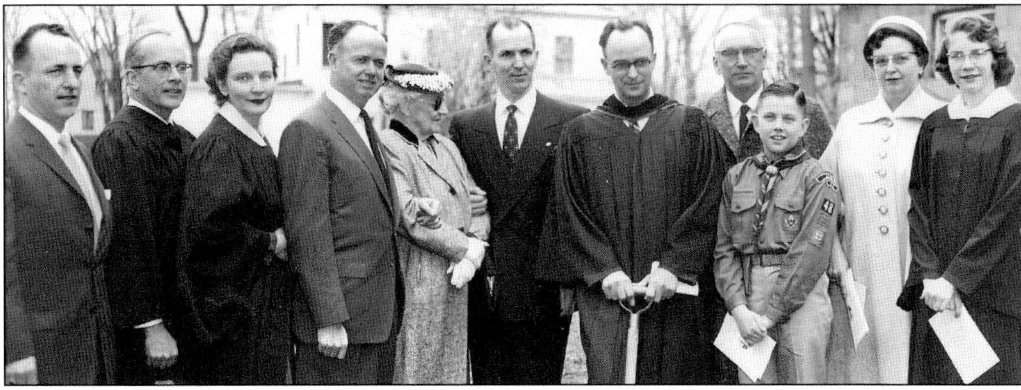

ALBION METHODISTS. Celebrating a new educational building at the Albion Methodist Church in 1959 are, from left to right, Donald Bloom, Arnold Vick, Elizabeth Vick, Jacob Schanals, Marion Collins, Richard Bloom, Rev. William Jessop, Milton Kast, Gary Breuilly, Hesper Scharett, and Lucille Burton. (Courtesy of Orleans County Department of History.)

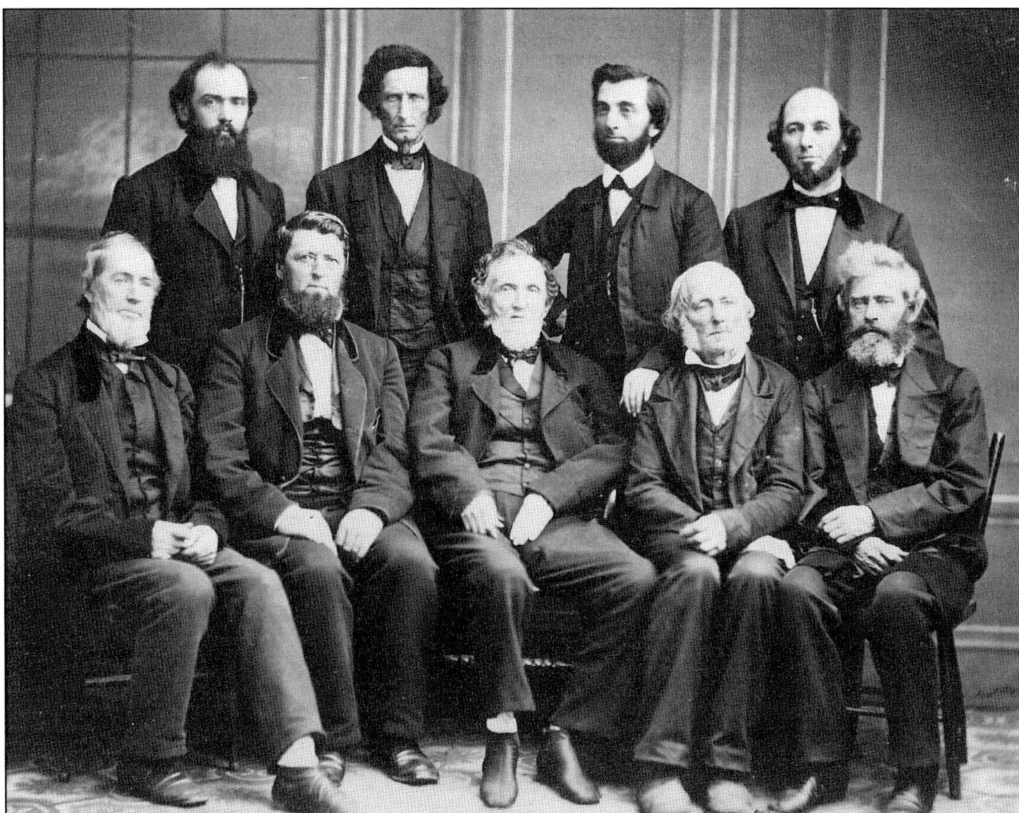

FIRST PRESBYTERIANS. These men are members of the session of the First Presbyterian Church of Albion in 1862. From left to right are the following: (first row) V. V. Bullock, deacon; and Henry Sears, Harvey Goodrich, ? St. Clair, and Asa Howard, all elders; (second row) Lucien Bingham, elder; James Wells, deacon; Henry Niles, pastor; and Origen Royce, elder. (Courtesy of Orleans County Department of History.)

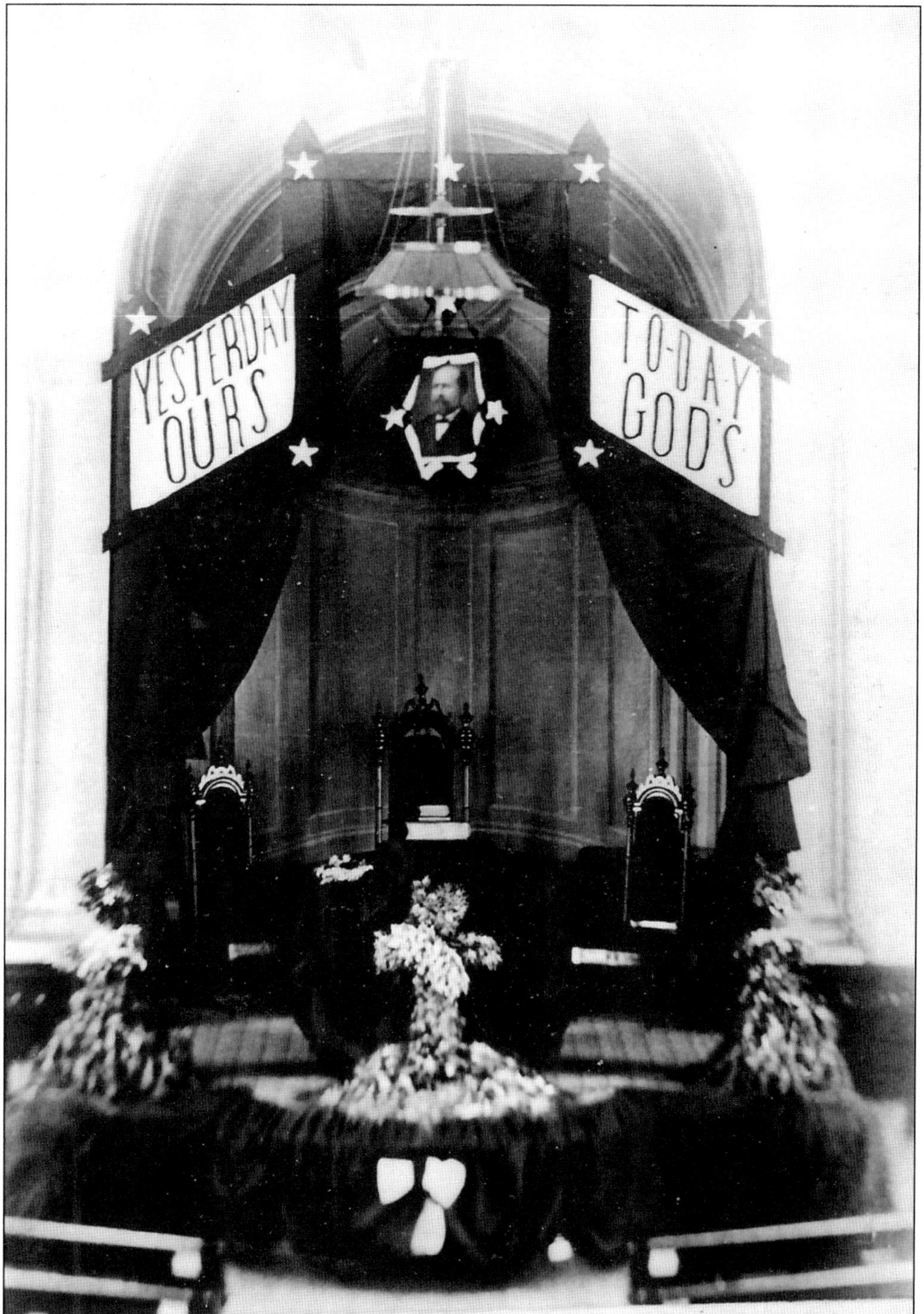

Honoring James Garfield. When Pres. James Garfield was assassinated on July 2, 1881, First Baptist Church honored him with a memorial service. The signs on either side of this special prop state, "Yesterday Ours" and "To-day God's." (Courtesy of Orleans County Department of History.)

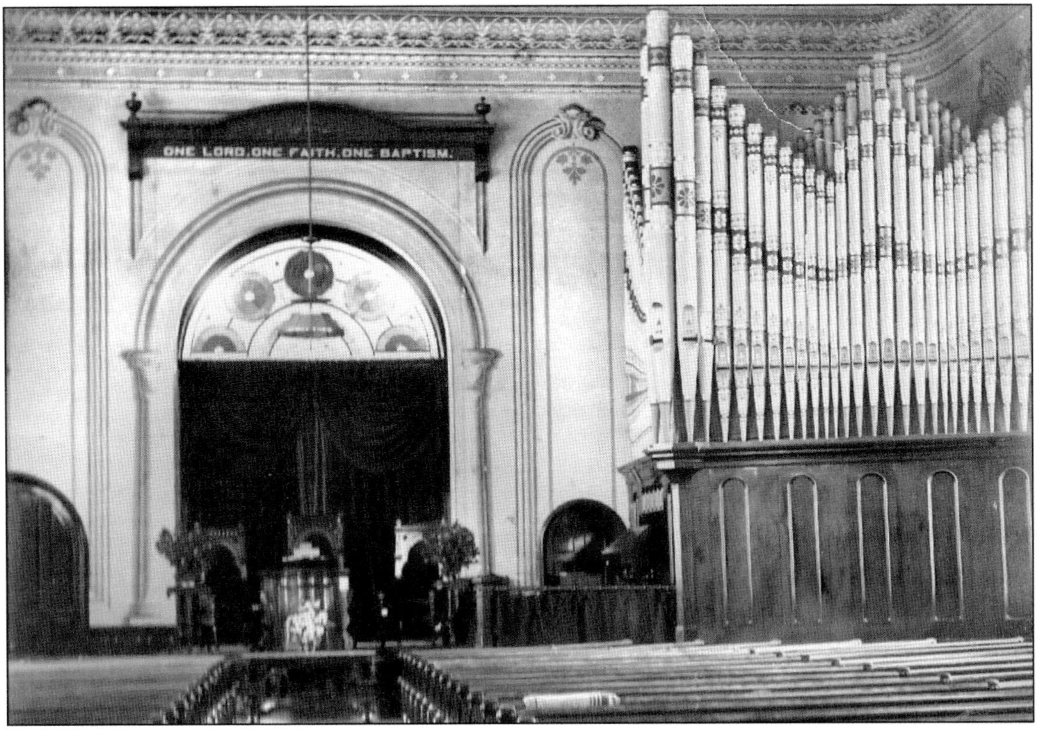

MASSIVE PIPES. These pipes were installed on the massive pipe organ inside the First Baptist Church in 1887. (Courtesy of Orleans County Department of History.)

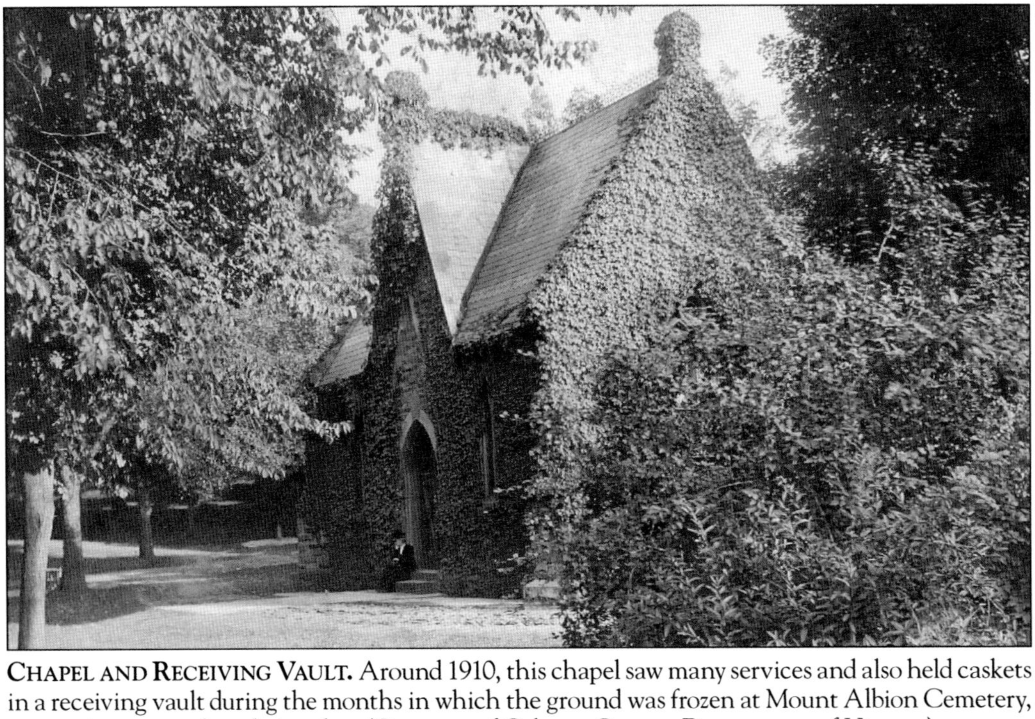

CHAPEL AND RECEIVING VAULT. Around 1910, this chapel saw many services and also held caskets in a receiving vault during the months in which the ground was frozen at Mount Albion Cemetery, preventing graves from being dug. (Courtesy of Orleans County Department of History.)

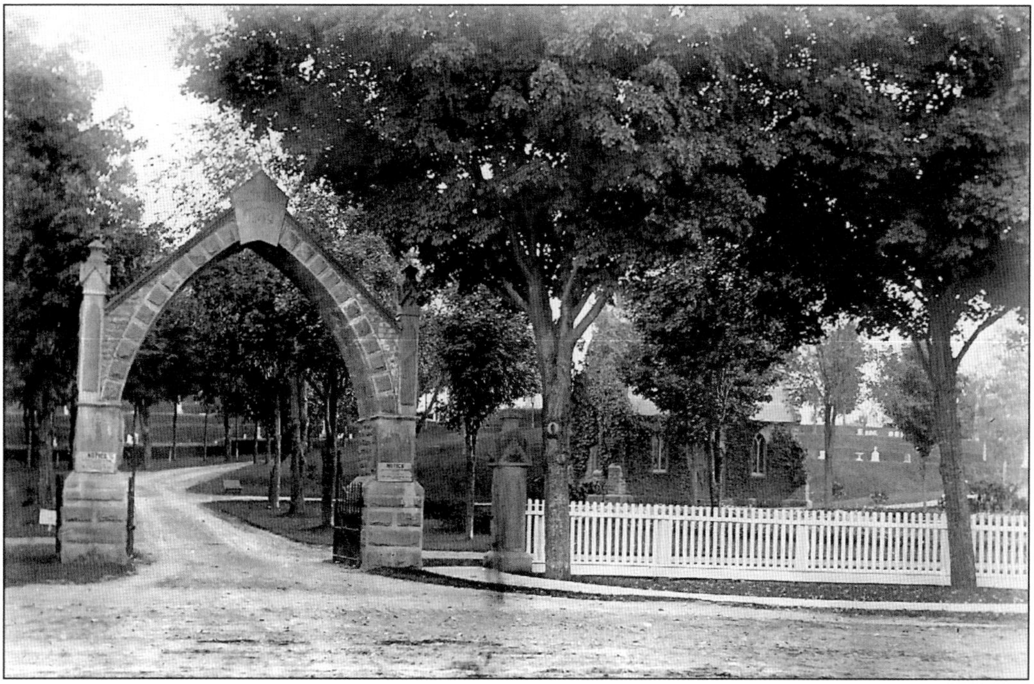

Entrance to Mount Albion Cemetery. The white picket fence in this view from around 1910 has been replaced with a wrought iron one. The cemetery is one of the most beautiful in the nation, with 100 acres of rolling hills offering a final resting place to those who have passed on. Maps are situated throughout the cemetery, directing visitors to the many lanes and scenic areas on the grounds. (Courtesy of Orleans County Department of History.)

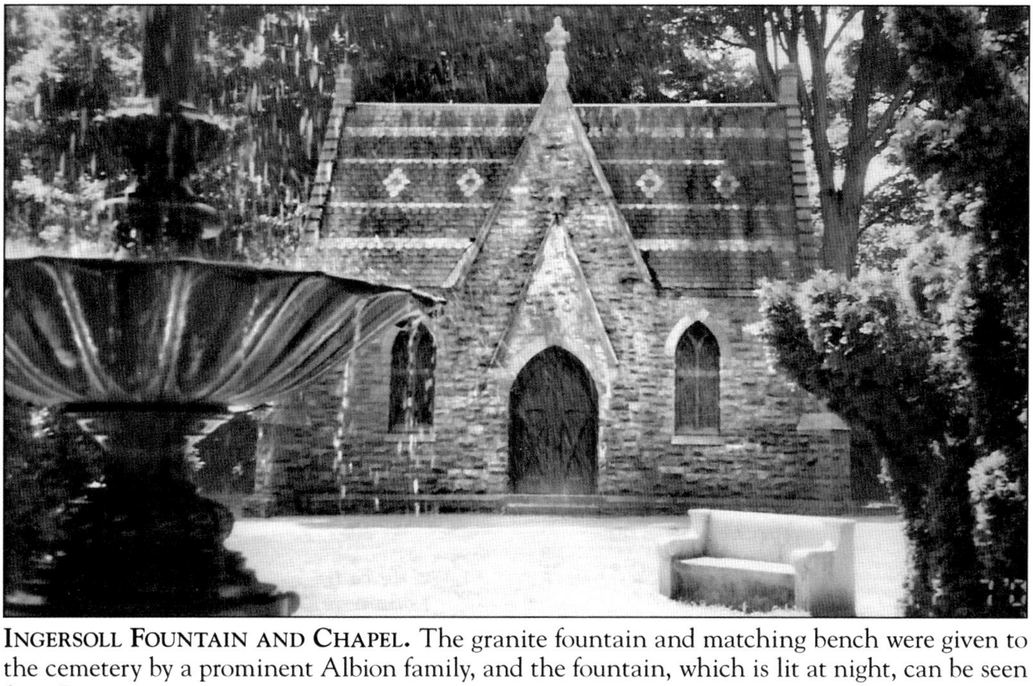

Ingersoll Fountain and Chapel. The granite fountain and matching bench were given to the cemetery by a prominent Albion family, and the fountain, which is lit at night, can be seen from Route 31.

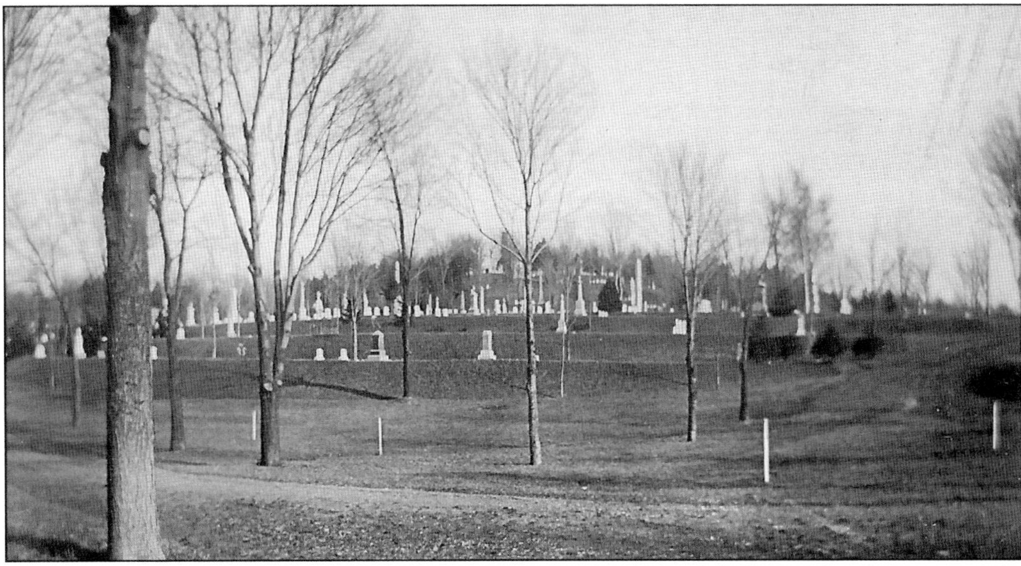

TIERED TERRACES. Mount Albion Cemetery features acres of high hills and lovely views. In this view from around 1910, the Soldiers and Sailors Monument is in the background. (Courtesy of Orleans County Department of History.)

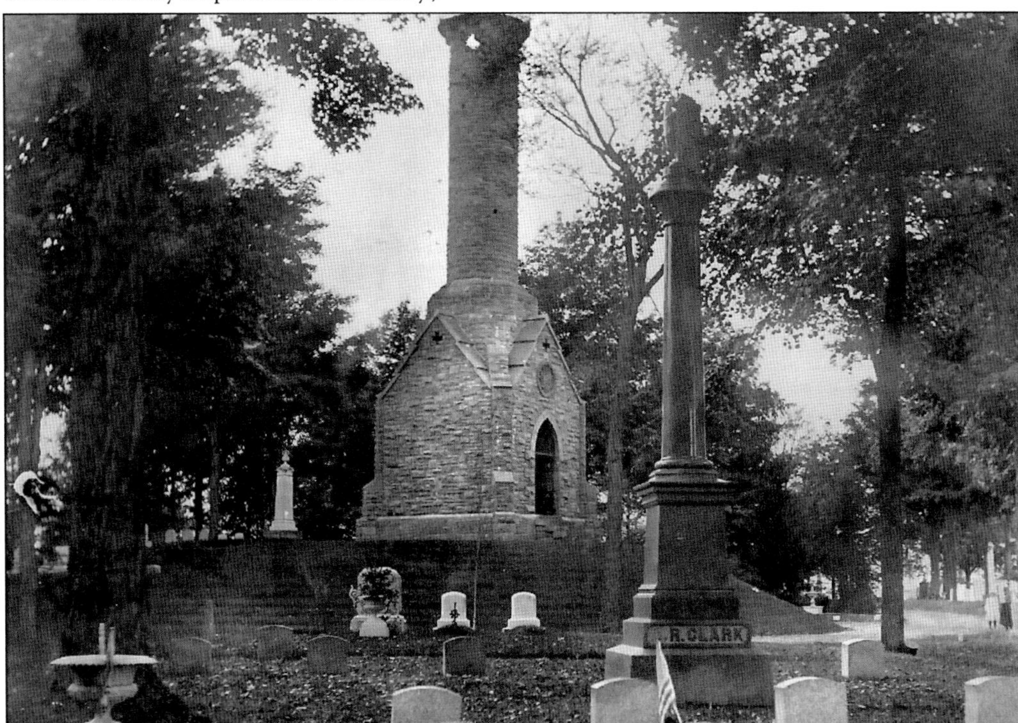

SOLDIERS AND SAILORS MONUMENT. Pictured around 1910, the Soldiers and Sailors Monument was built to honor the Civil War dead. People could use the stairway inside to reach the top and look out for miles. After the monument began to deteriorate in the 1960s, the Orleans County Historical Monument Corporation began restoring it, completing the work in 1976. (Courtesy of Orleans County Department of History.)

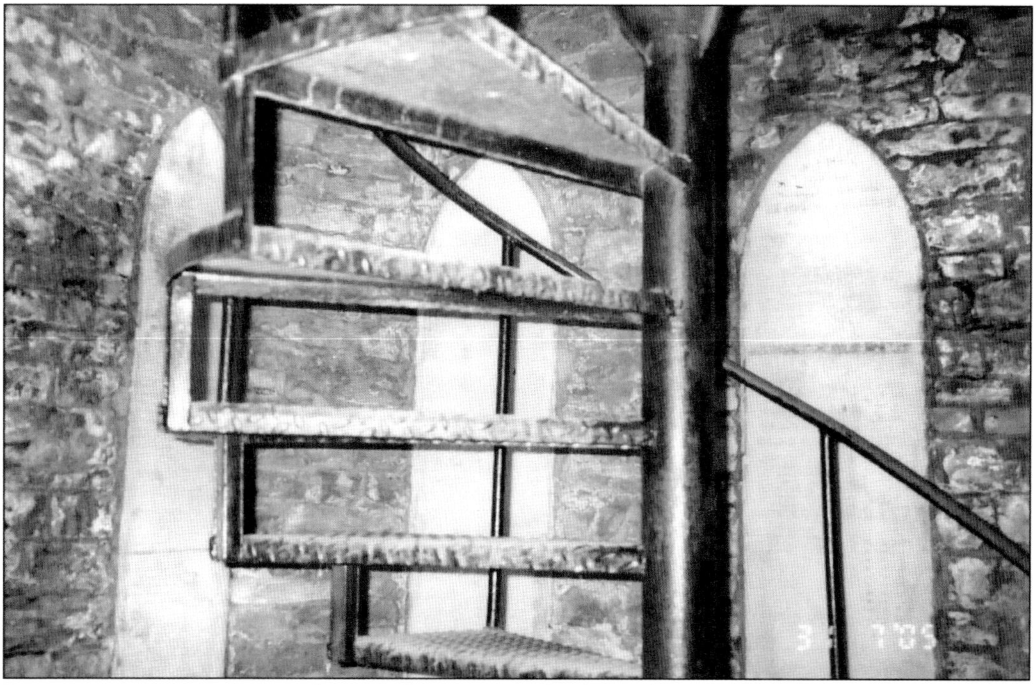

INSIDE THE MONUMENT. The circular staircase leads to the top. The climb up is somewhat daunting, as the stairs near the top are surrounded by only the dark shaft leading upward. At the base of the staircase are marble tablets engraved with the names of those who died in the Civil War from Orleans County.

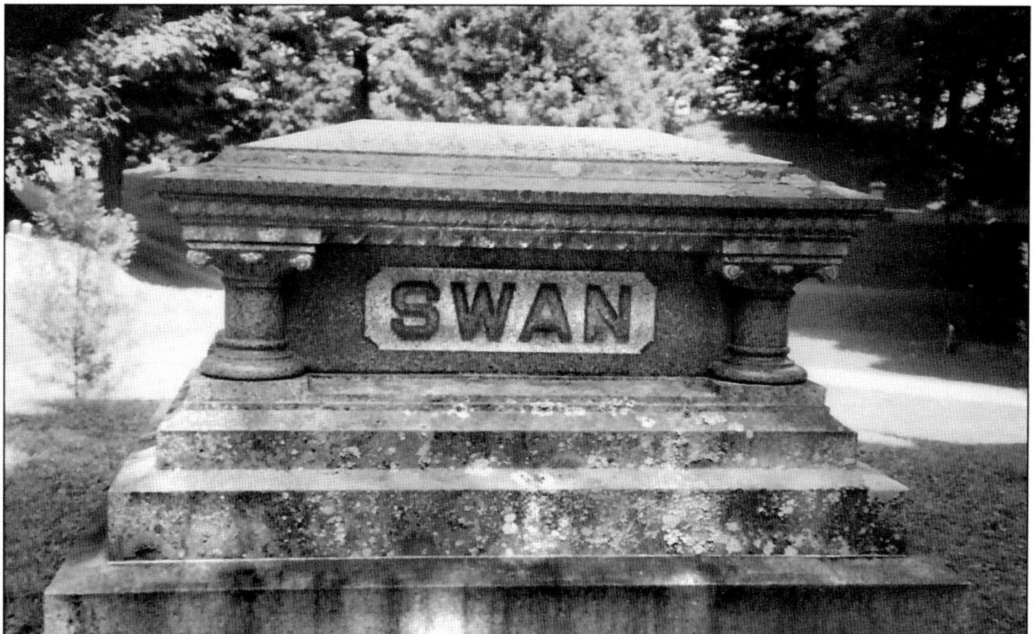

SWAN MEMORIAL. This is the memorial stone for William G. Swan and his family. Swan's father, interred in October 1843, became the first to be buried in Mount Albion Cemetery. (Courtesy of Donna Kay Belmont.)

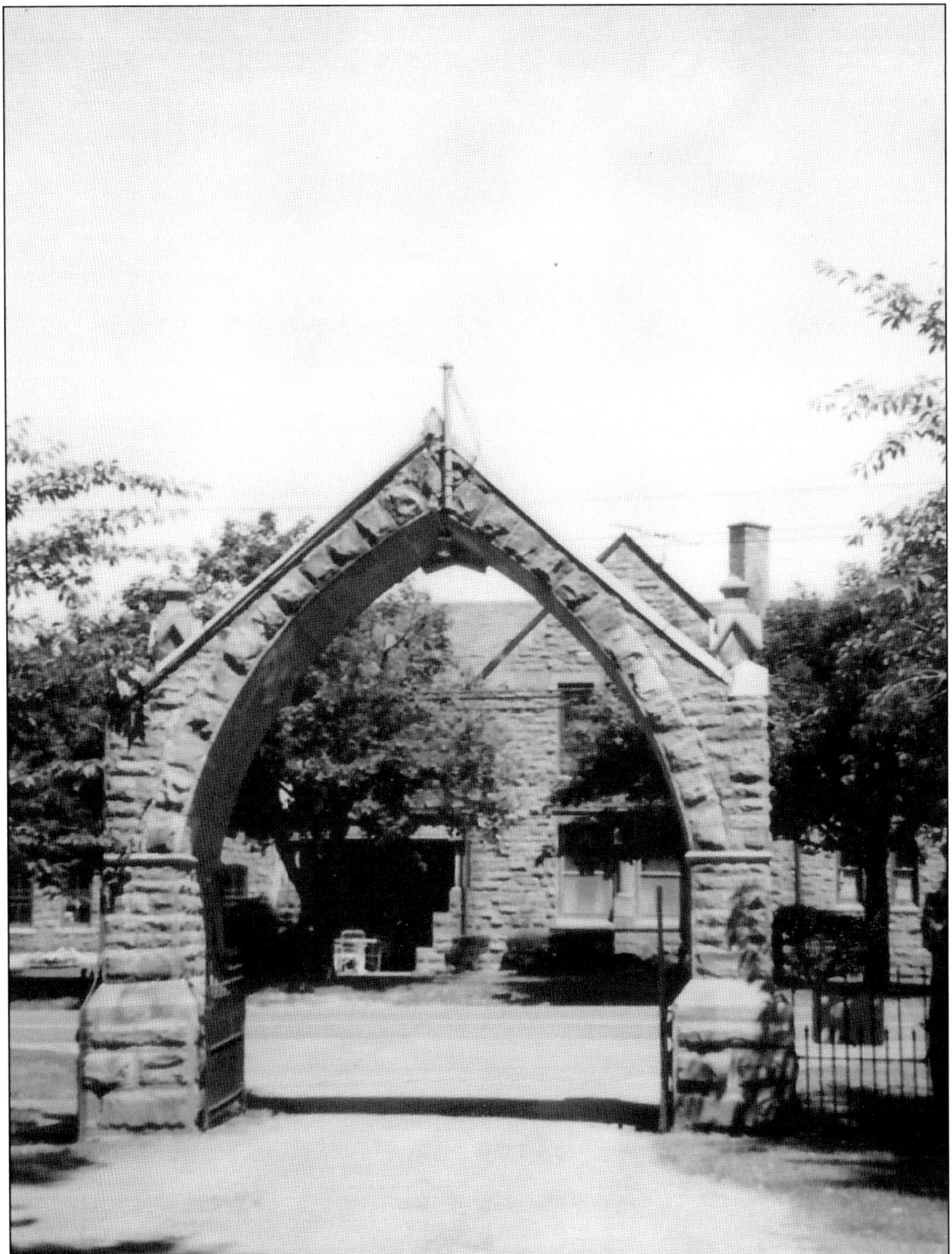

LEAVING THE CEMETERY. This arch is one of the exits from Mount Albion Cemetery on Route 31. The caretaker's residence is shown across the road. The white picket fences that surrounded the cemetery 100 years ago have been replaced with wrought iron.

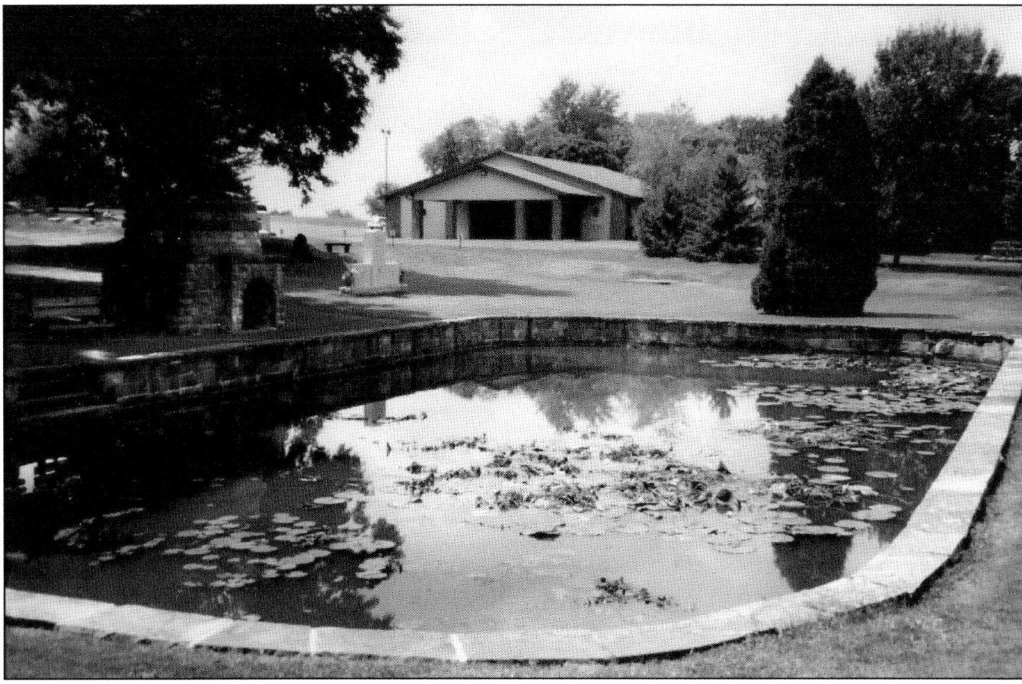

The Pond. One of the attractions at Mount Albion Cemetery is a large pond on the northwest corner of the cemetery. Filled with lily pads that bloom during the summer, the pond is a haven for frogs. Beside the pond is a springhouse.

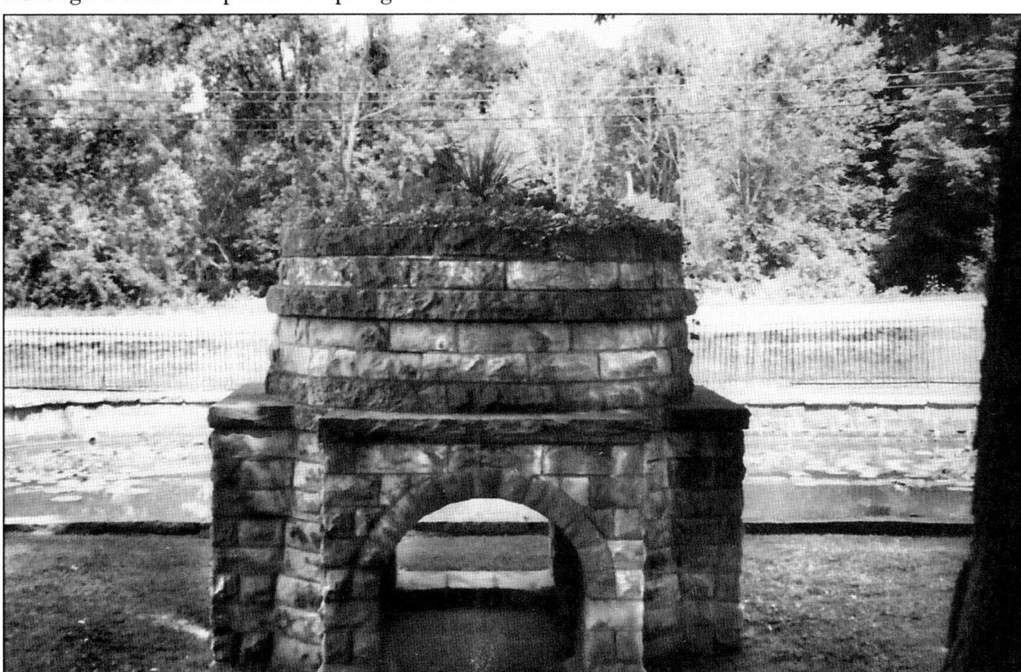

Springhouse. On the south edge of the pond is a gray Medina sandstone springhouse with a planter forming a roof over the spring that feeds the Lily Pond. Built in 1909, the pond was dedicated to volunteer men in 1982. (Courtesy of Donna Kay Belmont.)

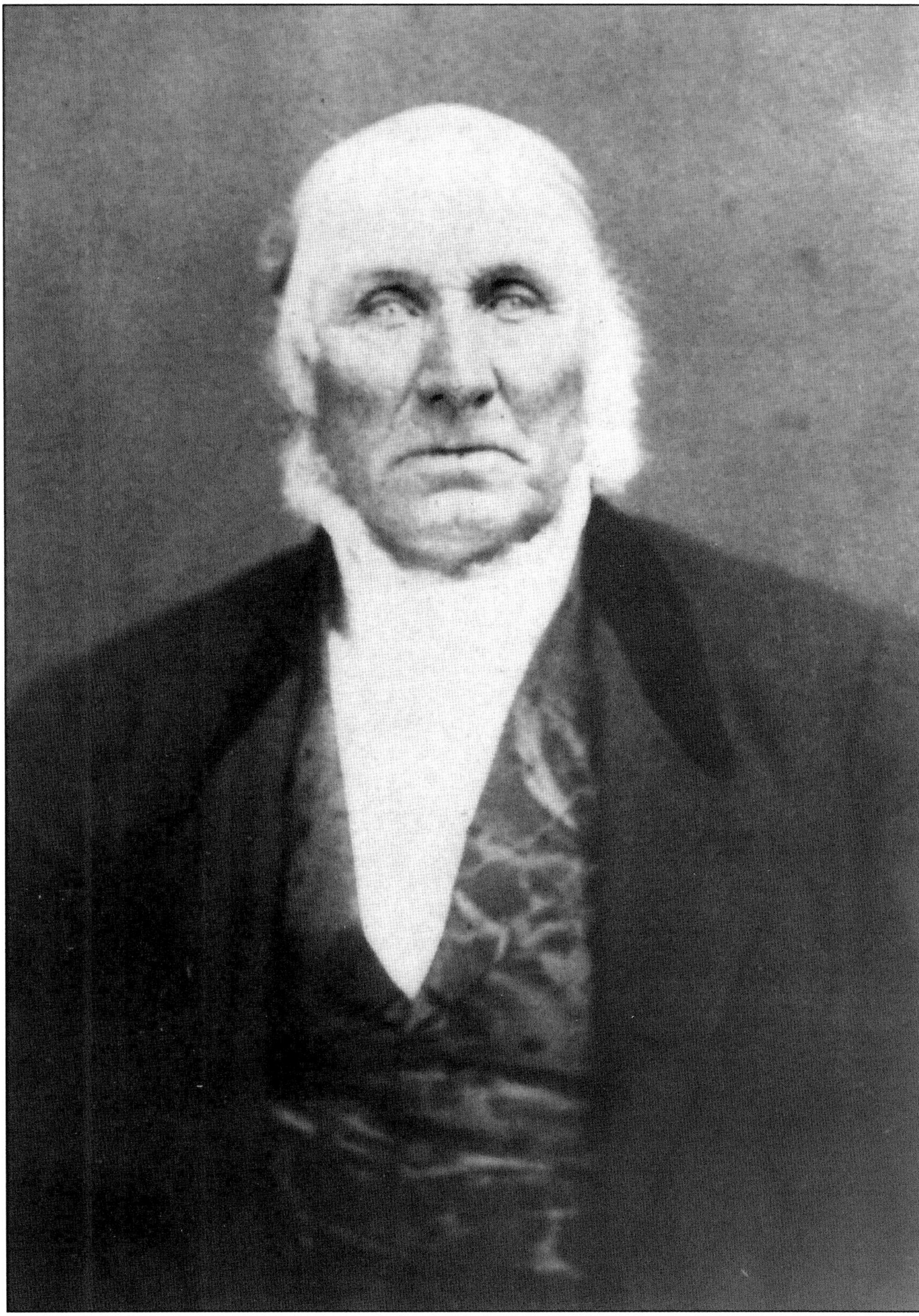

JOHN PROCTOR. The Universalist church in Childs was built by John Proctor and given to the First Universalist Society of Gaines in 1834. Proctor was founder of Fairhaven, first known as Proctor's Corners, now as Childs. (Courtesy of the Cobblestone Museum.)

Six

Childs and Gaines

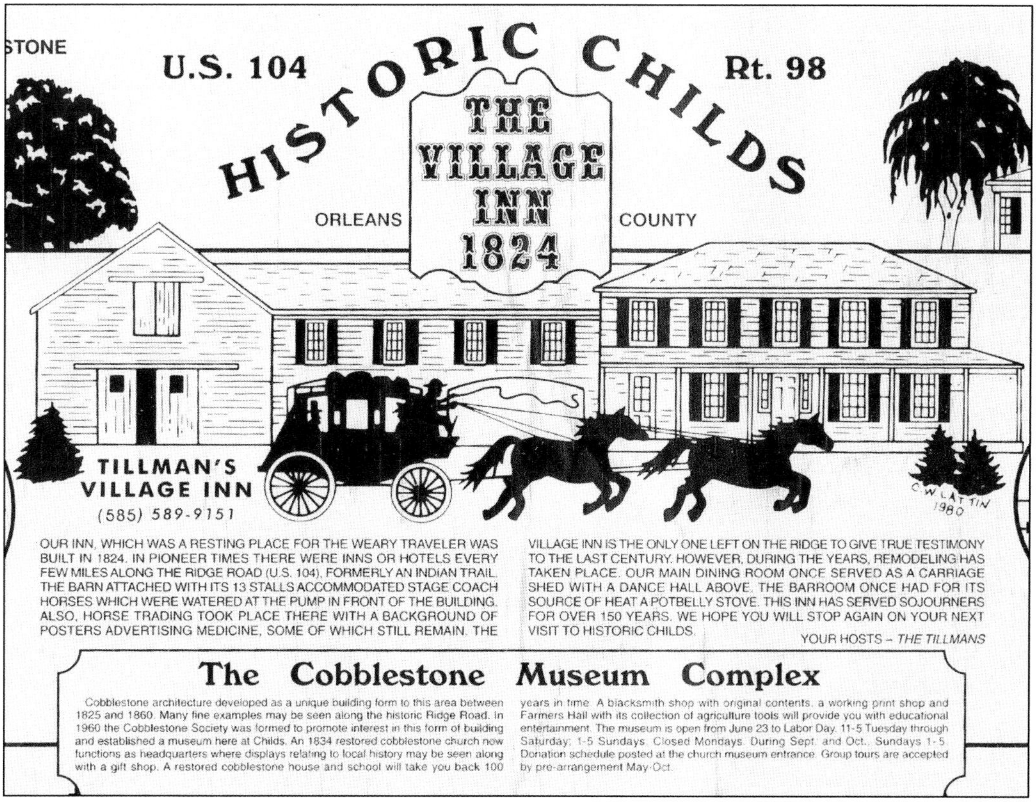

The Village Inn. This sketch, drawn by Orleans County historian C. W. Lattin, is part of the scene on the placemats of Tillman's Historic Village Inn. The inn, built on Ridge Road in 1824, was a resting place for travelers. The barn housed 13 stagecoach horses, which were watered at a pump in front of the building. The main dining room was once a carriage shed with a dance hall above. The barroom was once heated by a potbellied stove.

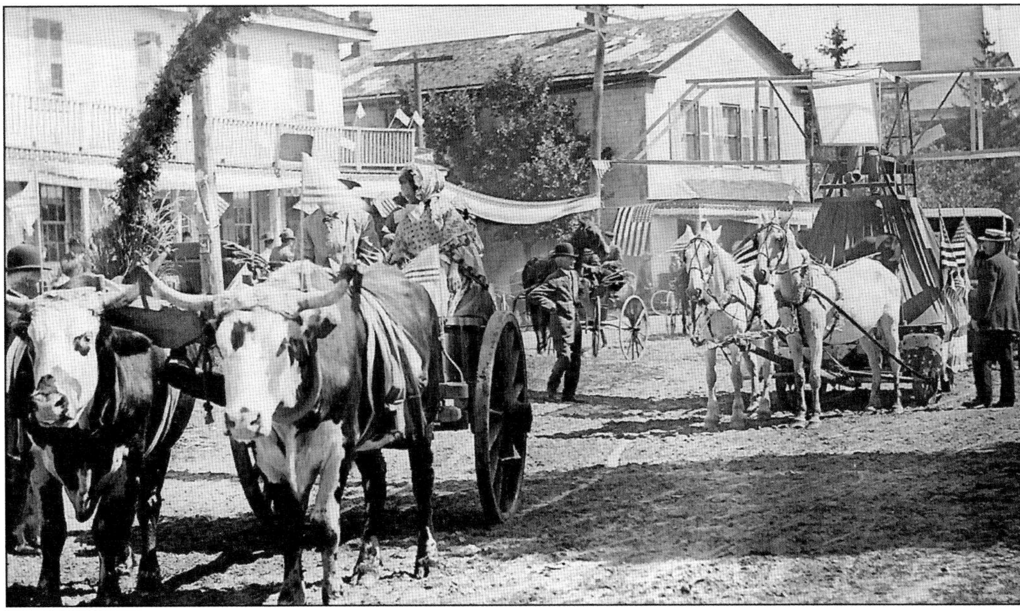

CELEBRATING 100 YEARS. In 1909, Gaines celebrated 100 years as a town. This photograph was taken on what is now the corner of Routes 104 and 98. On the left is the Village Inn, in the middle is a store that no longer exists, and behind the store is the Cobblestone Church. (Courtesy of the Cobblestone Museum.)

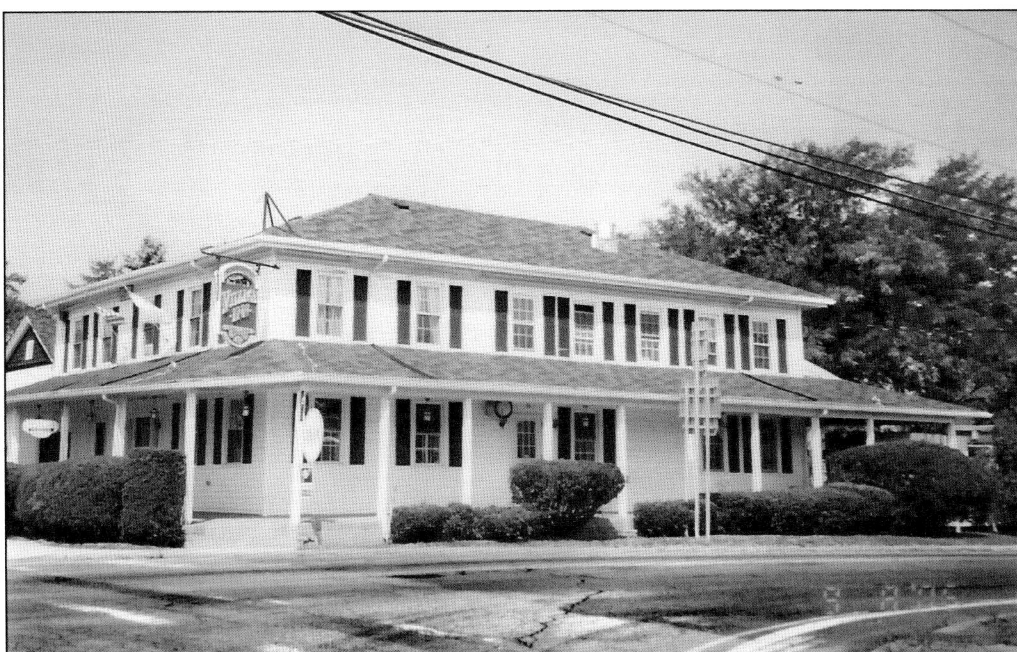

THE VILLAGE INN TODAY. Almost 200 years old, the Village Inn is tastefully updated and open for lunch and dinner. Its west room, which used to house stagecoach horses traveling on Ridge Road, is filled with photographs and memorabilia of a bygone era. This view, looking west across Route 98, was taken from Ridge Road.

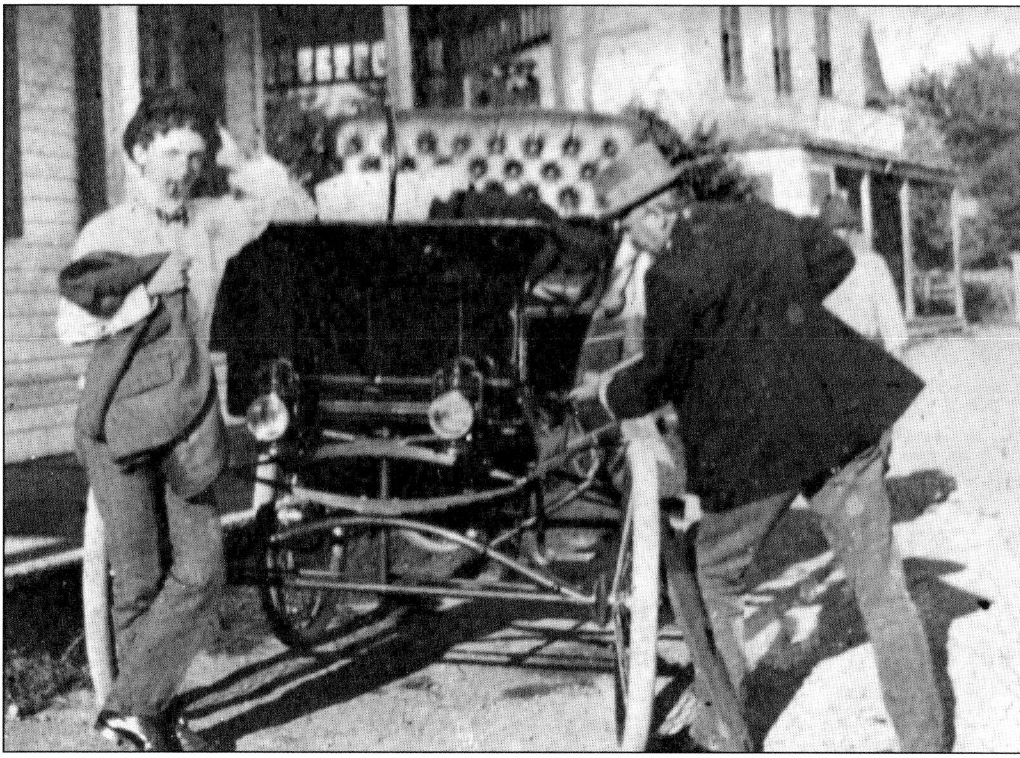

HORSELESS CARRIAGE. A. T. Blake (left) stares into the camera in 1899, as Dr. Sherwood makes an adjustment on his horseless carriage outside the Village Inn. (Courtesy of Mark Tillman.)

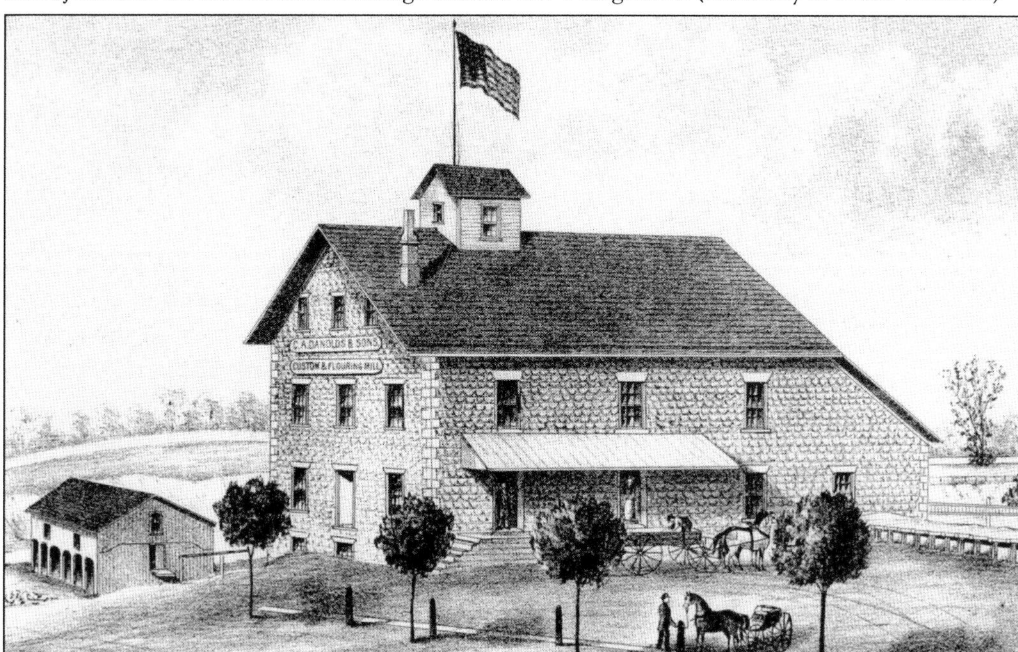

FLOUR MILL. This is a lithograph of the C. A. Danolds and Sons' Custom Flouring Mill at Eagle Harbor in 1879. (Courtesy of the Cobblestone Museum.)

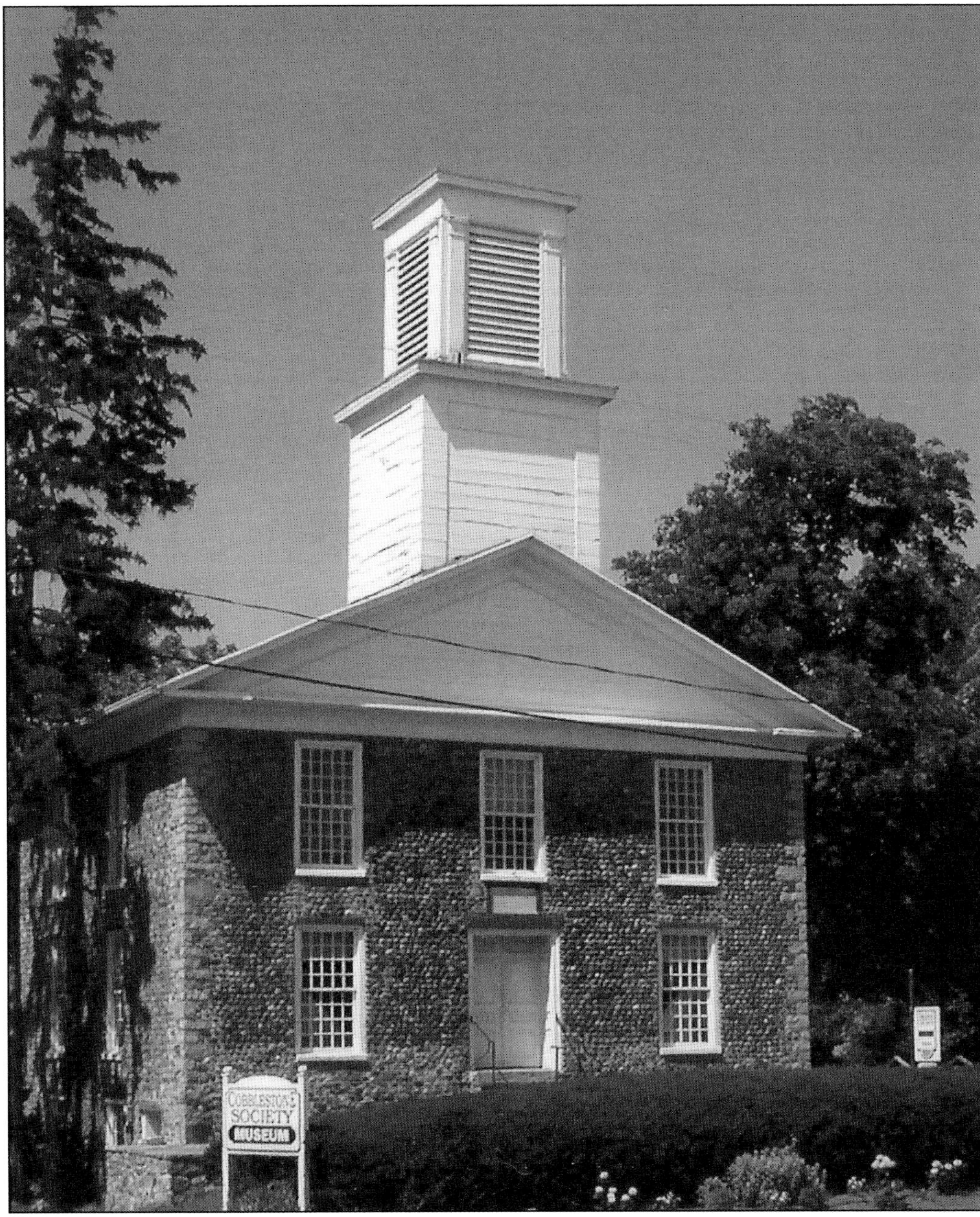

OLDEST COBBLESTONE CHURCH. Erected by John Proctor and given to the first Universalist Society of Gaines in 1834, this is the oldest cobblestone church in North America. In 1993, it was dedicated as a national historic landmark and is now a part of the Cobblestone Society Museum in Childs. The complex is open for viewing from May through October. (Courtesy of the Cobblestone Museum.)

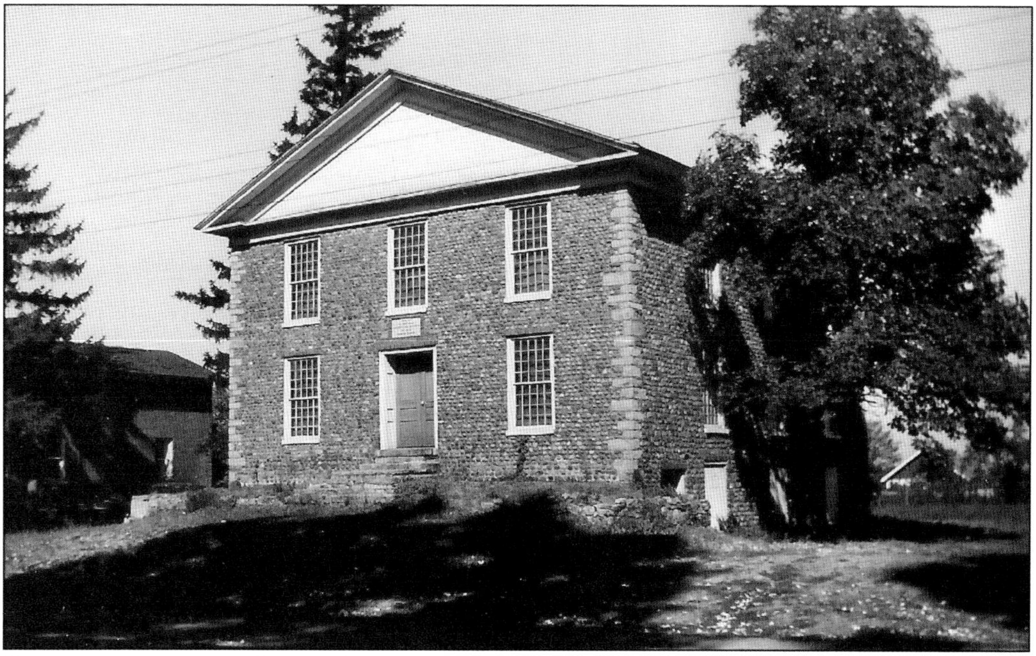

CHURCH WITHOUT TOWER. Taken on September 24, 1941, this photograph shows the Cobblestone Church in Childs. The old church tower was removed in 1919. The present tower was restored in 1966 in memory of Eva M. Brush. (Courtesy of the Cobblestone Museum.)

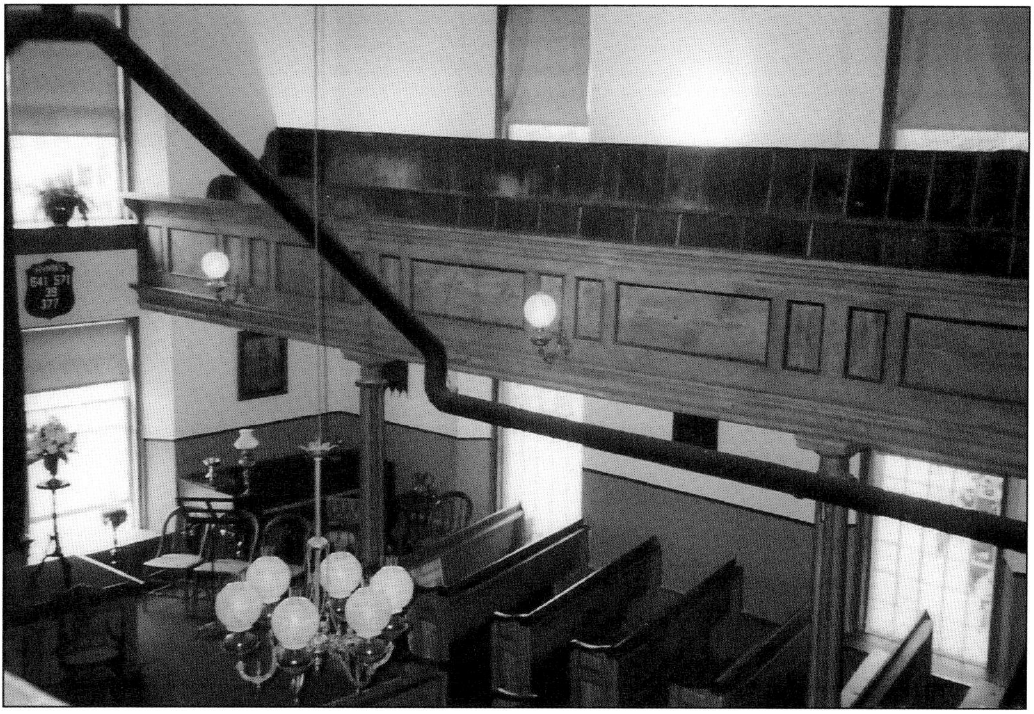

VIEW FROM THE LOFT. This view from upstairs looks down into the sanctuary of the Cobblestone Church. The pews are original, and the long one (top) has very narrow seats. The chandelier hanging over the pulpit was patented in 1864 for oil lamps.

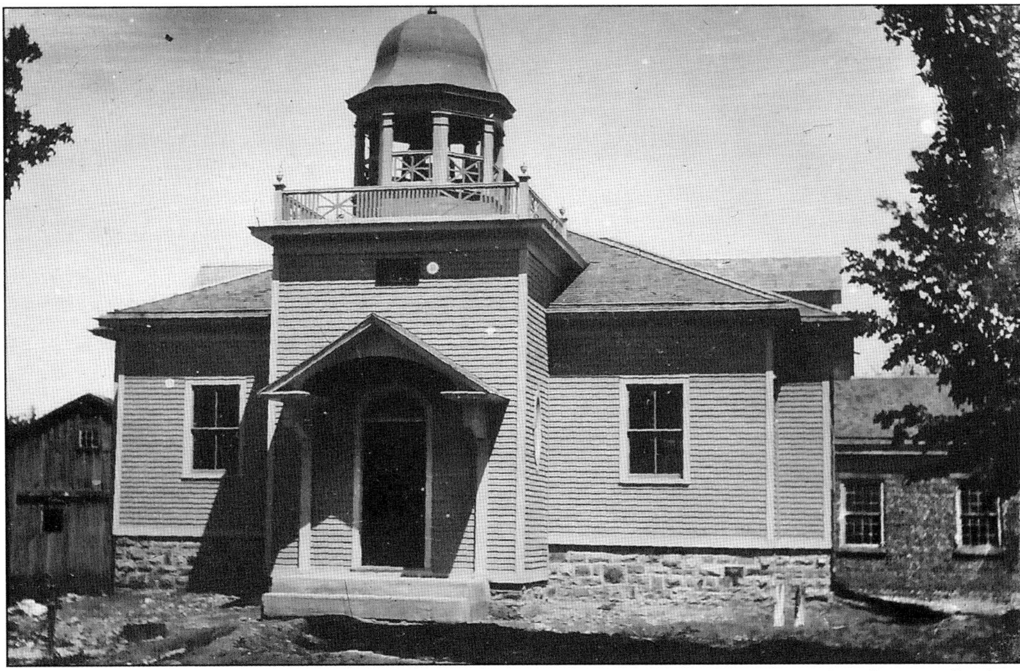

NEW SCHOOL, OLD SCHOOL. The building in the foreground is the new schoolhouse, built in Eagle Harbor in 1907. Behind it is the old cobblestone school, which was seen as outdated by that time. This is the only photograph of the former cobblestone school that is known to exist. (Courtesy of the Cobblestone Museum.)

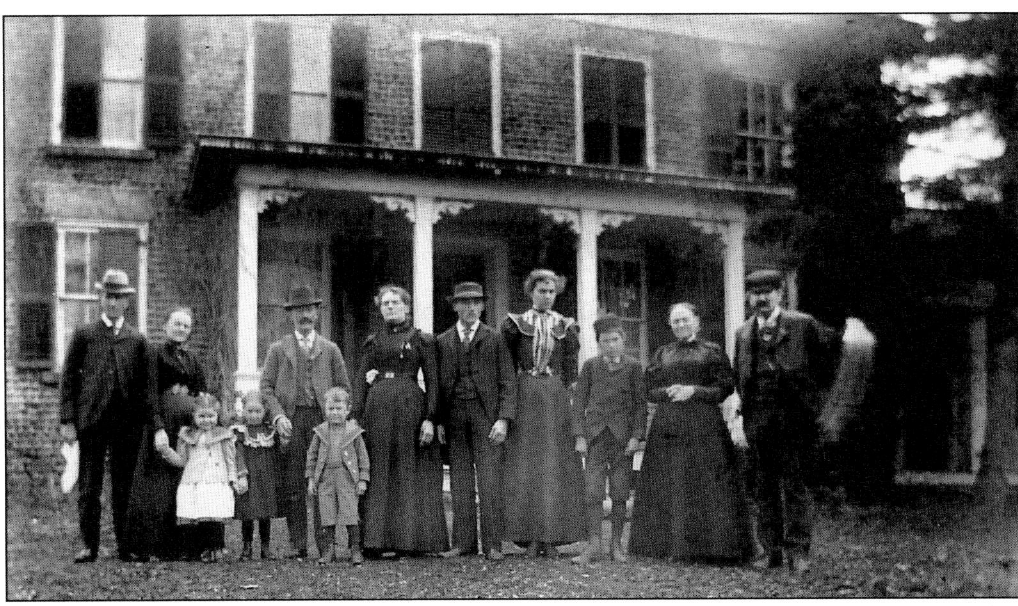

NEAR OTTER CREEK. Members of the Bartlett family are pictured around 1900 in front of their cobblestone house on Ridge Road, west of Otter Creek. From left to right are Grandpa Frank Lattin, May Lattin, Dorothy Lattin, unidentified child, Frank McGlenn, unidentified child, Lenny McGlenn, Mrs. and Mr. Bartlett, and three unidentified people. The house still stands, with some alterations. (Courtesy of the Cobblestone Museum.)

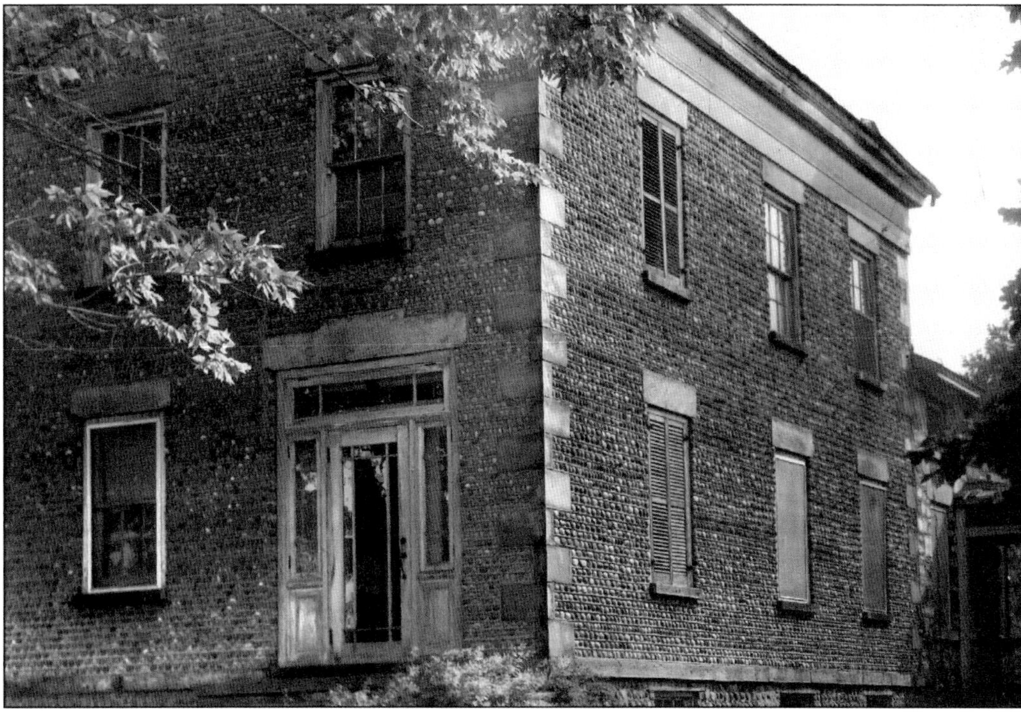

BACON-NEILANS HOME. This house, located on Route 98 north of Route 104, was the home of Moses Bacon. The north wall of the home is a different style from that of the other three walls, as can be seen in the photograph below. Three sides of the house have protruding stones, and the north side has stones in the depressed hexagonal pattern found only in Gaines. (Courtesy of the Cobblestone Museum.)

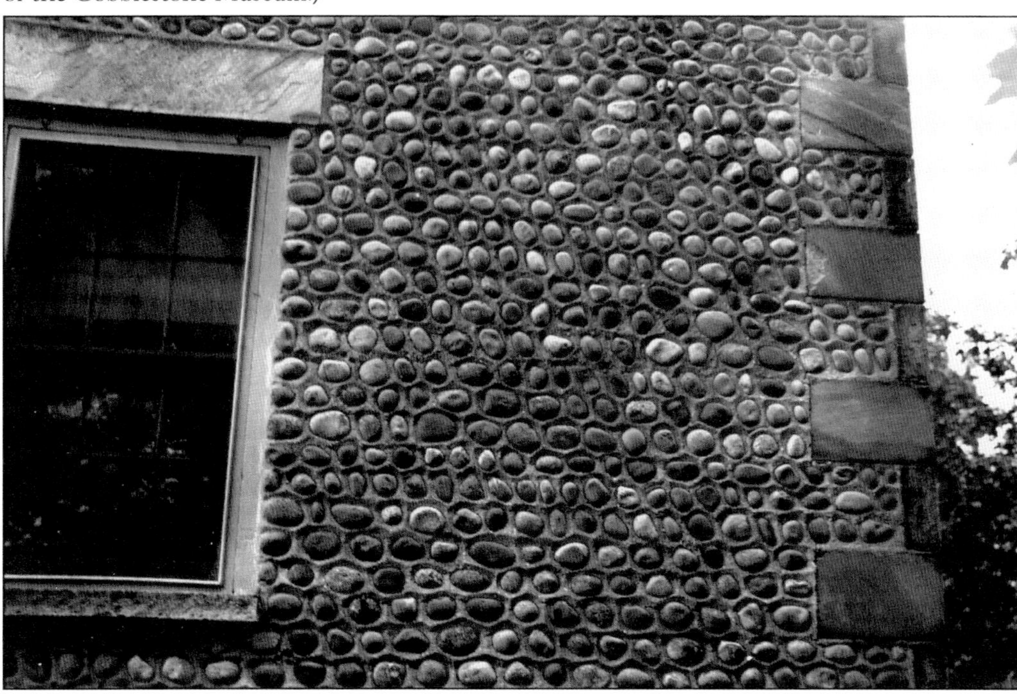

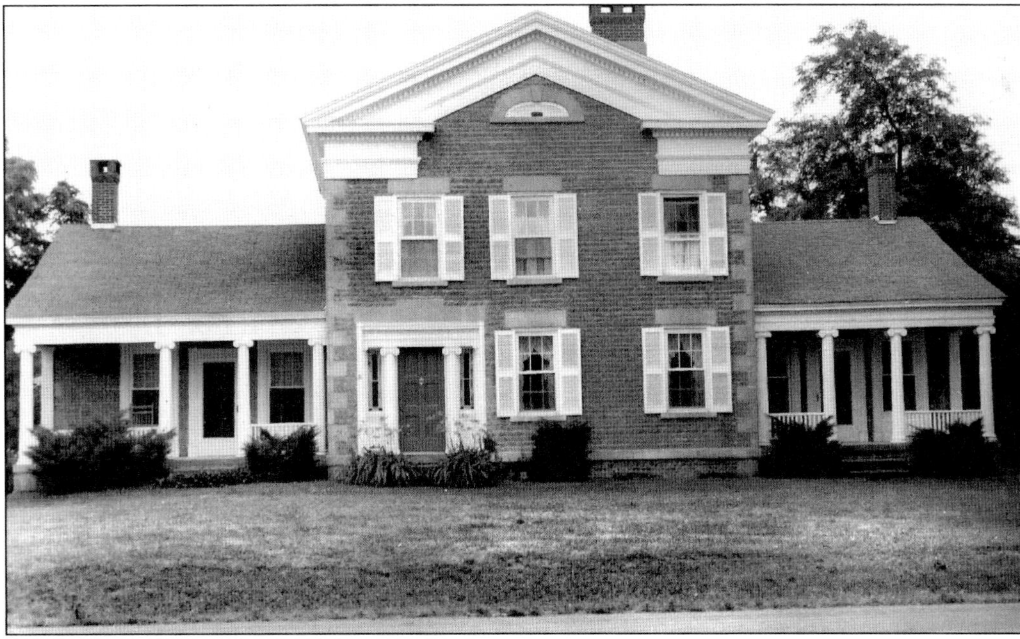

HERRINGBONE COBBLES. This unique home, at 13194 Ridge Road, is the former Florence Harmer House. It was done in a herringbone style, with the stones crisscrossing, in 1840. (Courtesy of the Cobblestone Museum.)

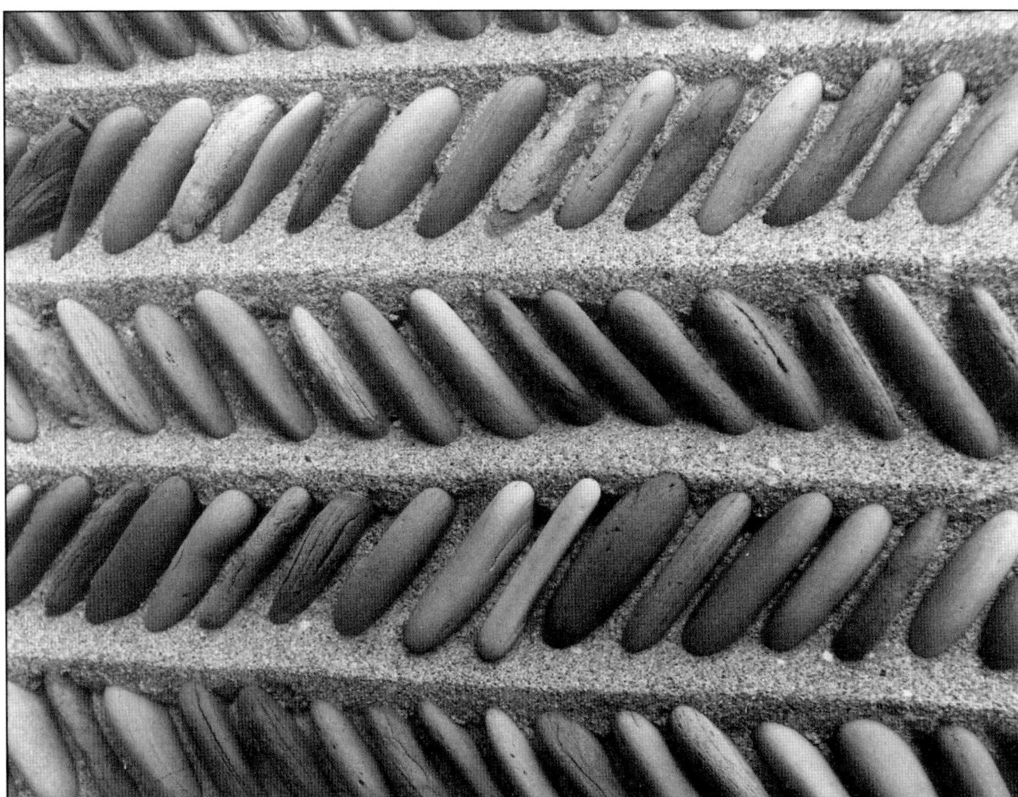

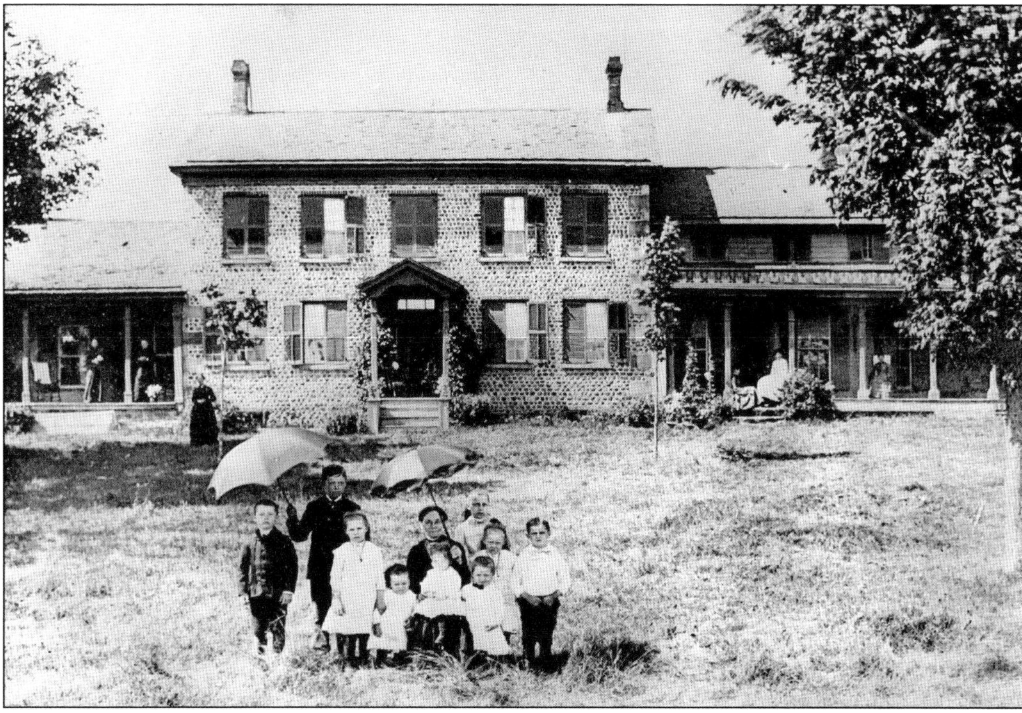

ZIG ZAG HOUSE. This was the Knapp family around 1900. The house, minus wings, is located on Zig Zag Road. (Courtesy of the Cobblestone Museum.)

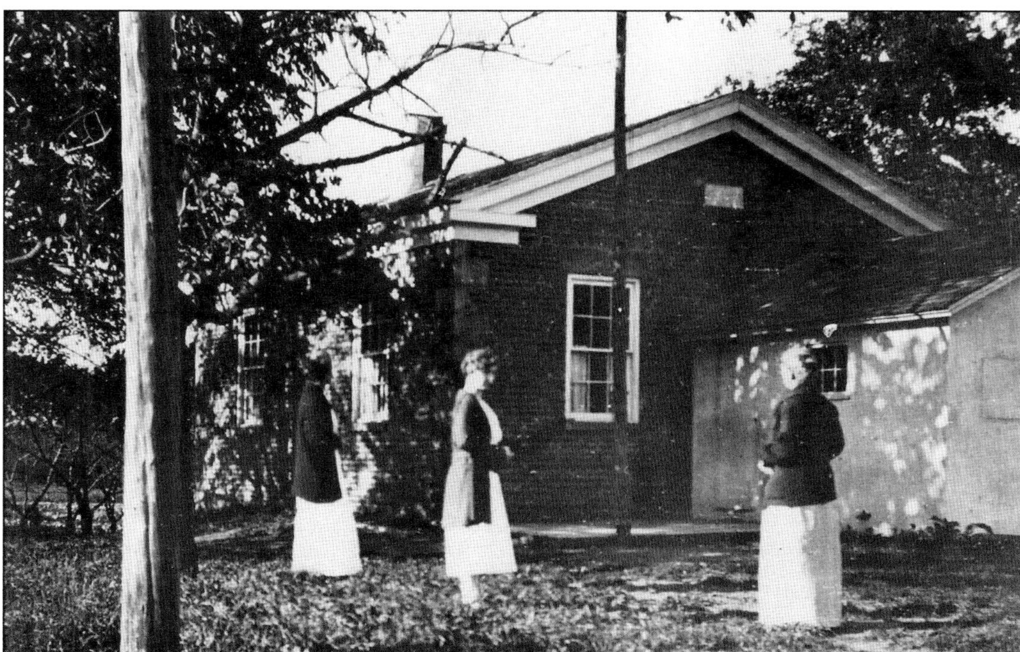

FIVE CORNERS SCHOOL. The woman in the center of this view from around 1910 is Florence Johnson. Five Corners is the area north of the canal at Routes 98 and 279. (Courtesy of the Cobblestone Museum.)

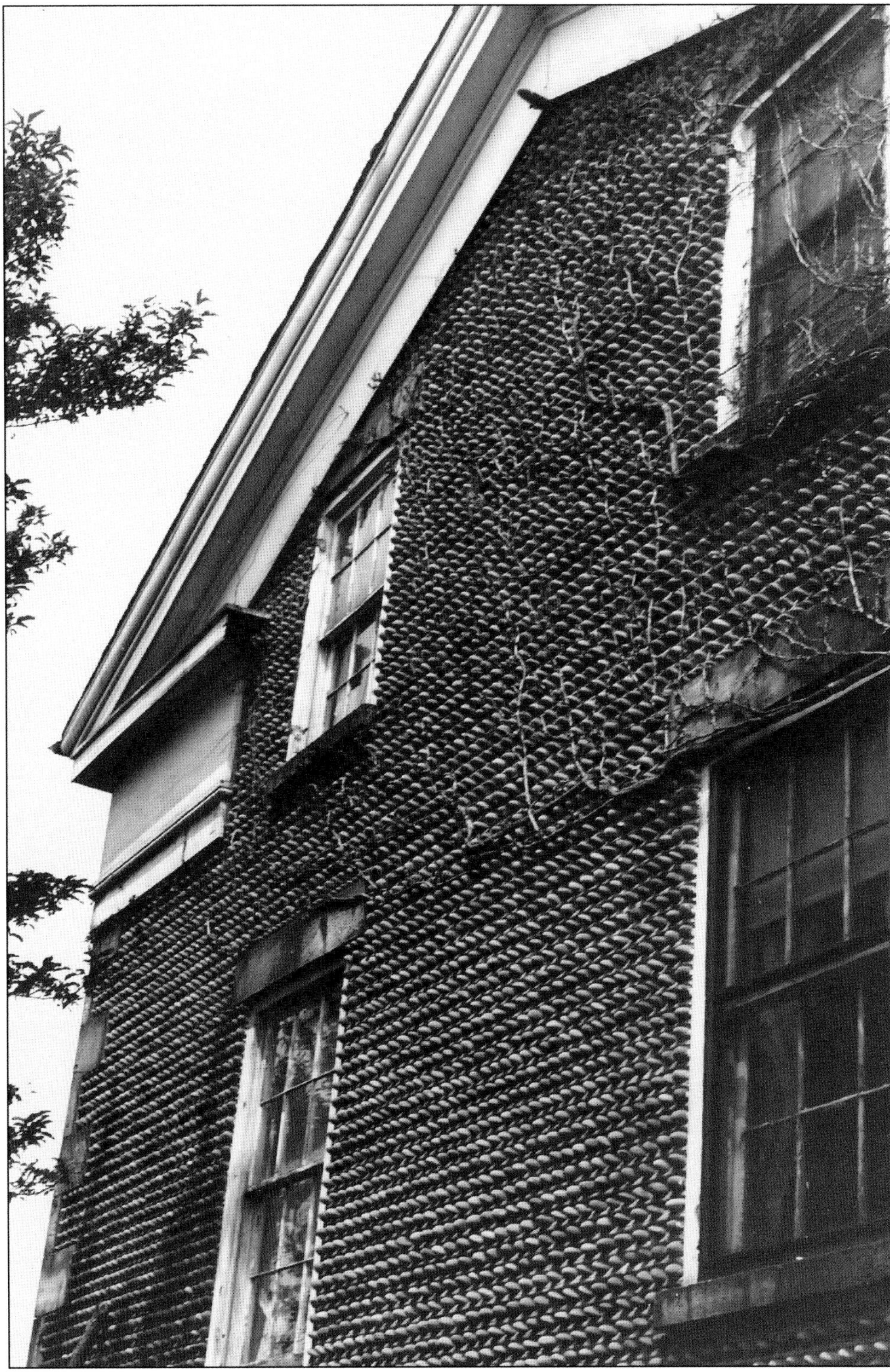

BACON-HEARD HOUSE. This house on Brown Road was built by Hosea Bacon. It was once known as Greystone Farm. (Courtesy of the Cobblestone Museum.)

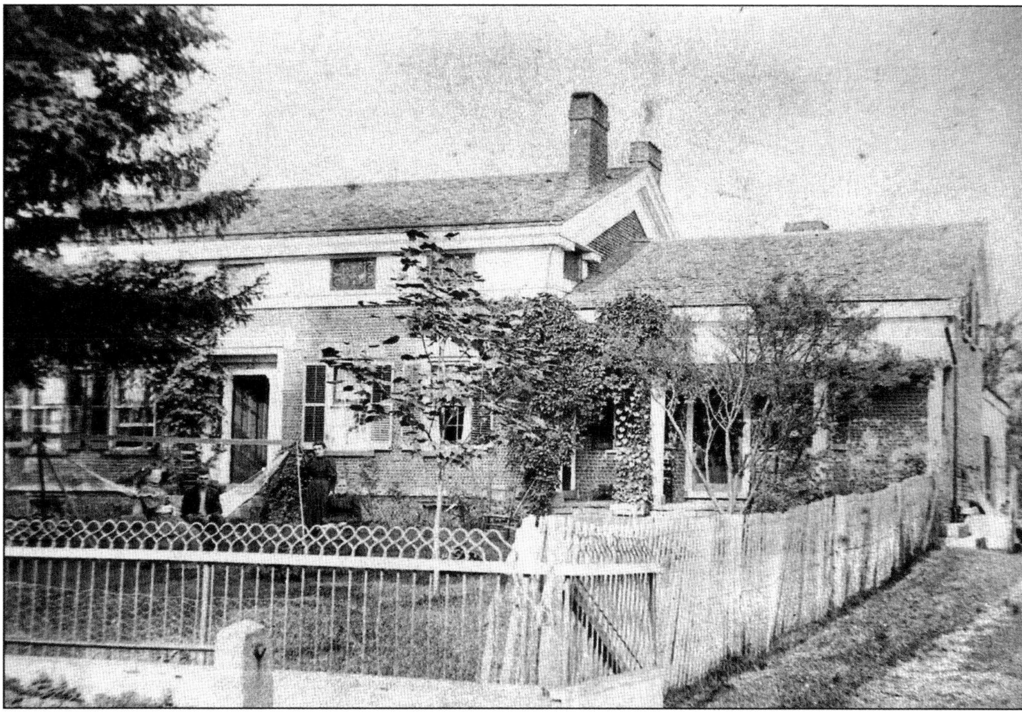

BACON-HEARD HOUSE. This photograph, taken around 1895, shows the cobblestone on Brown Road. The kitchen wing, at the right, was altered in the 1950s. The main portion of the house was built in 1852. (Courtesy of the Cobblestone Museum.)

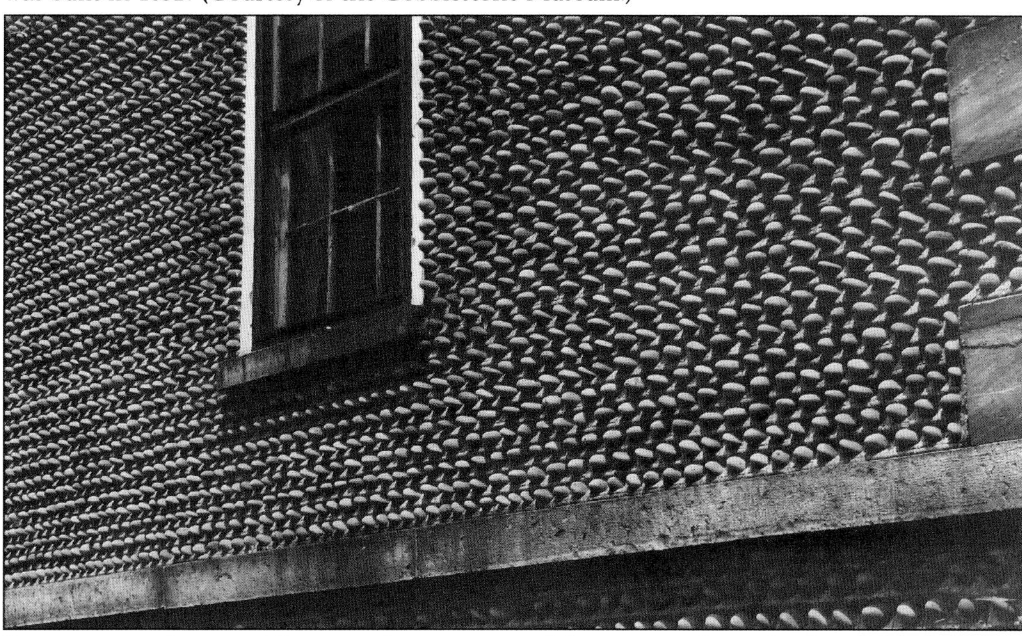

PROTRUDING STONES. This is a close-up view of the stonework on the Bacon-Heard House. Note how each stone juts out, with half the stone in the mortar and the other half protruding outward. This unique style wall was built by Werner Bacon, the 16-year-old son of Hosea Bacon. (Courtesy of the Cobblestone Museum.)

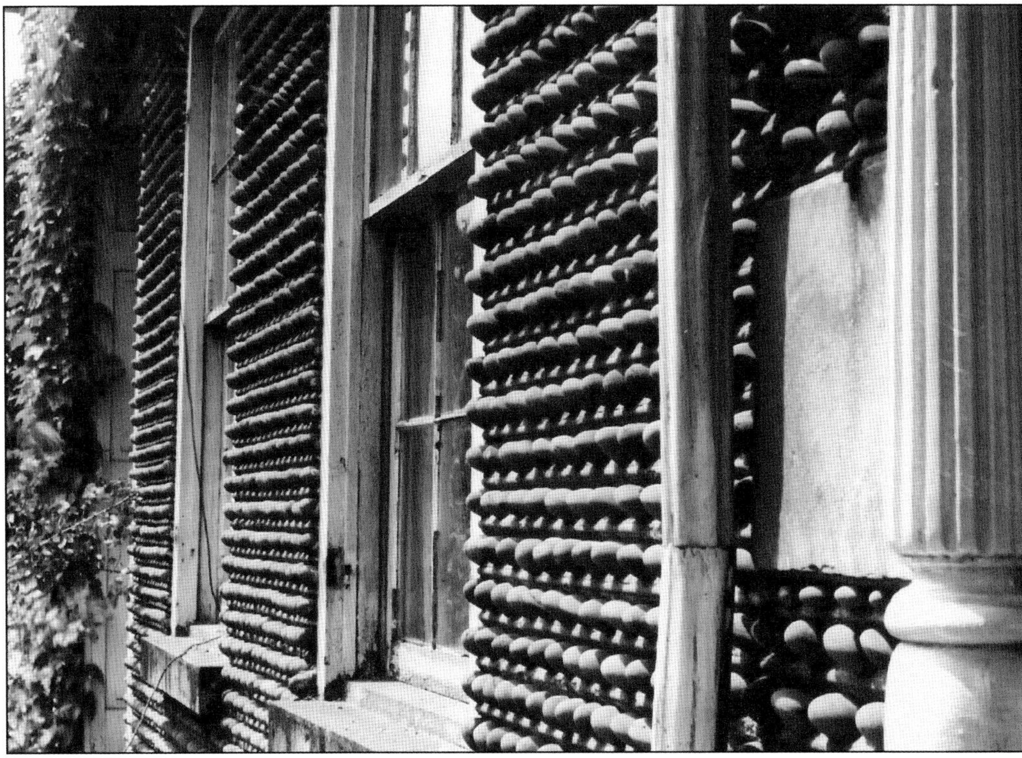

STONES RESEMBLE EGGS. This close-up view shows the stonework on the east side of the Bacon-Heard House. Usually the cobblestone work was more elaborate on the front of a house than it was on the rest of the structure. (Courtesy of the Cobblestone Museum.)

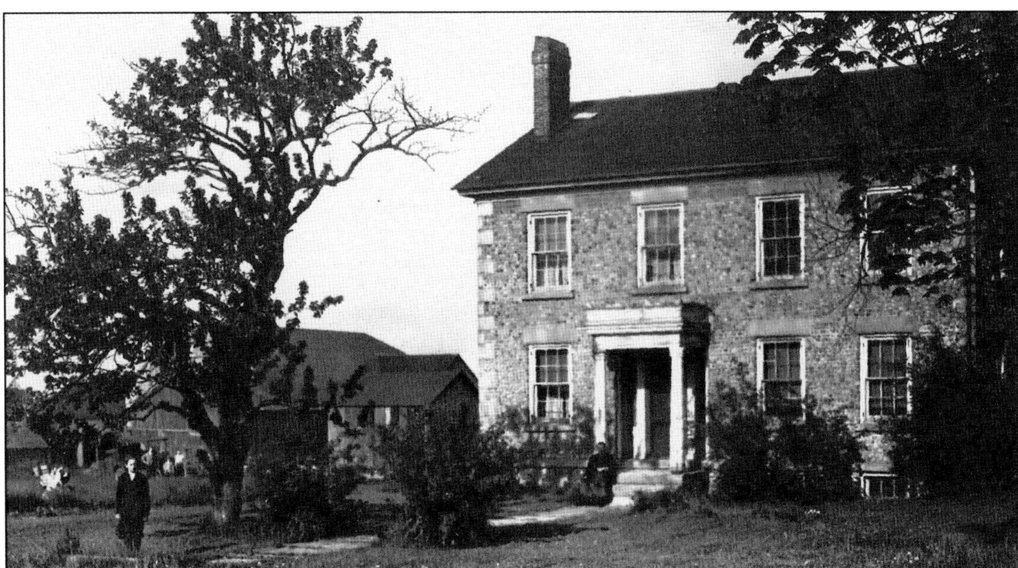

FERRIS FAMILY HOME. Located on Route 98 south of Five Corners, this house was built about 1840. This picture was taken around 1910, when the Ferris family lived here. (Courtesy of the Cobblestone Museum.)

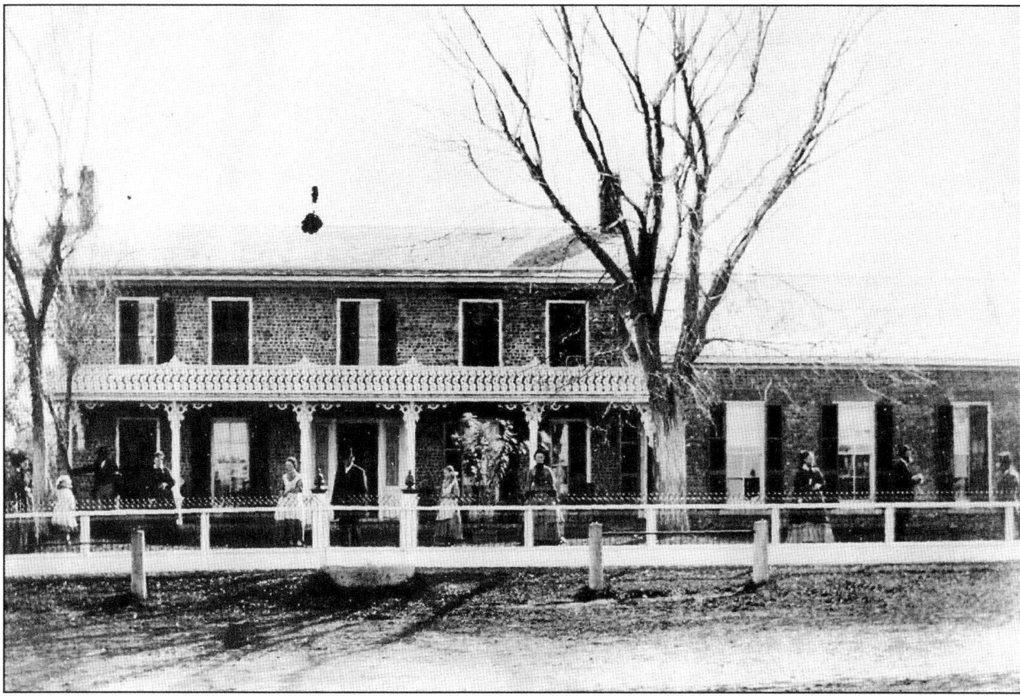

ANDERSON HOUSE. Members of the Anderson family enjoy a day outside their lavish Route 104 home around 1870. The main two-story section of the house was built in the 1830s, and the wing was added in 1859. (Courtesy of C. W. Lattin.)

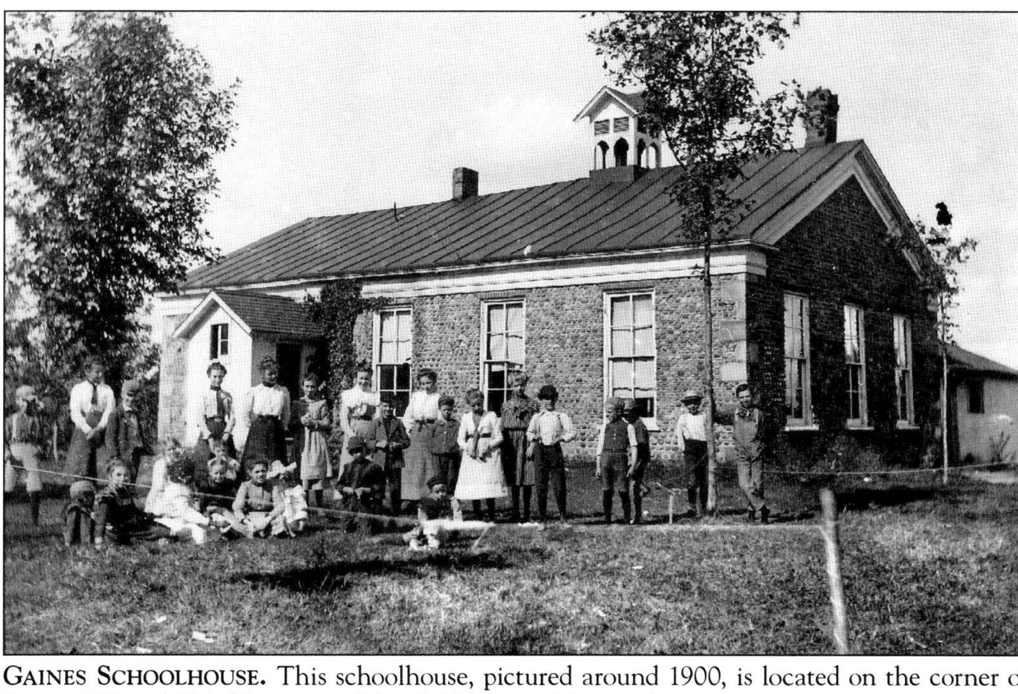

GAINES SCHOOLHOUSE. This schoolhouse, pictured around 1900, is located on the corner of Routes 279 and 104. (Courtesy of the Cobblestone Museum.)

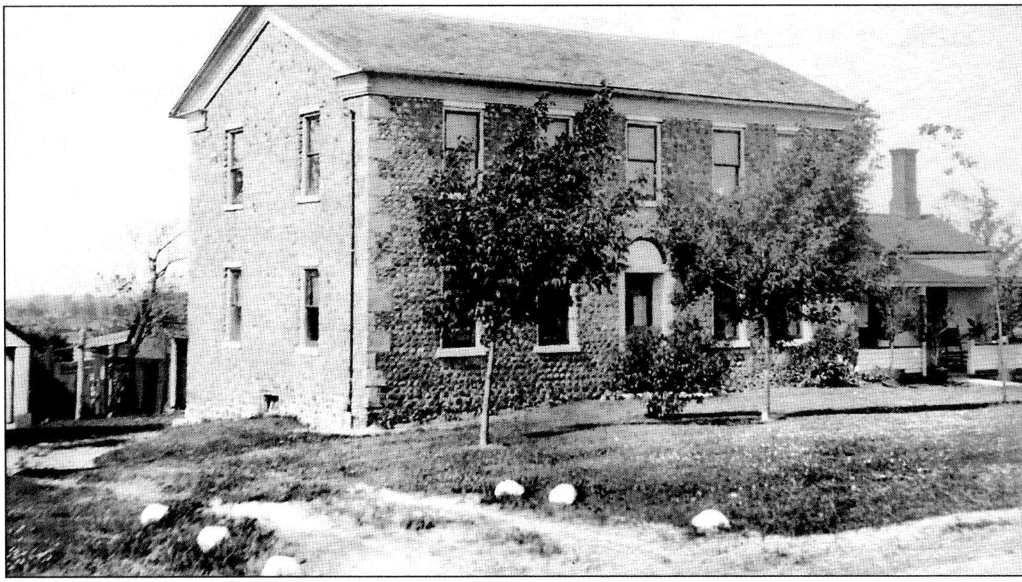

THE BILLINGS HOMESTEAD. The Billings Homestead, on Ridge Road, is pictured around 1930 (above) and in 1942 (below). In those dozen years, the home did not change much: the porch (right) has a different roofline, an outbuilding (back) has been added, and, of course, the trees are larger. The secret to maintaining a cobblestone house is to keep the roof in good repair. Cobbles are put on the inside as well as the outside of the building; thus, if water seeps in between them, it can destroy the wall. With a good roof, a cobblestone house could last forever. (Courtesy of the Cobblestone Museum.)

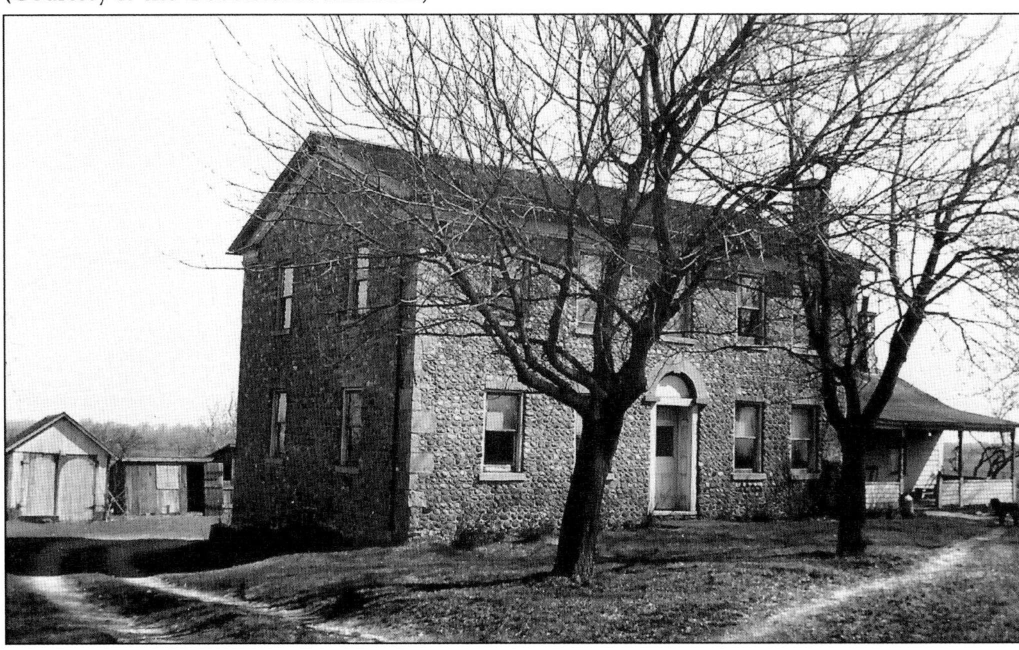

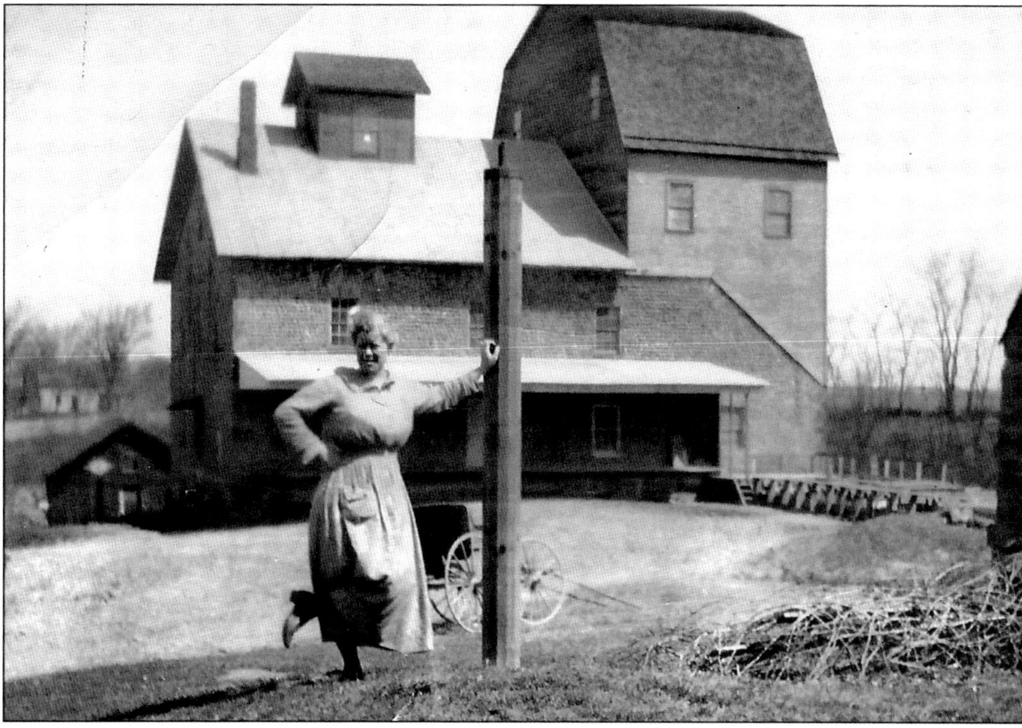

EAGLE HARBOR MILL. Mrs. Fox poses in front of the old Eagle Harbor Mill. (Courtesy of the Cobblestone Museum.)

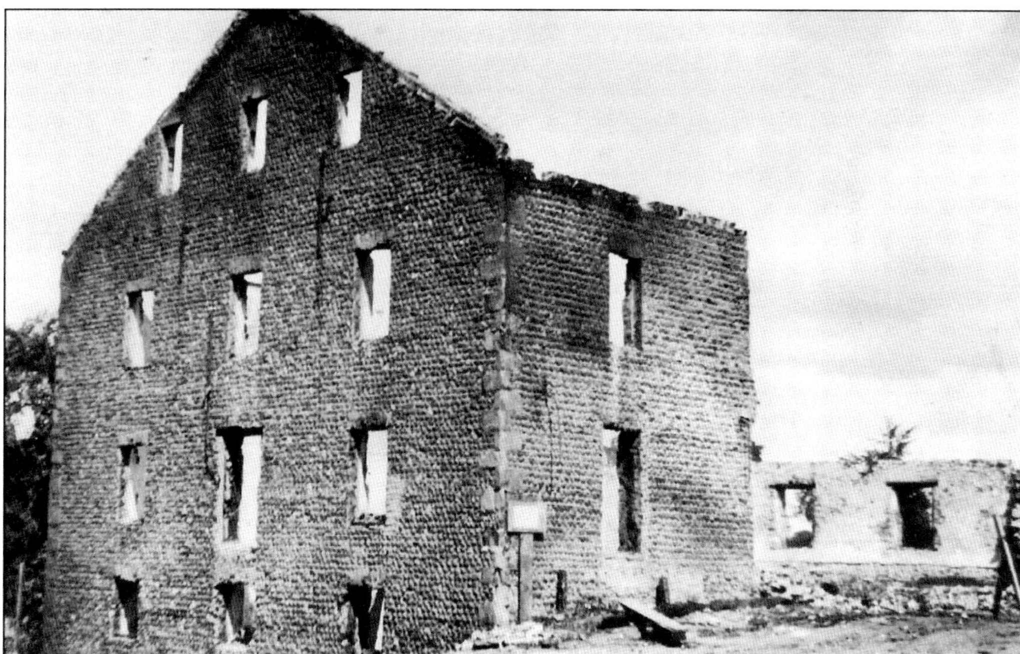

AFTER THE FIRE. Danolds's Mill was a cobblestone building on the east side of Eagle Harbor Road near Otter Creek. It burned in 1925, and its shell stood abandoned for many years before being leveled, except for one small section of wall. (Courtesy of the Cobblestone Museum.)

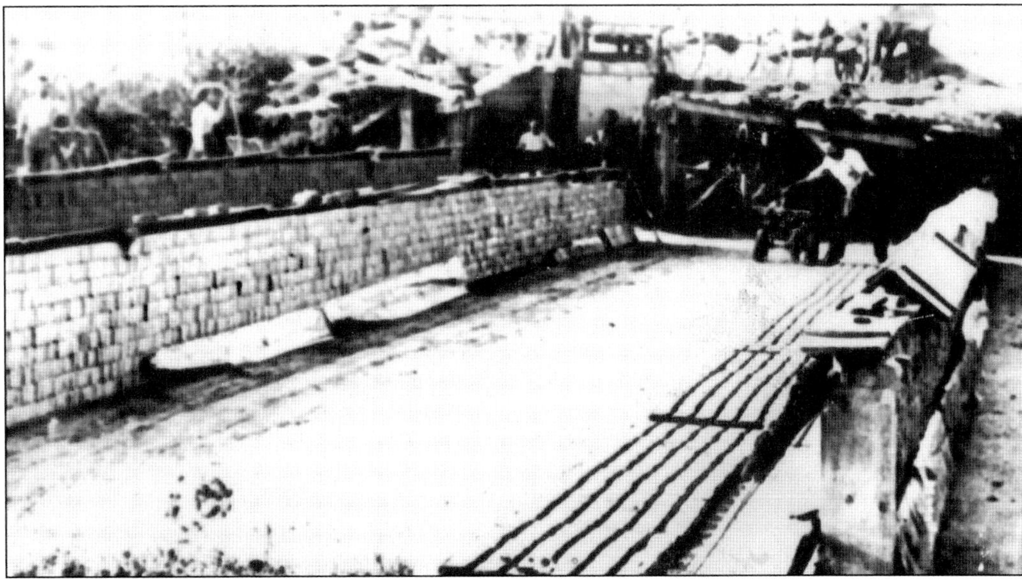

LAFLER BRICKYARD. This brickyard was on Route 98 in the town of Gaines. J. A. Lafler manufactured bricks used for the lintels of many of the homes in the area. (Courtesy of the Cobblestone Museum.)

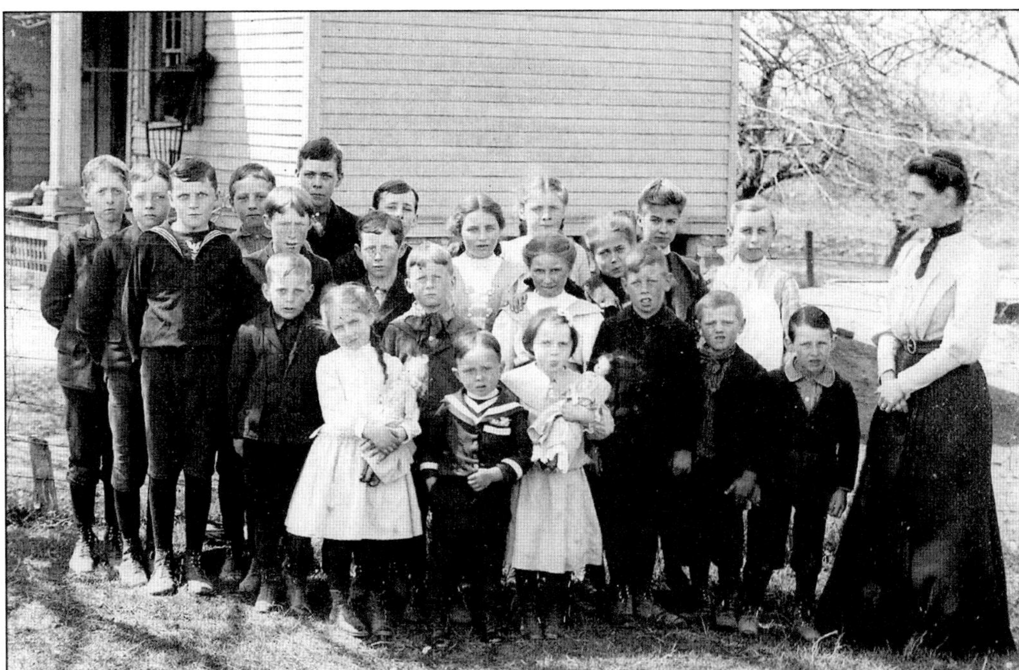

COBBLESTONE KIDS. These children attended class at the Cobblestone School around 1904. They stand alongside a neighboring home rather than the schoolhouse. Pictured here are Lillian Gmortall, Albert Houghton, Ruth Butler, Louie Satchels, Fred Bates, teacher Dora Bilby, ? Hughson, ? Cook, Berniece Ames, Edith Tiaver, Kenneth Butler, K. Cook, Kris Balcolm, L. Seringer, Gladys Butler, Bea Creishank, Walter Rowley, John Murray, Harold Barnum, Curtiss Murray, and Harold Bates. (Courtesy of the Cobblestone Museum.)

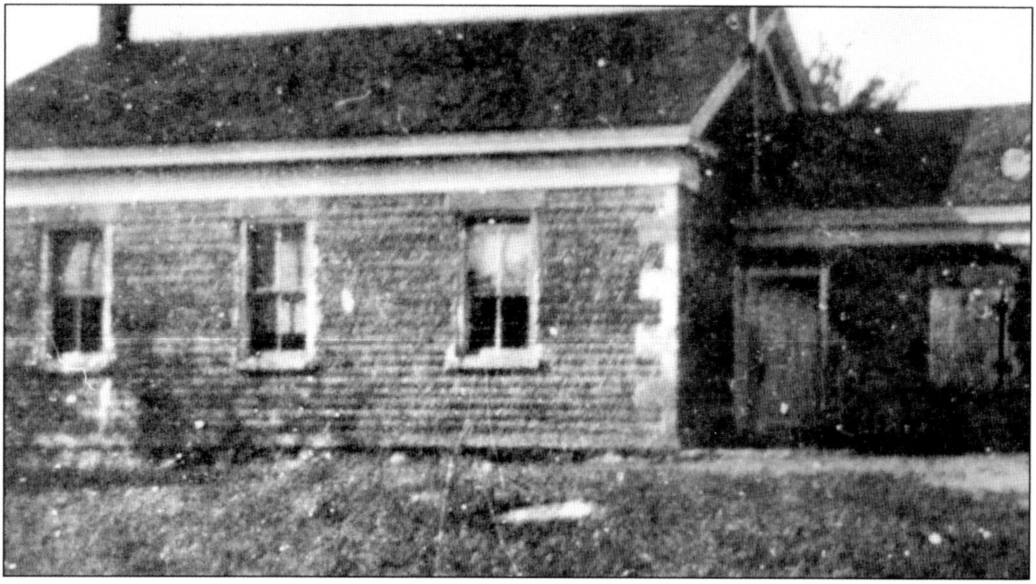

RICHES CORNERS SCHOOL. Cyrus Witheral of Gaines was the stonemason hired to build this school at the southwest corner of Riches Corners and Holley Roads in 1845. The school, done in the herringbone pattern, was built for a total cost of $550. It was torn down in 1959. (Courtesy of the Cobblestone Museum.)

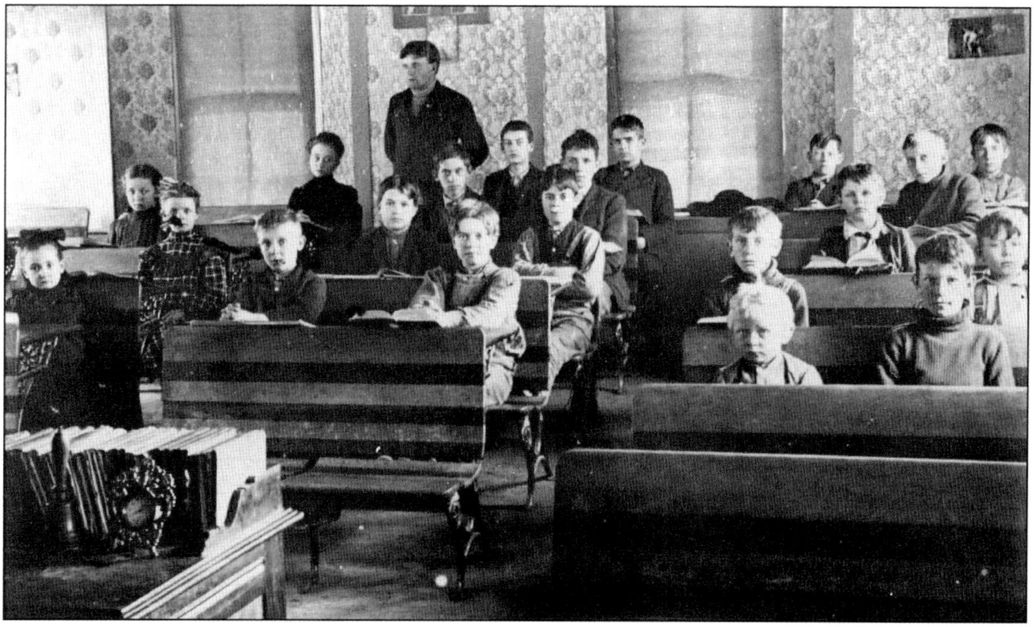

INSIDE THE RICHES CORNERS SCHOOL. Children were treated to a classroom with wallpaper after 1901. The building served not only as a school but also as a community center and a Sunday school. (Courtesy of the Cobblestone Museum.)

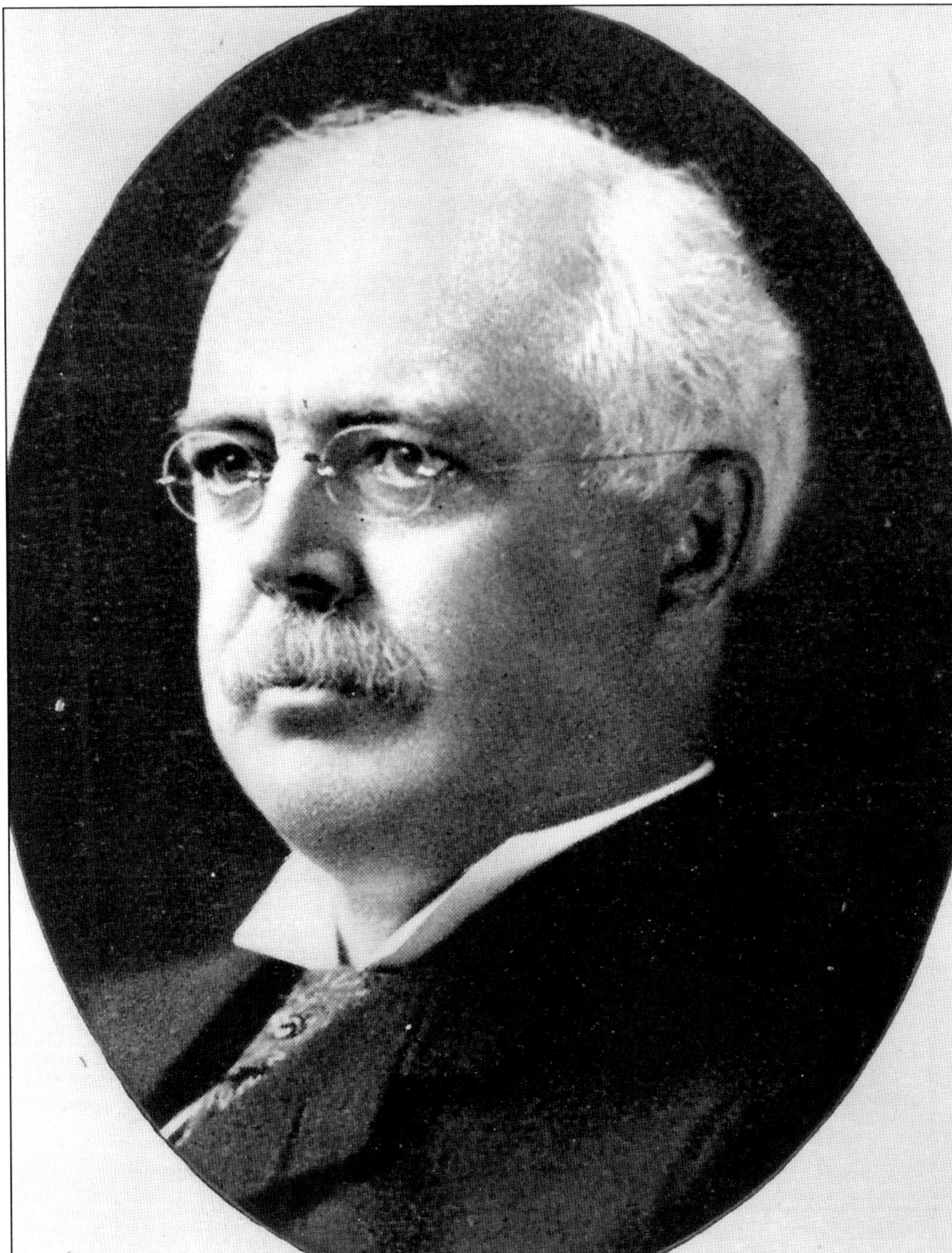

JOHN CUNNEEN. When he was 12 years old, John Cunneen came to America from Ireland and made a name for himself in Albion. He taught at the Childs Cobblestone School from 1870 to 1874 for $3.50 a week. He was elected New York State attorney general in 1902. (Courtesy of Orleans County Department of History.)

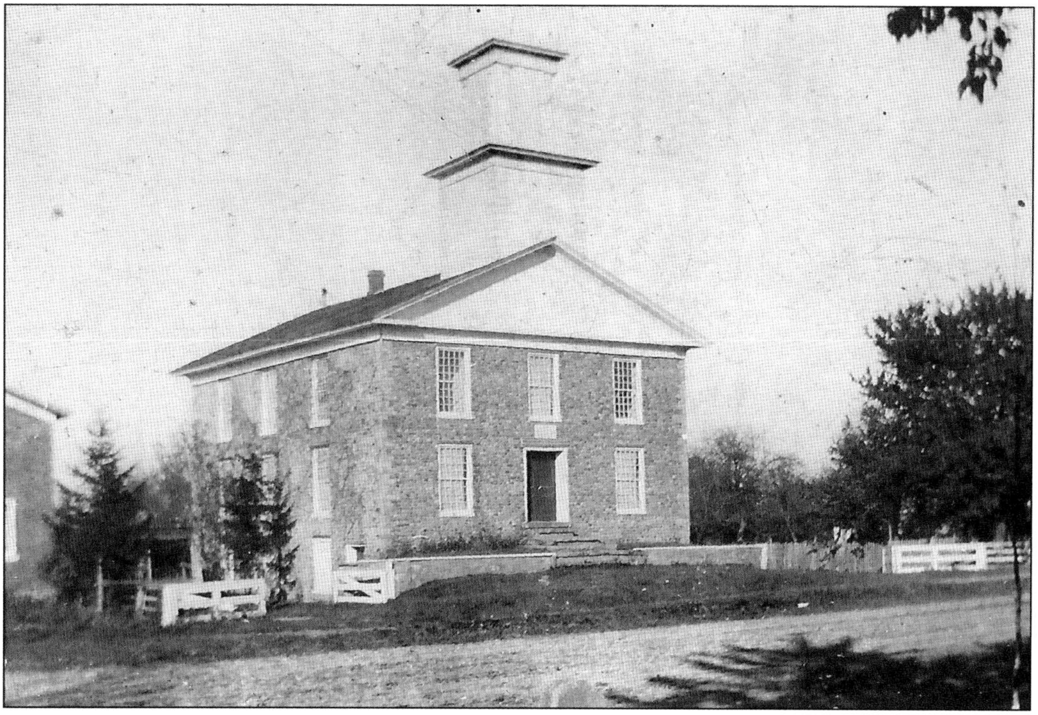

COBBLESTONE CHURCH. This photograph was taken about 1890, when Ridge Road was still made of dirt. (Courtesy of the Cobblestone Museum.)

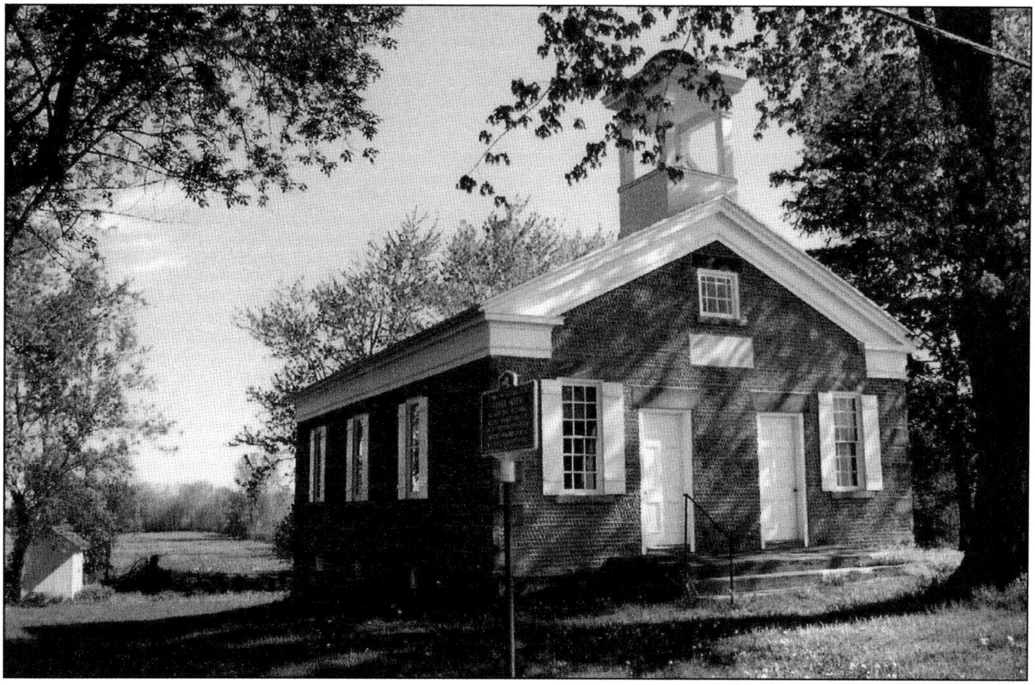

ONE-ROOM SCHOOLHOUSE. This cobblestone school was built of lake-washed stones in 1849. It is part of a series of buildings owned by the Cobblestone Museum in Childs, located on Route 104 near Route 98. Note the outhouse behind it. (Courtesy of the Cobblestone Museum.)

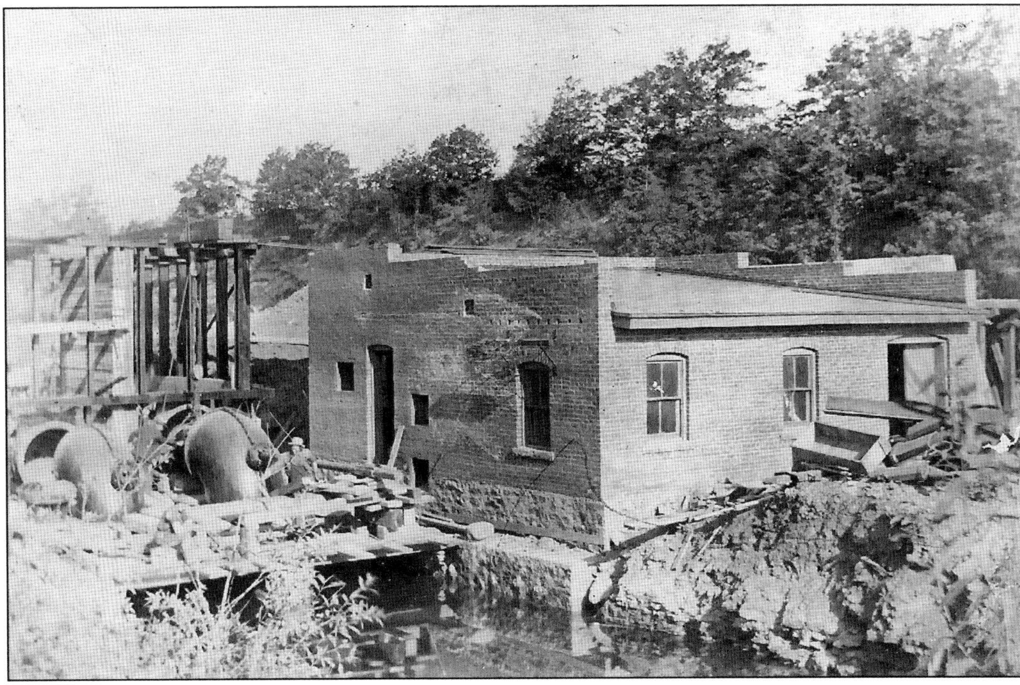

ALBION POWERHOUSE. This is the powerhouse at nearby Waterport, north of Albion. Here the Albion Power Company generated electricity using water from Oak Orchard River. (Courtesy of Orleans County Department of History.)

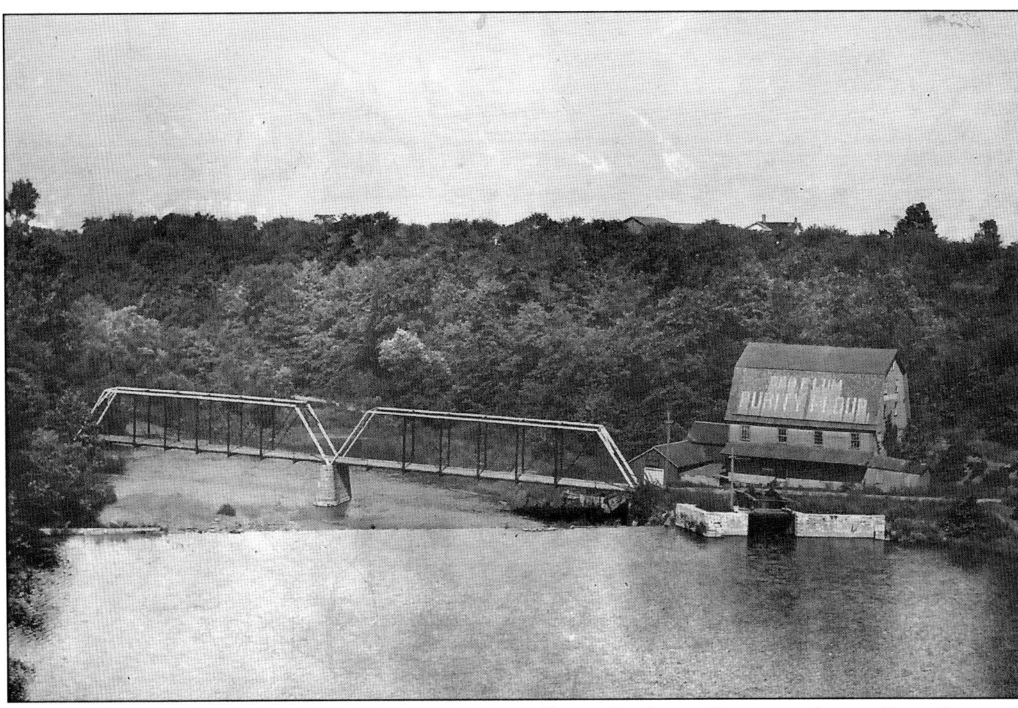

TWIN BRIDGES. These bridges led to Clark's Mills at Carlton, the site of a millpond east of Waterport. (Courtesy of Orleans County Department of History.)

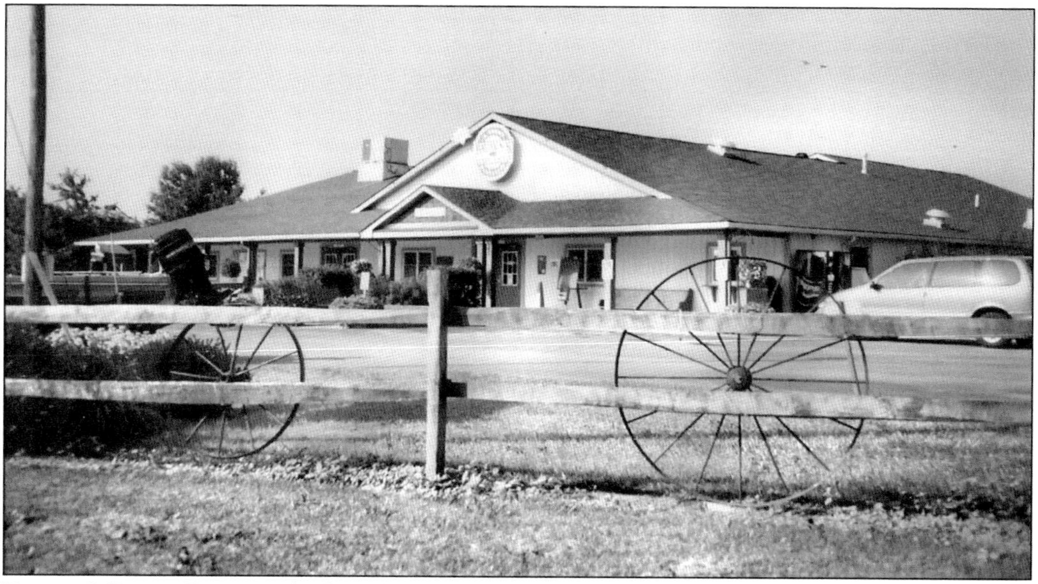

BROWN'S BERRY PATCH. The large building houses a store with fresh fruits and vegetables, jellies, and preserves. Brown's Berry Patch also has an indoor restaurant and an outdoor playground with a petting zoo, goats that travel up and over large walkways, and pumpkin-carving contests and hayrides in the fall.

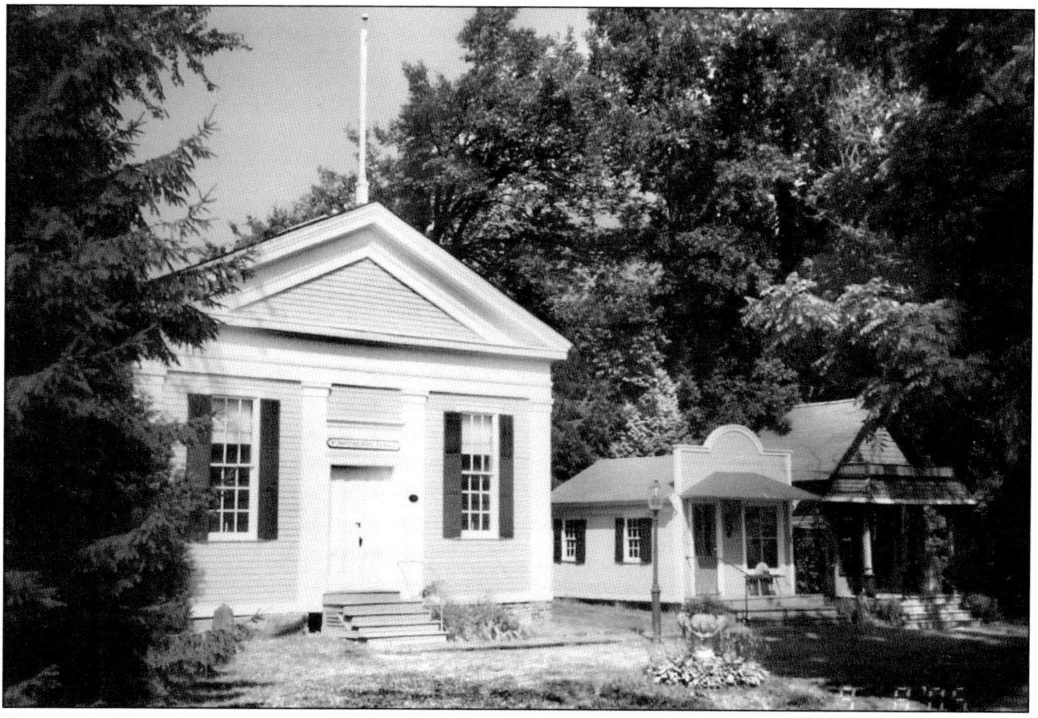

FARMERS HALL, HARNESS SHOP, AND PRINT SHOP. A short trip around the corner south on Route 98 from the Cobblestone Church are these three buildings. The Farmers Hall houses farm tools and artifacts used by area farmers many years ago. These buildings are part of the Cobblestone Museum complex.

ACKNOWLEDGMENTS

This book could not have been completed without the exhaustive help of C. W. "Bill" Lattin, Orleans County historian. He expended many hours finding vintage photographs and telling tales inspired by the old scenes. In addition, thanks are extended to Donna Kay Belmont, Mary Roth, Hollis Canham, Mark Tillman, and Tillman's Village Inn (which allowed use of the photographs on the walls), Sue Phillips of the Medina Book Shoppe, Susan Fuller, the Orleans County Department of History, and the Cobblestone Museum.

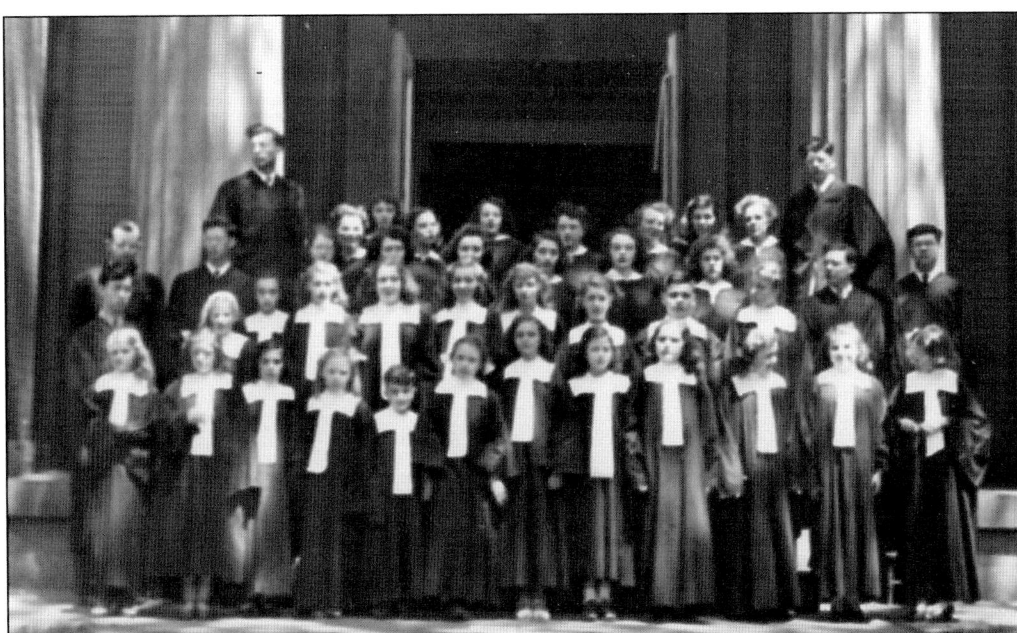

PRESBYTERIAN CHOIR. Members of the choir stand in front of the large pillars of the Presbyterian church. (Courtesy of Orleans County Department of History.)